Crisis Bargaining and the State

Crisis Bargaining and the State

The Domestic Politics of International Conflict

Susan Peterson

Ann Arbor

THE UNIVERSITY OF MICHIGAN PRESS

1999 1998 1997 1996   4 3 2 1

*Grateful acknowledgment is made to the following authors, publishers, and
journals for permission to reprint previously published materials.*

Portions of chapter 3 are reprinted from Susan Peterson, "The Domestic
Politics of Crisis Bargaining and the Origins of the Crimean War," in Jack
Snyder and Robert Jervis, eds., *Coping with Complexity in the International
System,* 1993, by permission of Westview Press, Boulder, Colorado.

Portions of chapter 4 are reprinted from Susan Peterson "How Democracies
Differ: Public Opinion, State Structure, and the Lessons of the Fashoda
Crisis," *Security Studies* 5, no. 1 (Fall 1995).

*Every effort has been made to trace the ownership of all copyrighted materials
in this book and to obtain permission for its use.*

A CIP catalog record for this book is available from the British Library.

Library of Congress Cataloging-in-Publication Data
Peterson, Susan, 1961–
    Crisis bargaining and the state : the domestic politics of
    international conflict / Susan Peterson.
        p.   cm.
    Includes bibliographical references and index.
    ISBN 0-472-10628-7 (hardcover : alk. paper)
    1. Diplomatic negotiations in international disputes.
    2. International relations—Decision-making.   3. Balance of power.
    4. National state. I. Title.
    JX4473.P47   1996
    327.2'09—dc20   95-41673
                                                                    CIP

Contents

Acknowledgments   vii

Chapter 1
    Introduction   1

Chapter 2
    Strategy and State Structure: The Domestic Politics of
        Crisis Bargaining   13

Chapter 3
    The Crimean War Crisis, 1852–54   47

Chapter 4
    The Fashoda Crisis, 1898   95

Chapter 5
    The Berlin Crisis, 1958–61   133

Chapter 6
    Conclusion   185

Index   203

Acknowledgments

I owe thanks to many people who helped make this book possible. My first debt is to Robert Jervis and Jack Snyder. As scholars, they provided insight and inspiration in their own work; as teachers, they gave much-appreciated advice and guidance over a period of many years. One other person made such an uncommon contribution that it is impossible to adequately thank him: Jonathan Mercer read more versions of this manuscript than he or I would care to remember. Without his friendship and professional counsel, this book would not exist.

Many others offered invaluable assistance. Ted Hopf and Mlada Bukovansky supplied a steady stream of advice and encouragement. James Richter, on whose interpretation of the Berlin crisis I rely heavily in chapter 5, provided extensive comments on the penultimate draft of the manuscript. Special thanks are also due to Andrew Cortell for his early efforts to tutor me on state structure and for his patient reading and insightful critiques of multiple drafts of the theoretical chapters. Many other individuals graciously read part or all of the manuscript. They include Harry Bliss, Neta Crawford, Eileen Crumm, John Garofano, Elizabeth Kier, Deborah Larson, Richard Ned Lebow, Thomas Risse-Kappen, Randall Schweller, Heather Scully, and one anonymous reviewer. Michaela Cahillane provided English translations of the French documents cited in chapter 4.

Generous financial support for this project was provided by the College of William & Mary, Smith College, the Eisenhower World Affairs Institute, and the John M. Olin Institute for Strategic Studies at Harvard University. To the Olin Institute, and especially to its director Samuel Huntington, go my additional thanks for a congenial and intellectually stimulating place to work during the two years of initial research.

Finally, I must express my gratitude to my family. In particular, I thank Heather Scully, whose primary contribution was to help me maintain a sense of humor and proportion. Without her help, I would have completed this book much sooner, but I hope she knows I am grateful for the delay. The book is dedicated with gratitude to my mother, Janet Chalke, for the quiet sacrifices she made so that her children might live lives of choice and opportunity.

1

Introduction

This book is about the domestic politics of crisis bargaining. It examines the ways in which the institutions of a state empower and constrain political leaders as they pilot their nation perilously close to the brink of war. To date, much of the academic study of international crises, like the debate within policy-making circles, has focused on the question, what is the best strategy to adopt in order to avoid both war and diplomatic defeat? A focus on the domestic context of crisis bargaining suggests that the answer hinges on the nature of the adversary: the same policy can have different consequences depending on the ways in which it interacts with existing debates within the target country. Those debates, in turn, are structured by the political institutions of the state.

Recent studies have touted the effectiveness of a "tit-for-tat" or "firm-but-fair" bargaining strategy in resolving international conflicts.[1] Such a strategy judiciously combines coercion and conciliation and responds in kind to an opponent's actions. While they agree on the need for a strategy of reciprocity, scholars and practitioners of foreign policy disagree about whether the initial response should be coercive or conciliatory. Deterrence theorists stress the "lessons of Munich" on the dangers of conciliation and, so, ordain a strategy that starts out "tough."[2] In contrast, cooperation theorists learned their lessons from World War I

---

1. For example, see Robert Axelrod, *The Evolution of Cooperation* (New York: Basic Books, 1985); Russell J. Leng and Hugh G. Wheeler, "Influence Strategies, Success, and War," *Journal of Conflict Resolution* 23, no. 4 (December 1979): 655–84; and Paul K. Huth, *Extended Deterrence and the Prevention of War* (New Haven: Yale University Press, 1988).

2. See Alexander L. George, David K. Hall, and William E. Simons, *The Limits of Coercive Diplomacy: Laos, Cuba, Vietnam* (Boston: Little, Brown, 1971); Charles Lockhart, *Bargaining in International Conflicts* (New York: Columbia University Press, 1979); and Glenn H. Snyder and Paul Diesing, *Conflict among Nations: Bargaining, Decision Making, and System Structure in International Crises* (Princeton: Princeton University Press, 1977).

and consequently worry about the dangers of escalation, not exploitation. They therefore advocate a strategy that starts out "nice."[3]
Neither strategy is consistently effective. An accommodative strategy invited exploitation at Munich but succeeded, at least initially, in the
1958–61 Berlin crisis. Similarly, the use of a coercive strategy, such as
the one that provoked escalation in 1914, has preceded the peaceful
resolution of many conflicts, including the Cuban missile crisis in 1962.
I argue that the success or failure of a strategy in resolving an
international crisis short of war and defeat depends on the nature of
the opposing government. State A's bargaining behavior interacts with
state B's policy-making process to produce B's policy response and,
ultimately, the outcome of the conflict. Two elements of the domestic
context are important: institutional structure and strategic beliefs. The
organization of foreign policy authority within a state determines the
channels through which crisis decision making occurs. Yet structure
only constrains or empowers; it alone does not explain behavior. How
one state responds to another state's actions depends on the strategic
beliefs of its leaders. Learning to avoid war, then, turns out to be a
matter of gauging the impact of one's own behavior on domestic debates within the opposing state.
This argument both challenges and integrates existing approaches
to the study of crisis bargaining. I dispute structural approaches that
suggest that domestic politics does not matter—that all states are strong
states when it comes to issues of national security. Most existing attempts to open the "black box" and examine decision making in international crises focus on either the role of decision-makers' beliefs or the
process of bargaining among domestic coalitions. I refute neither of
these analytic approaches. Rather, I integrate their insights and build on
them to argue that the institutional structure of the state generates a set
of governing conditions that determine when cognitive or bureaucratic
explanations prevail.

Rethinking the Role of the State

In recent years, international relations scholars have made a laudable
attempt to "bring the state back in" as a variable in explaining foreign

---

3. See Axelrod, *Evolution of Cooperation*; Charles E. Osgood, *An Alternative to War or Surrender* (Urbana: University of Illinois Press, 1962), chap. 5; and Richard Ned Lebow and Janice Gross Stein, "Beyond Deterrence," *Journal of Social Issues* 43 (winter 1987): 5–71. On the two approaches, see Robert Jervis, *Perception and Misperception in International Politics* (Princeton: Princeton University Press, 1976), chap. 3.

policy.[4] This is especially true in the area of foreign economic policy, where the state is treated as an actor in its own right and as a set of institutions that constrain individual and group action. These theories of the state focus on the influence of national political institutions and societal factors on foreign policy. They explain foreign policy continuity, because successive leaders face similar institutional constraints and imperatives. Since different institutional structures produce different policy outcomes, such theories also explain policy variation across states.

While the claim that "institutions matter"[5] in the making of trade, industrial, and monetary policy has been widely advanced and accepted for many years, the notion persists that politics stops at "the water's edge" on national security issues. As Bruce Bueno de Mesquita and David Lalman note, "Domestic politics has long been the stepchild of research into international conflict."[6] For example, in his 1978 study of raw materials investment policy, Stephen D. Krasner argued that societal cleavages are unimportant in "foreign political policy-making" because of the "independence of decisionmakers from particular pressures" within that realm.[7] He argued, in short, that the domestic structure of the state within this issue area insulates decision makers from private interests.

While this was largely true of the United States (the country in Krasner's study) prior to the Vietnam War, it is not true of all states at all times. For example, even during acute international crises like the 1852–54 Crimean crisis and the 1898 Fashoda showdown, the British cabinet was poorly insulated from societal pressures that entered the foreign policy-making process through Parliament. These pressures ultimately compelled more moderate cabinet members to fall into line behind a hard-line policy. In 1898, societal cleavages were so severe in France that the government fell in the midst of the Fashoda crisis. In addition to these societal pressures, there was a second domestic constraint on British

---

4. The quoted expression is from Peter B. Evans, Dietrich Rueschemeyer, and Theda Skocpol, eds., *Bringing the State Back In* (Cambridge: Cambridge University Press, 1985). Also see Peter J. Katzenstein, ed., *Between Power and Plenty: Foreign Economic Policies of Advanced Industrial States* (Madison: University of Wisconsin Press, 1978); and G. John Ikenberry, David A. Lake, and Michael Mastanduno, eds., *The State and American Foreign Economic Policy* (Ithaca: Cornell University Press, 1988).

5. The quoted phrase is from R. Kent Weaver and Bert A. Rockman, eds., *Do Institutions Matter? Government Capabilities in the United States and Abroad* (Washington, DC: Brookings, 1993).

6. *War and Reason: Domestic and International Imperatives* (New Haven: Yale University Press, 1992), 145.

7. *Defending the National Interest: Raw Materials Investments and U.S. Foreign Policy* (Princeton: Princeton University Press, 1978), 70, 346.

leaders in both crises: the foreign policy executive comprised a number of distinct offices, making the decision-making process a collective one. In short, not all states are strong states because national security is at stake. A complete understanding of crisis bargaining, contrary to conventional approaches, requires a theory of the state.

While the influence of domestic political factors on national security policy has been understudied, it has not been ignored. Early studies focused on differences in regime type—between democratic and totalitarian regimes, on the one hand,[8] and between parliamentary and presidential democracies, on the other.[9] Only recently and rarely, however, have domestic structural approaches to political economy, which focus on political institutions and the mechanisms that link state and societal actors, been adopted to the security arena.

Several works deserve mention. In his study of Russian and Soviet policy regarding nuclear testing and strategic defenses, Matthew Evangelista concludes that transnational relations and domestic structure in combination influence security policy.[10] Thomas Risse-Kappen similarly contends that the structure of the Soviet state allowed Western liberal internationalists to form transnational networks with "new thinkers" in the Soviet Union, leading to change in Soviet foreign policy and the end of the cold war.[11] Finally, Peter J. Katzenstein and Nobuo Okawara argue that the decentralized nature of the Japanese decision-making process and the lack of institutional autonomy granted to Japan's Defense Agency explain the comprehensive nature of Tokyo's security policy.[12]

8. See Henry Kissinger, "Domestic Structures and Foreign Policy," *Daedalus* 95 (1966): 503–29; and Norton E. Long, "Open and Closed Systems," in R. Barry Farrell, ed., *Approaches to Comparative and International Politics* (Evanston, IL: Northwestern University Press, 1966). For a recent and related argument, see Jack Snyder, *Myths of Empire: Domestic Politics and International Ambition* (Ithaca: Cornell University Press, 1991).

9. Kenneth N. Waltz, *Foreign Policy and Democratic Politics* (Boston: Little, Brown, 1967). For a recent work that distinguishes among democratic structures, see Thomas Risse-Kappen, "Public Opinion, Domestic Structure, and Foreign Policy in Liberal Democracies," *World Politics* 43, no.4 (July 1991): 479–512.

10. "The Paradox of State Strength: Transnational Relations, Domestic Structures, and Security Policy in Russia and the Soviet Union," *International Organization* 49, no. 1 (winter 1995): 1–38. On state structure, also see Evangelista's earlier work, *Innovation and the Arms Race: How the United States and the Soviet Union Develop New Military Technologies* (Ithaca: Cornell University Press, 1988).

11. "Ideas Do Not Float Freely: Transnational Coalitions, Domestic Structures, and the End of the Cold War," *International Organization* 48, no. 2 (spring 1994): 185–214.

12. "Japan's National Security: Structures, Norms, and Policies," *International Security* 17, no. 4 (spring 1993): 84–118.

These studies demonstrate that domestic factors have begun to penetrate the field of security and strategic studies. However, domestic structural arguments have not been applied to the study of crisis bargaining.[13] Borrowing from the field of international political economy, I develop a theory about institutional constraints on politicians during acute international crises. Applying such a theory of the state to crisis bargaining provides a crucial test of the role of domestic institutions in the making of foreign policy. Since external constraints on actors' behavior are strongest when national security is threatened, international crises provide a difficult test for theories of domestic and bureaucratic politics.[14]

The Argument

It is easy to argue after the fact that sticks are better used against the Hitlers of the world, and carrots are better used against the Lord Greys. But such *post hoc* analyses often seem *ad hoc*. What is needed is a theory that integrates the domestic and the international or strategic levels of analysis to determine which strategy is appropriate in which situations and against what kinds of opponents.

In the following chapters, I identify four different types of states based on differences in the organization of foreign policy authority. These are ideal types. In general, the more concentrated foreign policy authority is within the executive branch and the more autonomy the executive enjoys from the legislative body, the less likely crisis decision making is to enter the domestic political arena. Conversely, the more dispersed executive authority is among different offices and the less freedom the executive enjoys from a national legislature, the more likely it is that domestic factors and processes will matter. In short, domestic structure determines the arena within which foreign policy making oc-

---

13. A partial exception is James D. Fearon, "Domestic Political Audiences and the Escalation of International Disputes," *American Political Science Review* 88, no. 3 (September 1994): 577–92. The importance of domestic structure to bargaining and negotiation is also noted in Robert D. Putnam, "Diplomacy and Domestic Politics: The Logic of Two-Level Games," *International Organization* 42, no. 3 (summer 1988), 448–50; and in the essays by Barry Eichengreen and Marc Uzan, Miles Kahler, Peter B. Evans, Helen Milner, and John S. Odell, in Peter B. Evans, Harold K. Jacobson, and Robert D. Putnam, eds., *Double-Edged Diplomacy: International Bargaining and Domestic Politics* (Berkeley: University of California Press, 1993).

14. For related arguments, see Graham T. Allison, *Essence of Decision: Explaining the Cuban Missile Crisis* (Boston: Little, Brown, 1971), 276; Benjamin Miller, "Explaining Great Power Cooperation in Conflict Management," *World Politics* 45, no. 1 (October 1992): 1–46; and Arnold Wolfers, *Discord and Collaboration: Essays on International Politics* (Baltimore: Johns Hopkins University Press, 1962), 13–14.

curs. It also determines whose preferences will matter in crisis decision making.

In what I refer to as a type I state, one with a unitary foreign policy executive free of legislative control, responsibility for crisis policy making resides in a single chief executive. In nineteenth-century Russia, for example, Czar Nicholas I had sole jurisdiction over foreign policy. Mid-twentieth-century America provides a second, if very different, example of a type I state. Before the U.S. war in Vietnam, presidents enjoyed significant autonomy on national security issues from both Congress and their own cabinets and national security apparatuses.[15]

In these unitary, autonomous states, the success or failure of the opposing state's bargaining strategy depends on the ways in which it interacts with the chief executive's beliefs. During the diplomatic crisis preceding the Crimean War, the initially conciliatory British strategy confirmed the czar's hard-line beliefs. His image of Britain as an ally that would cooperate, or that at the very least would not ally against Russia, was reinforced by early British restraint. By the time London shifted to more coercive rhetoric and tactics, the crisis had progressed toward war. A similar story can be told about the U.S. decision-making process in the 1958–61 Berlin crisis, although the outcome differed markedly. While both the Eisenhower and the Kennedy administrations were characterized by internal disagreement between "hawkish" and moderate factions, the tactical beliefs of the two successive presidents largely determined U.S. response to Soviet bargaining behavior. Indeed, the most significant shift in U.S. policy—from early signs of conciliation to later coercion—was the result of a change in leadership following the 1960 presidential election.

At the opposite extreme, domestic factors have the greatest influence in type IV states, where foreign policy authority is dispersed within the executive branch and the legislature performs an oversight function. Nineteenth-century Britain provides the closest thing to a perfect example of this type of state. Domestic pressures entered the foreign policy-making process through Parliament and indirectly shaped the policy preferences of individual cabinet members. Additionally, policy decisions were the collective product of elite bargaining within the cabinet.

Again, state structure determines the decision-making process. In the type IV state, where the foreign policy executive is diffuse and lacks autonomy from the legislature, policy-makers' preferences reflect the

---

15. This characterization of state structure does not hold for other issue areas. On the need for a highly differentiated conception of state structure, see Ikenberry, Lake, and Mastanduno, *The State and American Foreign Policy*.

influence of societal pressures, and national policy is the product of internal bargaining and coalition building among elites. In short, policy response depends on the domestic distribution of power and the ways in which the opponent's actions interact with domestic debates. In the Crimean War crisis, initial Russian coercion undermined the arguments of moderate politicians like Prime Minister Aberdeen and Foreign Secretary Clarendon and reinforced those of hard-liners like Home Secretary Palmerston and John Russell, leader of the House of Commons. St. Petersburg's coercive policy ultimately shifted the balance of power in London toward a more coercive response, and the crisis escalated toward war. In the Fashoda crisis later in the century, French coercion similarly eroded the arguments of Britain's soft-line prime minister, Salisbury, and pushed British strategy into the arms of more hard-line elements of the cabinet.

Between these two ends of the spectrum lie two other types of states. In type II states, a unitary executive is subject to significant legislative oversight. In the Third French Republic, the government depended on Parliament for its legitimacy and survival. In contrast to Britain, however, crisis decision making in turn-of-the-century France was centered in the office of the foreign minister, Théophile Delcassé.

While the success or failure of an opponent's bargaining strategy against a type II state depends on the policy preferences of a single chief executive, those preferences reflect and are altered by societal pressures that enter the decision-making process through the national legislature. For example, Britain's unyielding stance in the 1898 Fashoda crisis succeeded because it convinced the hard-line foreign minister that he would have to retreat without significant British concessions. Since French governments relied on a parliamentary majority, however, Delcassé was not free from domestic pressures. His policy preferences reflected continued assaults by the media, public opinion, and interest groups. Even after French retreat became inevitable, Delcassé attempted to stall in order to appease those members of Parliament and the public who favored continued resistance.

Finally, a type III state is one in which executive authority for foreign policy is dispersed among a number of offices but no effective national legislature exists. I argue that the Soviet Union—considered in many ways to be a strong, monolithic state—was actually a type III state; while Soviet leaders in the post-Stalin era enjoyed significant autonomy from a largely symbolic representative body, decision-making authority within the Politburo and the Secretariat of the Central Committee of the Communist Party was diffuse. Khrushchev was, at best, a first among equals.

In such a state, national policy reflects an internal process of coalition building among elites. An adversary's bargaining behavior influences the outcome of the crisis by influencing the domestic balance of power between advocates of coercion and accommodation. Initial U.S. restraint in the Berlin crisis reinforced the arguments of the relatively moderate leader, Khrushchev, against his hard-line opposition. The later shift to coercion by the United States aroused the general secretary's domestic opponents and shifted the balance in favor of a more coercive policy response.

Chapter 2 draws on existing literature on state structure, mostly from the field of international political economy, to develop these hypotheses. The argument suggests that existing approaches to the study of crisis bargaining drawn from cognitive psychology and bureaucratic politics theory provide complementary, not competing, explanations. The institutional structure of the state intervenes between the external environment and foreign policy and determines when each decision-making theory applies.

Theoretical Contributions

My argument about the domestic politics of crisis bargaining has implications for three debates within the field of international relations. First, the findings of this study reinforce the recent shift from an emphasis on structural or systemic causes of state behavior to a focus on the domestic politics of international relations.[16] My research suggests that neither level—international or domestic—is sufficient to explain the outcome of international crises. While observation tells us that "domestic politics and international relations are often somehow entangled," our theories are just beginning to "[sort] out the puzzling tangles."[17]

This book is one attempt to do just that in the area of crisis bargaining. It fits within a growing literature on the interaction of ideas, institutions, and state behavior.[18] Unlike this literature, much of which focuses

---

16. For recent work on domestic politics, see especially Evans, Jacobson, and Putnam, *Double-Edged Diplomacy*; and Snyder, *Myths of Empire*. The classic systemic analysis remains Kenneth N. Waltz, *Theory of International Politics* (New York: Random House, 1979).

17. Putnam, "Diplomacy and Domestic Politics," 427.

18. For other arguments, see Jeff Checkel, "Ideas, Institutions, and the Gorbachev Foreign Policy Revolution," *World Politics* 45, no. 2 (January 1993): 271–300; Judith Goldstein, *Ideas, Interests, and American Trade Policy* (Ithaca: Cornell University Press, 1993); James G. Richter, *Khrushchev's Double Bind: International Processes and Domestic Coalition Politics* (Baltimore: Johns Hopkins University Press, 1994); Risse-Kappen, "Ideas Do Not Float Freely"; and Kathryn Sikkink, *Ideas and Institutions: Developmentalism in Brazil and Argentina* (Ithaca: Cornell University Press, 1991).

either on American foreign economic policy or on the foreign policy of the former Soviet Union, my approach is explicitly comparative. Furthermore, I examine both sides in an interactive conflict, rather than seeking to explain only one state's foreign policy.

The second debate is between deterrence and cooperation theorists over the causes and management of international conflict. How can policy makers signal their resolve without setting in motion a spiral of escalation? My argument resolves this dilemma by focusing on the nature of the adversary.[19] Domestic political factors provide an important source of actors' preferences, a largely unexplored issue in many game theoretic treatments of international conflict. Domestic politics provides a crucial indicator of whether an opponent is the type assumed by deterrence or by cooperation theory. My argument thus provides an answer to the question of what sequence or combination of bargaining tactics succeeds in what kinds of situations and against what kinds of opponents.

The final contribution of this study is to that body of work that seeks to explain the outcomes of international crises. Most studies focus on the impact of bargaining behavior on information processing during a crisis.[20] These studies assume that policy makers learn from their opponent's actions and use those lessons in making future policy choices. In contrast, I argue that the bargaining process differs from state to state. True, national leaders in all states interpret their opponent's behavior according to their preexisting beliefs. In states in which the foreign policy executive is not a single, unitary actor with total autonomy from legislative oversight, however, the bargaining process enters the political arena. In the Crimean War crisis, for instance, the British foreign secretary, Lord Clarendon, provided the swing vote for a reversal of British policy. But his advocacy of coercion was not based on a change in beliefs or an adjustment in his expectations of the Russian adversary. Rather, Clarendon altered his policy preference, shifting the balance in favor of coercion, because Russia's early intimidation tactics had focused strong domestic pressures on him.

This suggests that an emphasis on state learning, on how and why decision-makers' beliefs change, is insufficient to explain crisis resolution. Although useful in describing and explaining how individuals adapt to a changing international environment, an analysis that focuses on individual learning cannot account for the behavior of nation-states because it ignores domestic politics. To accurately explain and predict

---

19. See Jervis's discussion of the nature of the adversaries in *Perception and Misperception*, chap. 3.

20. See Lockhart, *Bargaining in International Conflicts*; and Snyder and Diesing, *Conflict Among Nations*.

national policy, we must also consider the interaction between the domestic and international arenas. Sometimes elites learn. At other times, however, societal pressures influence policy-makers' preferences and alter national policy, even though individuals' beliefs remain constant.[21]

Policy Implications

My argument also has practical consequences for managing international conflict. Understanding how one state's policy influences another's response during a severe conflict is a first step toward preventing the escalation of crises toward war. From the Persian Gulf to Bosnia, from Somalia to Haiti, the brief history of "the new world order" suggests that conflict will continue to plague the international system. By better understanding the complex relationship among bargaining behavior, state structure, and strategic preferences, national leaders can learn to effectively manage these conflicts in a new but less certain era.

Most simply, my argument suggests that politicians should not follow the advice of students and practitioners of crisis management who argue that one particular strategy is always best. Understanding the conditions under which different strategies are effective is crucial to peaceful conflict resolution. One important condition is the domestic nature of the adversary. Whether it is the United States seeking to influence reform in Russia, China, Iraq, or Haiti, or Russia trying to influence the behavior of former Soviet republics, the same principle applies: foreign policy actions interact with domestic debates in other states.

My argument also challenges the notion, prevalent in arms control and a wide range of other bargaining and negotiation issues, that domestic political factors impede cooperation. Rather, as this book shows, domestic political division may also encourage compromise. If it can reinforce the arguments of those elements in the opposing state that already seek compromise, a carefully crafted foreign policy may take advantage of domestic opposition to an adversary's government to facilitate a cooperative outcome.

Finally, the domestic institutional approach of this book suggests

---

21. On learning, see George W. Breslauer and Philip E. Tetlock, eds., *Learning in U.S. and Soviet Foreign Policy* (Boulder, CO: Westview, 1991). Although that volume recognizes the importance of domestic politics, its focus is on belief change. For other works that question the emphasis on learning, see Charles Glaser, "Political Consequences of Military Strategy: Expanding and Redefining the Spiral and Deterrence Models," *World Politics* 44, no. 4 (July 1992): 497–538; and Matthew Evangelista, "Cooperation Theory and Disarmament Negotiations in the 1950s," *World Politics* 42, no. 4 (July 1990): 502–28.

that the recent trend toward increased democratization in Eastern Europe and Latin America may not necessarily mean a more peaceful international order, as many students of democracy and war had hoped. Instead, it suggests that we need to focus on the nature of the political institutions that are created in new states, particularly the organization of foreign policy authority. In short, some democracies may be more prone than others to the ill effects of public opinion and nationalist sentiment. I return in chapter 6 to these and other implications of the argument.

Plan of the Book

The next chapter discusses four explanations for the success or failure of bargaining strategies—systemic, cognitive, motivated bias, and bureaucratic politics. It also presents my own argument, which uses domestic structure to predict the decision-making process and the outcome of international crises. The chapter concludes with an examination of the study's methodology—the variables, case selection, and testing methods. Chapters 3, 4, and 5 test these five approaches as explanations of the 1852–54 Crimean War crisis, the 1898 Fashoda crisis, and the 1958–61 Berlin crisis, respectively. These case studies examine the institutional structure and decision-making process in each state involved in the three dyadic crises. The concluding chapter examines the pattern of outcomes in these cases and further implications for theory and policy.

2

Strategy and State Structure: The Domestic Politics of Crisis Bargaining

Although much of the debate about the causes of crisis escalation and war has focused on bargaining behavior, strategy alone cannot predict whether a crisis will be resolved by war, compromise, diplomatic defeat, or victory. In this chapter, I explore several explanations of the relationship between bargaining and the outcome of international crises, including international structural approaches, cognitive psychology, motivational psychology, and bureaucratic politics. I then advance my own argument that the institutional structure of the state determines the explanatory value of existing cognitive and bureaucratic hypotheses. Finally, I present the methodology of the study—the variables, case selection, and testing methods.

Existing Explanations

Because my argument integrates the insights of other approaches to crisis decision making, I begin by examining existing theories.

International Structure

The international structure—the disputants' capabilities, intentions, and interests—forms the context within which crisis bargaining occurs. As such, many students of international crises argue, structure determines the effectiveness of different bargaining strategies. A state's preferences reflect its capabilities, interests, and intentions. According to this systemic or structural view, the militarily superior state, like the nation with greater interests at stake, wins a crisis by employing an initially coercive strategy that credibly demonstrates its superior resolve and capabilities. An initially nice strategy, in contrast, leads to escalation because it fails to illuminate the comparative resolve of the adversary states.[1]

---

1. Snyder and Diesing, *Conflict among Nations*, esp. chaps. 2–3. Also see James D. Morrow, "Capabilities, Uncertainty, and Resolve: A Limited Information Model of Crisis Bargaining," *American Journal of Political Science* 33, no. 4 (November 1989): 941–72.

Many game theoretic and other structural approaches examine the influence of the intentions of the adversary on the effectiveness of different sequences of bargaining tactics.[2] A state attempting to deter challenges to the status quo has greater interests at stake in a conflict and therefore can make more credible threats to stand firm.[3] In this view, initially coercive and initially conciliatory strategies sometimes succeed and sometimes fail depending on the goals and motivations of the opponent against whom they are used. Starting "high"[4] is more effective for states seeking to preserve the status quo in the international system. Early coercion demonstrates the state's resolve to stand firm in the face of aggression. Starting "low" is a more appropriate strategy for states seeking to revise the status quo, since accommodation offers a means of addressing the underlying issues and sources of conflict.[5]

At first glance, structural explanations seem to provide a compelling explanation for the success of states' policies in resolving international crises short of war or diplomatic defeat. In the 1898 Fashoda crisis, for example, an initially coercive British strategy succeeded against a militarily weaker and revisionist French foe because it convinced the French foreign minister, Théophile Delcassé, that he could not succeed against his stronger, more resolved British opponent.

Two major problems with structural approaches remain. First, structural theories often generate inaccurate or indeterminate predictions. For example, an initially coercive strategy sometimes fails to persuade a weaker opponent to concede. In the 1852–54 Crimean case, Russia's heavy-handedness in the early phase of the conflict convinced British policy makers that the czar was hostile and aggressive. This view persisted and the crisis escalated toward war despite the fact that, as the French became increasingly wary of allying with London against St. Petersburg, the balance of power shifted in favor of Russia. It can be

---

2. This factor was originally emphasized by Jervis in *Perception and Misperception*, chap. 3. Also see Stephen M. Walt, *The Origins of Alliances* (Ithaca: Cornell University Press, 1987); and Randall L. Schweller, "Tripolarity and the Second World War," *International Studies Quarterly* 37, no. 1 (March 1993): 73–104.

3. Robert Jervis, *The Meaning of the Nuclear Revolution: Statecraft and the Prospect of Armageddon* (Ithaca: Cornell University Press, 1989), 29–35; Thomas C. Schelling, *Arms and Influence* (New Haven: Yale University Press, 1966), 69–78; Snyder and Diesing, *Conflict among Nations*, 184–85.

4. For purposes of this discussion, "high" and "low" refer to the location of a specific tactic along a continuum of bargaining moves, with a highly coercive move labeled "high" and a strongly accommodative tactic labeled "low."

5. For a similar argument, see Evan Luard, "Conciliation and Deterrence: A Comparison of Political Strategies in the Interwar and Postwar Periods," *World Politics* 19, no. 2 (January 1967): 167–189.

argued that Russia did not possess a significant military advantage in 1852, since the British Navy countered the enormous Russian advantage in land forces. This response raises two additional questions. First, how much superiority is enough? If an initially coercive strategy succeeded when used by the militarily superior United States in the 1948 Berlin crisis or the 1962 Cuban missile crisis, why did a similar strategy fail when implemented by Russia in the conflict that precipitated the Crimean War? Second, what is the proper strategy to use against an equally armed and resolved competitor?

In addition to these theoretical difficulties, all structural explanations of the outcome of international crises suffer from a fundamental methodological problem. It is nearly impossible to avoid tautology when describing the value structures of the parties to a conflict; by definition, the state that wins the crisis is the more resolved.

It is easy to understand why structural arguments frequently devolve into post hoc attempts to derive states' preferences from the outcome of the conflict. For example, if France had succeeded in securing significant concessions from the British over Fashoda, the crisis could not, by definition, have been a game of Bully in which Britain was the more resolved party. Similarly, if Britain had backed down in the Crimean War crisis, the conflict could not have been a Prisoner's Dilemma in which both sides preferred war to capitulation. It is difficult to determine the structure of a conflict independent of its outcome, and it is impossible to disprove a structural argument in which actors' preferences are derived from the outcome.

By examining the sources of states' preferences, we can avoid tautological and post hoc analyses. Structural approaches assume interests and intentions. Actually calculating these payoffs—examining their source and how they are altered by another state's actions in a specific case—requires us to examine both domestic political factors and decision-makers' perceptions of the interests at stake in a conflict.[6] In short, structural theories can only generate determinate predictions once other theories at lower levels of analysis provide states' preferences.

The Fashoda case nicely illustrates these difficulties. It is generally assumed that Britain had greater interests at stake than did France.[7]

---

6. For similar arguments, see Robert Jervis, "Rational Deterrence: Theory and Evidence," *World Politics* 41, no. 2 (January 1989): 183–207; and Helen Milner, "International Theories of Cooperation Among Nations: Strengths and Weaknesses," *World Politics* 44, no. 3 (April 1992): 466–96.

7. See Richard Ned Lebow, *Between Peace and War: The Nature of International Crisis* (Baltimore: Johns Hopkins University Press, 1981), 320–26; Lockhart, *Bargaining*

Nevertheless, it is hard to support this assertion without reference to the outcome of the conflict—British victory—or the prestrategic interests of the British or French states. To avoid the first, a tautology, we must examine the second, which requires an analysis of the domestic process by which preferences are aggregated and the national interest formed. As chapter 4 demonstrates, a major reason why Britain resolved to stand firm over an abandoned piece of swampy territory in East Africa was that British public opinion prevented compromise. French public opinion was indifferent, allowing Delcassé to back down. Many scholars focus on decision-making variables to address these problems with international structural explanations.

The Decision-Making Process

Decision-making explanations for the outcome of international crises examine how cognitive and domestic political factors effect states' interests and preferences. Cognitive approaches contend that an adversary's beliefs determine the effectiveness of state strategy. Theories about the role of domestic political factors in crisis bargaining come in two varieties. The indirect variant focuses on the influence of domestic political weakness on the information-processing and decision-making abilities of policy makers, while the direct version emphasizes the impact of an opponent's behavior on coalition politics and the domestic incentives of actors.

Cognitive Explanations
Cognitive psychology's most important contribution to international relations has been the lesson that decision makers tend to assimilate new information to their preexisting beliefs about international politics and about the intentions of specific actors within the system.[8] The content of the belief system—whether hard-line, soft-line, or somewhere between these two poles—determines a policy-maker's initial interpretation of the opponent's bargaining strategy.[9] The "stickiness" of the belief system—

---

in International Conflicts, 22; and Snyder and Diesing, *Conflict among Nations*, 123–24, 508, 524.

    8. See Alexander George, "The 'Operational Code': A Neglected Approach to the Study of Political Leaders and Decision-Making," *International Studies Quarterly* 13 (June 1969): 190–222; Ole Holsti, "Cognitive Dynamics and Images of the Enemy: Dulles and Russia," in David J. Finlay, Ole Holsti, and Richard R. Fagen, eds., *Enemies in Politics* (Chicago: Rand McNally, 1967), 25–96; and Jervis, *Perception and Misperception*, chap. 4.

    9. For applications of cognitive psychology to crisis bargaining, see Steven W. Hoagland and Stephen G. Walker, "Operational Codes and Crisis Outcomes," in Lawrence S.

the degree to which the decision-maker's beliefs are resistant to change—determines the extent to which the decision maker adjusts his or her subsequent expectations and behavior during the bargaining process. Different decision makers can be located along a continuum ranging from the irrational bargainer, who possesses a rigid belief system, to the rational bargainer, who adjusts his or her beliefs about the opponent based on the adversary's bargaining behavior.[10] Even in the latter case, however, the decision-maker's underlying beliefs remain unchanged.

These assumptions of cognitive psychology lead to the prediction that different sequences of coercive and accommodative tactics are successful in different situations depending on the psychological makeup of the target—the content and stickiness of his or her beliefs. An initially coercive strategy will succeed against rational hard-liners but will fail against more conciliatory bargainers. Similarly, an initially conciliatory strategy will succeed against a soft-liner but will fail against a hawkish opponent.

It is not difficult, in retrospect, to trace the effect of cognitive factors on crisis bargaining. British Home Secretary Palmerston's interpretation of Russian actions and his advocacy of a hard-line response in the Crimean War crisis was consistent with his distrust of the czar and his view of international relations, while Prime Minister Aberdeen's conciliatory policy prescriptions flowed from his soft-line belief system. In fact, similar consistencies can be found in all three crises studied. In nearly every instance, decision makers interpreted the actions of others according to their preexisting beliefs. Nevertheless, there are three fundamental problems with an exclusively cognitive approach.

First, current applications of cognitive psychology to crisis bargaining are unable to make determinate predictions about how external bargaining behavior interacts with a decision-maker's beliefs, because they focus exclusively on the difference between "hawks" and "doves." A hard-liner may interpret a state's coercive actions as evidence that the adversary is hostile and expansionist or as proof that it is bluffing. More important, a hard-liner may be personally intent on unlimited

Falkowski, ed., *Psychological Models in International Politics* (Boulder: Westview Press, 1979); Lockhart, *Bargaining in International Conflicts*, 47–51; Snyder and Diesing, *Conflict among Nations*, esp. 286; and J. Philip Rogers, "Crisis Bargaining Codes and Crisis Management," in Alexander L. George, ed., *Avoiding War: Problems of Crisis Management* (Boulder: Westview Press, 1991).

10. Snyder and Diesing, *Conflict among Nations*, 333–37; Lockhart, *Bargaining in International Conflicts*, 52–57. For explanations of why people persevere in their beliefs beyond the point at which those beliefs are supported by the evidence, see Richard Nisbett and Lee Ross, *Human Inference* (Englewood Cliffs, NJ: Prentice-Hall, 1980), chap. 8.

expansion or may merely be testing his or her opponent. Only in the latter case is the hawkish bargainer willing to back down when he or she meets resistance.

Second, according to a purely cognitive approach, decision-makers' policy preferences should rarely diverge from their preexisting beliefs. In fact, such divergences are common. In the Crimean War crisis, the dovish British foreign secretary, Lord Clarendon, eventually advocated coercion despite his faith in the good intentions of the Russian czar. Throughout the 1958–61 Berlin crisis, the relatively moderate Khrushchev maintained his belief in the inherent goodwill of President Eisenhower and Secretary of State Dulles, but he nonetheless shifted to coercive tactics.

Third, without a theory of the process of policy formation, it is impossible to explain the policy response of a *state* during an international crisis based on the cognitive structure of individual leaders. Whether a particular strategy successfully alters an opposing state's behavior also depends on the distribution of power within the adversary's government. For example, given the gulf between Palmerston's beliefs and policy preferences, on the one hand, and Aberdeen's and Clarendon's, on the other, it is necessary to look at the domestic policy process to explain the content of British policy on the eve of the Crimean War. In only two of the six states examined in this study does a single decision maker determine a state's foreign policy.

Domestic Politics and Motivated Bias

Some domestic political approaches emphasize the role of motivated bias or decisional conflict—the influence of a volatile domestic situation on perceptions in a crisis. Decisional conflict, the "simultaneous opposing tendency within the individual to accept and reject a given course of action," produces psychological stress.[11] In any decision in which there are competing interests at stake and uncertainty as to the outcome, the policy maker will experience decisional conflict and psychological stress that impair his or her decision-making abilities.[12] Domestic political factors enter the model as a source of threat or conflict. Three major domestic sources of threat—the weakness of a state's political system, the domestic political weakness of its leaders, and the existence of intra-elite competition for power—can convince leaders of the need to pursue

---

11. Irving L. Janis and Leon Mann, *Decision Making* (New York: Free Press, 1977), 46–50, quote at 46.

12. Alexander L. George, *Presidential Decisionmaking in Foreign Policy* (Boulder: Westview Press, 1980), chap. 2.

confrontational policies to shore up their government, coalition, or own political future.[13]

Once he or she realizes that there are serious risks involved in either doing nothing or undertaking any available policy option, the decision maker is likely to engage in "defensive avoidance" of the conflict. An individual who adopts this coping mechanism gives up searching for a solution, even though he or she remains dissatisfied with the available options. The individual then avoids information that will stimulate anxiety about the decisional conflict.[14] Policy makers may also overestimate the likelihood that their confrontational policies can succeed. They come to believe that the adversary will not resist or, if it does, that their own state can win the war at a relatively low cost. In short, national leaders engage in "gross self-deception or wishful thinking."[15]

Motivational psychology hypothesizes that emotional needs—specifically those created by strong threats to the government, coalition, or ruler—drive information processing. The ability of national leaders to accurately perceive an opponent's bargaining strategy depends on the strength or weakness of the government, coalition, or ruler. These perceptions, in turn, determine the success or failure of a particular bargaining strategy. An initially coercive policy will fail against a vulnerable adversary whose domestic interests lead him or her to ignore or resist threats and to view aggressive policy options as both feasible and necessary. Such an opponent will be insensitive to threats and warnings in the initial phase of the crisis and will misperceive later conciliatory offers.[16] In short, early coercion may lead the domestically vulnerable actor to overestimate the hostility of the opponent in subsequent bargaining rounds.

---

13. Richard Ned Lebow, "The Deterrence Deadlock: Is There A Way Out?" in Robert Jervis, Richard Ned Lebow, and Janice Gross Stein, *Psychology and Deterrence* (Baltimore: Johns Hopkins University Press, 1985), 184–87. For a work that argues for the use of "regime fragmentation" and "vulnerability" as indicators of foreign policy, see Joe D. Hagan, "Regimes, Political Oppositions, and the Comparative Analysis of Foreign Policy," in Charles F. Hermann, Charles W. Kegley, Jr., and James N. Rosenau, eds., *New Directions in the Study of Foreign Policy* (Boston: Allen & Unwin, 1987).

14. George, *Presidential Decisionmaking*, 25, 28–47; Janis and Mann, *Decision Making*, 52–64.

15. Lebow, *Between Peace and War*, 119–47, 169–92, quote at 169. Also see Lebow, "Deterrence Deadlock," 182.

16. Proponents of a motivated bias approach focus on the first hypothesis. See Richard Ned Lebow, "Deterrence: A Political and Psychological Critique," in Paul C. Stern, Robert Axelrod, Robert Jervis, and Roy Radner, eds., *Perspectives on Deterrence* (New York: Oxford University Press, 1989); Lebow and Stein, "Beyond Deterrence"; and Janice Gross Stein, "Deterrence and Reassurance," in Philip E. Tetlock, Jo L. Husbands, Robert Jervis, Paul C. Stern, and Charles Tilly, eds., *Behavior, Society, War*, vol. 2 (New York: Oxford University Press, 1991).

A motivated bias explanation of the outcome of international crises highlights the importance of domestic political factors in the bargaining process. However, it suffers from three problems. First, testing for the effects of motivated bias presents serious methodological obstacles. Discerning whether domestic vulnerability or simple greed motivates a state turns out to be a messy job. As Robert Jervis notes, even Saddam Hussein's 1990 attack on Kuwait was partially motivated by domestic weakness.[17] Furthermore, it is difficult to establish a test for the presence of motivated misperception that effectively eliminates the influence of cognitive biases as an alternative explanation, since the predictions of the two approaches are often identical.[18] In the Crimean case, for example, it is hard to tell whether Aberdeen's accommodative preferences and his continued faith in the Russian czar were the result of wishful thinking, the prime minister's soft-line beliefs, or both.

This example raises a second—theoretical—difficulty. Existing applications of the concept of motivated bias to crisis decision making predict that domestically vulnerable actors will pursue confrontational, not conciliatory, policies. In theory, however, national leaders could also be motivated by their domestic insecurities to believe that their opponents want compromise. They could wishfully think that their own strategy has succeeded in influencing the adversary, who will now concede. This reasoning prevents the generation of determinate predictions about the behavior of domestically vulnerable actors.

Finally, motivated misperception is not as common as the literature suggests. Among the cases in this study, there is only limited empirical evidence of the pathologies predicted by a decisional conflict approach, and domestically vulnerable states sometimes respond cooperatively to initially coercive bargaining tactics. Lord Clarendon, Théophile Delcassé, and Nikita Khrushchev were all domestically vulnerable leaders at the time international crisis enveloped their governments. All three national leaders should have exhibited similar behavior, but motivational psychology cannot explain cases like Fashoda, in which Delcassé capitulated despite his own and his government's extreme vulnerability. Although Clarendon did not back down in the Crimean War crisis, there is no evidence that motivated bias led him to defy Russian threats or ignore Russian concessions. In fact, the British foreign minister clearly recog-

17. Robert Jervis, "Political Implications of Loss Aversion," *Political Psychology* 13, no. 2 (1992), 194.

18. See Jervis, *Perception and Misperception*, esp. 120–22; Lebow, *Between Peace and War*, 111–19; Stein, "Deterrence and Reassurance"; and Philip Tetlock and Ariel Levi, "Attribution Bias: On the Inconclusiveness of the Cognition-Motivation Debate," *Journal of Experimental Social Psychology* 18, no. 1 (January 1982): 68–88.

nized Russian overtures in the latter part of the crisis, was aware of the consequences of his own actions, and consciously chose to escalate the crisis for domestic political reasons. Khrushchev's public statements in the Berlin crisis are also not entirely consistent with the predictions of decisional conflict theory. Though the Soviet leader responded to U.S. threats in the second phase of the crisis with new threats of his own, it is not clear that he was engaging in defensive avoidance. Many of Khrushchev's statements continued to describe U.S. leaders as "realists" who were forced reluctantly to a more coercive stance. Nevertheless, Khrushchev may have engaged in wishful thinking by exaggerating the willingness of the United States to compromise.

While historians frequently cite domestic political factors as prominent causes of war, these factors are consistently ignored by political scientists' analyses of crisis bargaining.[19] Motivational psychology, despite its shortcomings, attempts to close this gap between history and theory. Bureaucratic politics theory, an approach that moves beyond the impact of domestic factors on perceptions and allows an independent causal role for domestic political incentives, remedies some of the problems facing decisional conflict theory.

Bureaucratic Politics
Early students of bureaucratic politics recognized that a state's foreign policy influenced another state through its impact on the domestic political process. However, the theory's focus on the influence of a decision-maker's role or position on his or her attitudes and policy preferences masks its two most predictively accurate and prescriptively useful propositions—that individual decision makers are driven by domestic political imperatives and that the process of coalition building influences the content of a state's foreign policy.[20]

Bureaucratic politics theory provides a persuasive motivation for individuals' actions similar to that pointed to by decisional conflict theorists. What Glenn H. Snyder and Paul Diesing refer to as the "rational component" of bureaucratic politics theory describes the domestic imperatives faced by national leaders who are attempting to forge a policy response during an international conflict: "Any politician who wishes to participate in public action is thus faced with the imperative of maintaining or increasing his power, authority, influence. . . . This is a rational

---

19. Jack S. Levy makes a similar criticism in "Domestic Politics and War," *Journal of Interdisciplinary History* 18, no. 4 (spring 1988): 653–73.

20. Allison, *Essence of Decision*; Robert J. Art, "Bureaucratic Politics and American Foreign Policy: A Critique," *Policy Sciences* 4 (1973): 467–90.

imperative in the sense that it is a prerequisite for any participation in government."[21] Indeed, international crises are "two-level games" or "nested games" in which decision makers face both domestic and international audiences for their policy choices.[22]

For this reason, state A's bargaining strategy influences state B's by changing the incentives and power resources of B's key domestic actors. Unlike a motivated bias approach, in which the value conflicts of policy makers unconsciously impair their information-processing skills, a bureaucratic approach predicts that leaders consciously change their policy stance in response to a changed domestic environment. For example, Evangelista has found that U.S.-Soviet disarmament negotiations in the 1950s failed not because U.S. leaders misperceived Soviet intentions but because they refused to compromise for domestic political reasons.[23] In the Crimean crisis, the British foreign minister also responded primarily to domestic incentives when shaping his policy stance. Clarendon clearly recognized Russian overtures in the second phase of the conflict and consciously rejected them for domestic political reasons.

The second proposition of bureaucratic politics theory holds that the process of domestic bargaining and compromise influences the content of a state's foreign policy. Graham Allison and Morton H. Halperin have argued that nation A's foreign policy will influence nation B in the desired direction when the strategy increases the influence of those members of nation B who already want to cooperate.[24] The international environment affects foreign policy by influencing domestic coalitions. Jeff Frieden argues, for instance, that the destruction of overseas competition in the 1930s increased the influence of internationalist elements within the United States, leading to a more open foreign economic policy after World War II.[25]

The ultimate influence of external factors on domestic politics oc-

---

21. Snyder and Diesing, *Conflict among Nations*, 354.

22. Putnam, "Diplomacy and Domestic Politics"; George Tsebelis, *Nested Games: Rational Choice in Comparative Politics* (Berkeley: University of California Press, 1990).

23. "Cooperation Theory and Disarmament Negotiations."

24. "Bureaucratic Politics: A Paradigm and Some Policy Implications," in Raymond Tanter and Richard H. Ullman, eds., *Theory and Policy in International Relations* (Princeton: Princeton University Press, 1972), esp. 65; Morton H. Halperin, *Bureaucratic Politics and Foreign Policy* (Washington, DC: Brookings, 1974), 102.

25. "Sectoral Conflict and U.S. Foreign Economic Policy, 1914–1940," *International Organization* 42, no. 1 (winter 1988): 59–90. For related arguments, see Peter Gourevitch, *Politics in Hard Times: Comparative Responses to International Economic Crises* (Ithaca: Cornell University Press, 1986); and Thomas Risse-Kappen, "Did 'Peace Through Strength' End the Cold War? Lessons from the INF," *International Security* 16, no. 1 (summer 1991): 162–88.

curs when one state's behavior precipitates a change of government within the opposing state. In his study of the lessons of strategic bombing, Ernest R. May finds that the bombing of Italy and Japan in World War II and Korea in the 1950s "worked relatively little change in the positions or attitudes of individuals. . . . What was crucial in each case was not changes of heart but the fact that events brought into power men not committed to the earlier course of action."[26] One state's bargaining strategy influenced another's policy response by increasing the power of those already inclined to compromise.

During an international crisis, the injunction to influence the domestic process in the adversary's government translates into a requirement to weaken hard-liners and strengthen soft-liners.[27] By forging a bargaining strategy that encourages the formation of a "grand majority" or "majority coalition" favoring compromise, a state can prevent its own diplomatic defeat or the escalation of the crisis to war.[28]

Bureaucratic politics theory's emphasis on coalition building explains some of the puzzles left by structural, cognitive, and motivated bias approaches. Decision-makers' policy preferences sometimes diverge from their preexisting beliefs because of the domestic constraints and opportunities created by an adversary's behavior. Yet two problems remain. First, bureaucratic politics theory cannot provide determinate predictions about the interaction of strategy and domestic coalitions. Theoretically, one state's coercive strategy may strengthen the domestic position of hard-liners within the adversary's government by demonstrating aggressiveness, and conciliatory moves may strengthen soft-liners because the tactics show a willingness to compromise. The opposite is equally logical, however: by compelling a nation to concede, a coercive strategy may strengthen soft-liners, and conciliatory moves may strengthen hard-liners, who may demand further concessions. Determining the direction of influence requires knowledge of the domestic balance of power between hard-liners and soft-liners.

Second, existing bureaucratic approaches cannot explain why the effects of domestic politics are so visible in some cases, like Victorian England, and largely absent in others, such as czarist Russia, or why domestic pressures operate differently in the United States than in other democracies, like France or Britain. The answers to these questions lie in the organization of decision-making authority within the state.

---

26. *"Lessons" of the Past* (New York: Oxford University Press, 1973), chap. 5, quote at 130–31.

27. Snyder and Diesing, *Conflict among Nations*, 516.

28. See Charles E. Lindblom, *Politics and Markets* (New York: Basic Books, 1977); and Snyder and Diesing, *Conflict among Nations*, 349–50.

The Argument: State Structure and the
Decision-Making Process

Cognitive psychology and bureaucratic politics theory provide powerful hypotheses on the relationship between bargaining behavior and the outcome of international crises. However, neither approach alone explains the decision-making process in the three crises examined. There are clearly some cases, such as nineteenth-century Russia, in which a single decision maker, such as the czar, formulates a policy based on his or her own beliefs; in others, such as the case of Britain in the Crimean and Fashoda crises, policy is a product of domestic coalition building. These states are distinguished by their different institutional structures.

State Strength

Domestic structural explanations focus on the influence of national political institutions and societal factors on foreign policy. The most prevalent structural approach in the political economy literature examines "state strength," the degree to which power is dispersed among governmental institutions and the extent of control that the state exercises over society.[29] One argument about state strength compares the links between state and society in the United States and France. Decision making within the distinctively weak United States is a product of a decentralized state infiltrated by private actors. The stronger French state is characterized by a more highly centralized state apparatus dominating a decentralized private sector, has access to more policy instruments, and exhibits a greater capacity to implement its policy preferences.[30]

Critics assail this argument's reliance on a single, undifferentiated conception of state structure. They persuasively argue that the U.S. state has significantly greater autonomy in some arenas and that France

29. See Peter Hall, *Governing the Economy: The Politics of State Intervention in Britain and France* (New York: Oxford University Press, 1986); Katzenstein, *Between Power and Plenty*; Peter J. Katzenstein, "International Relations and Domestic Structures: Foreign Economic Policies of Advanced Industrial States," *International Organization* 30, no. 1 (winter 1976): 1–45; Krasner, *Defending the National Interest*; and Eric A. Nordlinger, *On the Autonomy of the Democratic State* (Cambridge: Harvard University Press, 1981).

30. In Katzenstein, *Between Power and Plenty*, see Peter J. Katzenstein, "Conclusion: Domestic Structures and Strategies of Foreign Economic Policy"; Stephen D. Krasner, "United States Commercial and Monetary Policy: Unravelling the Paradox of External Strength and Internal Weakness"; and John Zysman, "The French State in the International Economy." Also see Nordlinger, *On the Autonomy of the Democratic State*, 104–5; and Risse-Kappen, "Public Opinion."

is not immune to societal preferences. In other words, the overall domestic political structures of the United States and France may not be so different.[31]

Instead, the capacity of each state to make decisions and implement policy varies across issue areas. For example, Michael Mastanduno argues that different institutional settings within the United States explain different policy outcomes in three areas of U.S. industrial policy during the 1980s.[32] As many students of state structure argue, it is necessary to examine state power within a specific arena. The same state that enjoys significant autonomy in forging monetary policy may be highly constrained in its ability to develop and implement a unified industrial policy. In what follows, I examine one issue area—decision making in severe foreign policy crises—usually thought to be immune from the effects of domestic politics.

The Organization of Foreign Policy Authority

A state's ability to respond in an international crisis depends on the organization of foreign policy-making authority, measured across two dimensions.[33] First, the ability of the state to respond in a conflict depends on the *structure of the foreign policy executive.* Here, I refer to the number of various offices of the state that have responsibility for making foreign policy during a crisis. The greater the number of government offices with decision-making authority, the more "diffuse" the

---

31. G. John Ikenberry, "The Irony of State Strength: Comparative Responses to the Oil Shocks in the 1970s," *International Organization* 40, no. 1 (winter 1986); Ikenberry, Lake, and Mastanduno, *The State and American Foreign Economic Policy*; Helen Milner, *Resisting Protectionism: Global Industries and the Politics of International Trade* (Princeton: Princeton University Press, 1988); Ezra Suleiman, *Private Power and Centralization in France: The Notaires and the State* (Princeton: Princeton University Press, 1987), chap. 14.

32. "Do Relative Gains Matter? America's Response to Japanese Industrial Policy," *International Security* 16, no. 1 (summer 1991): 73–113. Also see Michael M. Atkinson and William D. Coleman, "Strong States and Weak States: Sectoral Policy Networks in Advanced Capitalist Economies," *British Journal of Political Science* 19 (1989): 47–67; and Krasner, "United States Commercial and Monetary Policy."

33. For related arguments, see Andrew Philip Cortell, "Industry and State: Institutional Constraints on Industrial Policy in the United States" (paper presented to the American Political Science Association, Chicago, September 1992); Peter Hall, "Policy Innovation and the Structure of the State: The Politics-Administration Nexus in France and Britain," *Annals of the American Academy of Political and Social Science* 466 (March 1983): 43–59; David Lake, *Power, Protection, and Free Trade: International Sources of U.S. Commercial Strategy, 1887–1939* (Ithaca: Cornell University Press, 1988); and John Zysman, *Governments, Markets, and Growth: Financial Systems and the Politics of Industrial Change* (Ithaca: Cornell University Press, 1983).

decision-making structure and the less freedom of action enjoyed by the chief executive.[34]

For example, a unitary executive ruled nineteenth-century Russia. A coterie of advisors surrounded the Russian czar, but Nicholas I alone determined the course of Russian foreign policy. Ironically, the U.S. executive is also largely a unitary actor when it comes to crisis decision making. While large numbers of agencies and bureaucracies populate the executive branch of the U.S. government, leading to its usual characterization as weak and decentralized, postwar U.S. presidents have enjoyed a remarkable degree of freedom in the international arena. Although the president may seek advice from his staff, his cabinet officers, or the National Security Council, ultimate authority within the executive branch rests within the office of the president. A relatively unitary executive, albeit one seriously constrained by Parliament, also shaped foreign policy in the Third French Republic. While collective cabinet decision making characterized the overall executive element of the government, the minister of foreign affairs typically enjoyed significant, but not total, freedom of action in foreign policy making.

Decision making in foreign policy crises was diffuse in three of the states examined in this study. A multitude of cabinet ministers collectively determined British policy in the nineteenth century. Foreign policy was no exception: prior to both the Crimean and Fashoda conflicts, the individual heads of various cabinet-level departments actively participated in the policy-making process. The Soviet Union, in contrast, is commonly viewed as a highly centralized state with a unitary leader.[35] In one important respect, however, leadership politics within the Communist Party—the Politburo and the Secretariat of the Central Committee—more closely resembled the cabinet politics of nineteenth-century Britain than it resembled the distribution of juridical authority in the Soviet Union's predecessor state, czarist Russia. In the post-Stalinist era, although a single dictator continued to rule the Soviet Union, the structure of the Soviet state required that this individual seek the support of his colleagues in the Party leadership. Decision making within this group reflected the diffuse interests of its fifteen to twenty-five members. Although the Soviet foreign policy-making process was less collective than that of Victorian Britain, the Soviet leader of the 1950s was not a unitary executive.

---

34. On this point, see Hall, "Policy Innovation," 46; Katzenstein, "Conclusion"; and Stephen Skowronek, *Building a New American State: The Expansion of National Administrative Capacities 1877–1920* (Cambridge: Cambridge University Press, 1982), 20.

35. For example, see Evangelista, *Innovation and the Arms Race.*

Juridical authority for foreign policy making was shared, if unequally, among members of the Party elite.[36]

A second element, the *degree of executive autonomy from the legislature*, also defines the organization of foreign policy authority. The greater the executive's autonomy, the less control the legislature can exert over the content of a state's foreign policy during an international crisis. A national legislature may exert control in two related ways.[37] First, in theory the legislature may possess the authority to make policy during a crisis. In the six cases studied, however, the legislature did not possess such authority. The American case is illustrative. The congressional authority to declare war, which is specifically granted by the U.S. Constitution, gives the legislature the potential to control executive action during a conflict. In practice, however, Congress largely abdicated its foreign policy-making powers in pre-Vietnam era conflicts.[38] Second, and more likely, the executive may be responsible to and dependent on the representative branch for its tenure in office, as was true in the nineteenth-century British and French parliamentary systems.

A foreign policy executive that is not constrained by legislative activity is considered "autonomous." The governments of Russia and the Soviet Union, for example, enjoyed significant autonomy in both respects from any representative element of government. Even in the Soviet Union, where a national legislature existed, the legislative body neither possessed foreign policy-making powers nor held the survival of the government in its hands.

As the most representative element of the national government, the legislative body serves as a conduit for societal pressures on the executive. The less autonomy the chief executive enjoys from the legislature, the greater role interest groups, political parties, and public opinion may play in the decision-making process. When the representative branch plays a role in decision making in a crisis—either directly, through policy

---

36. On the process of political struggle within the Politburo, see George W. Breslauer, *Khrushchev and Brezhnev as Leaders: Building Authority in Soviet Politics* (London: Allen & Unwin, 1982); Harry Gelman, *The Brezhnev Politburo and the Decline of Detente* (Ithaca: Cornell University Press, 1984); Carl Linden, *Khrushchev and the Soviet Leadership: 1957–1964* (Baltimore: Johns Hopkins University Press, 1966); Sidney Ploss, *Conflict and Decision-Making in Soviet Russia* (Princeton: Princeton University Press, 1965); Snyder, *Myths of Empire*, chap. 6; and Michel Tatu, *Power in the Kremlin*, trans. Helen Katel (London: Collins, 1969).

37. I am grateful to Andrew Cortell for pointing out this distinction.

38. Cecil V. Crabb, Jr., and Pat M. Holt, *Invitation to Struggle: Congress, the President, and Foreign Policy*, 3d ed. (Washington, D.C.: Congressional Quarterly Press, 1989), chap. 5.

making, or indirectly, by determining the survival of the government—other domestic actors become important.

Some students of domestic institutions may find my analysis of state structure too narrow for either of two reasons. First, many studies of foreign economic policy seek to measure the degree of state autonomy vis-à-vis society more directly than I do.[39] In the area of crisis decision making, however, I argue that private actors can only exercise binding influence through a national legislature. Since, by definition, crises are characterized by a shortened decision frame and a heightened threat to the national interest, decision making is restricted to a relatively small group of people regardless of state structure. This allows societal groups fewer points of access to the state. While not all states are strong states simply because national security is at stake, the nature of an international crisis precludes the large-scale participation of private actors that may occur in other issue areas. To the extent that other issue areas share the characteristics of crisis decision making—particularly the perception of time constraints and heightened threat—my conception of state structure may also provide an appropriate measure of the state's ability to act in those areas.

Both issues—whether there are additional avenues for societal influence during a crisis and whether my argument is generalizable to other issue areas—are empirical questions.[40] Many observers of international negotiation contend that national leaders must win ratification from domestic constituents for an international agreement.[41] However, these arguments fail to clarify which groups matter or when and how they influence policy making. I present a falsifiable argument on how such groups enter the decision-making process and in what kinds of states they exercise greatest influence.

A second objection to my use of state structure might be that it neglects the role of social norms or political culture.[42] Both the social consensus for containment shared by U.S. elites during the 1950s and the social legitimacy that the Orthodox Church bestowed on the czarist government in the nineteenth century set the bounds for state action.

---

39. Atkinson and Coleman, "Strong States and Weak States"; Cortell, "Industry and State"; Katzenstein, "Conclusion." For an argument that political economy models of state autonomy may not be useful for studying national security issues, see Matthew Evangelista, "Issue-Area and Foreign Policy Revisited," *International Organization* 43, no. 1 (winter 1989), 152.

40. Thanks to John Odell for his comments on this point.

41. Putnam, "Diplomacy and Domestic Politics"; Evans, Jacobson, and Putnam, *Double-Edged Diplomacy*.

42. For works that include these "soft" dimensions of domestic structure, see Katzenstein and Okawara, "Japan's National Security"; and Risse-Kappen, "Ideas Do Not Float Freely."

The role of social norms can be subsumed within existing definitions of state structure, including my own. If political culture is unique to a specific country and if it is causally important, it will shape the institutions of the state; that is, the political culture will be reflected in the state's political institutions and in the quasi-juridical rules that govern relations between state and societal actors.[43] Determining the organization of foreign policy authority gives concrete form to a potentially slippery concept: if social norms are important, they should limit the autonomy of decision makers through their influence on the institutions of the state.

Together, these two variables—the structure of the executive and the degree of executive autonomy from the legislature—constitute a single measure of the organization of authority for crisis decision making. Table 1 summarizes the coding of the six states examined.

A few final caveats about these variables are necessary. First, it is possible and (as I argue later in this chapter, in the discussion of this study's methodology) necessary to measure both variables prior to and independently of a state's behavior during a crisis and the outcome of the conflict. Second, both variables are more accurately measured along continua, although for simplicity I often discuss them as dichotomous variables. Finally, while it is possible to determine the organization of decision-making authority in any given period, these elements of state structure are not fixed. A comparison of the two British cases, for example, reveals that electoral reform, the development of a stronger party system, and the transition from a "parliamentary system" to a "cabinet system" intervened between the 1852–54 Crimean War crisis and the 1898 Fashoda crisis. As a result of these changes, the British cabinet was no longer entirely dependent on Parliament for its tenure. The more disciplined the parties became and the more strongly they could influence members' votes, the less powerful an influence Parliament could exert.[44] Similarly, the U.S. president enjoyed far more autonomy in 1958–61 than he does today. Executive-legislative relations changed significantly following the 1965 escalation of the U.S. war in Vietnam. By the time of the passage of the War Powers Resolution in 1973 over President Nixon's veto, the United States had entered a new period in relations between the White House and Capitol Hill. Congress can and does interject itself into current debates on foreign policy during an

43. For a related argument, see Goldstein, *Ideas, Interests, and American Trade Policy*.

44. John P. Mackintosh, *The British Cabinet* (Toronto: University of Toronto Press, 1962). On the tendency of structures to change over time, see G. John Ikenberry, "Conclusion: An Institutional Approach to American Foreign Economic Policy," in Ikenberry, Lake, and Mastanduno, *The State and American Foreign Economic Policy*.

TABLE 1. The Organization of Foreign Policy Authority: Coding the Cases

State and Time Period	Structure of Foreign Executive	Degree of Executive Autonomy
Russia		
1852–54	unitary	autonomous
United States		
1958–61	unitary	autonomous
France		
1898	unitary*	nonautonomous
Soviet Union		
1958–61	diffuse	autonomous
Britain		
1898	diffuse	nonautonomous
Britain		
1852–54	diffuse	nonautonomous

*Note that these are continuous, not dichotomous, variables, and that the French foreign policy executive was not entirely unitary. See the discussion in chap. 4.

international crisis, a role it largely abdicated before Vietnam.[45] I return in chapter 6 to the subject of institutional change.

Hypotheses on the Decision-Making Process

The institutions of the state, specifically the organization of foreign policy authority, determine how national policy is made during a crisis. In general, the more concentrated decision-making authority within the executive element of the government and the greater autonomy the foreign policy executive enjoys from the legislature, the less influence domestic political factors will have on the evolution and outcome of international crises. In short, the structure of executive authority and the extent of legislative oversight determine the explanatory power of cognitive and bureaucratic hypotheses on the bargaining process.

Figure 1 presents specific hypotheses on the process by which crises are resolved in four ideal-type states. I next examine in detail the policy-making process within each of the four types of states. In each section, I introduce specific hypotheses, based on my conception of state structure, about when the predictions of cognitive psychology and bureau-

---

45. For example, see the discussion of the Persian Gulf crisis in Andrew P. Cortell and James W. Davis, Jr., "The Domestic Impact of International Rules and Norms" (paper presented at the annual meeting of the American Political Science Association, New York, September 1994).

Degree of Executive Autonomy from the Legislature
Autonomous   Nonautonomous

	Type I	Type II
Unitary	*cognitive explanation*: the beliefs of a single chief executive determine how the state responds to an opponent's bargaining strategy	*societal constraints*: national policy is formulated by a single chief executive whose preferences reflect public and legislative pressures
Diffuse	Type III *elite coalition building*: the state's response to an opponent's bargaining behavior is determined by intra-elite bargaining	Type IV *elite coalition building subject to societal constraints*: national policy is the outcome of compromise and coalition building among elites whose preferences reflect societal pressures

Structure of the Foreign Policy Executive (left margin label)

Fig. 1. Hypotheses on the bargaining process

cratic politics theory are most useful in explaining a state's policy response during an international crisis. These hypotheses are of two types: first, I present hypotheses on the influence of state structure on the bargaining processes; and second, I offer hypotheses on the ways in which the decision-making process, bargaining strategy, and policy preferences interact to produce policy outcomes.

A Unitary, Autonomous Foreign Policy Elite: The Russian and American Cases

Domestic political forces influence the course of crisis bargaining in all states except those (type I) where a single chief executive has jurisdiction over foreign policy and enjoys near total autonomy from legislative scrutiny. In a unitary, autonomous state, the success or failure of an adversary's bargaining strategy depends on the strategic beliefs of the chief decision maker. In other words, a cognitive explanation is the most compelling. The adversary's strategy interacts with the executive's beliefs to produce the policy response. In the cases in this book, unitary, autonomous executives led two otherwise very different states—nineteenth-century Russia and the twentieth-century United States.

Structure alone does not explain outcome. By identifying the relevant actors and the pressures they face, structural factors predict the channels through which policy is made. In a political system led by a unitary, autonomous executive, few domestic worries besiege the chief policy maker. The primary source of leaders' initial policy preferences is their beliefs about the nature of international politics, the specific adversary they face in a particular conflict, and the appropriate instruments of international influence. The extent to which these preferences are subsequently altered by the constraints and opportunities of the international system depends on the persistence of the belief system. In short, knowing the structure of a state tells us that the decision-making process is cognitive; knowing the beliefs of the relevant actors allows us to predict the state's policy response.[46]

Cognitive explanations of international crises distinguish between hard-liners, who view the international system as inherently conflictual, and soft-liners, who see a more harmonious world characterized by the presence of common interests between states.[47] There are, of course, basic assumptions, or "core" beliefs, shared by most or all members of a policy elite.[48] Within these bounds, decision makers differ on "intermediate" beliefs about the domestic structure and dynamics of the opponent, the adversary's risk propensity, and the requirements for maintaining national security, as well as on "peripheral," or tactical, beliefs about the efficacy of the use of force in international politics.[49] In the United States of the 1950s, for example, the social consensus for containment virtually guaranteed a hostile image of the Soviet Union. Members of the foreign policy elite differed, however, in their estimation of the Soviet Union's willingness to take risks and of the relative efficacy of coercion and negotiation. The argument presented here focuses on differences in tactical and intermediate beliefs. While essential to understanding the ways policy makers interpret the actions of others, the distinction between hard-liners and soft-liners is insufficient to predict the effect a state's bargaining behavior will have on the opponent's policy response.

By definition, hawks are preoccupied with the need to preserve the power position of their state. They believe in the efficacy of force and the threat of its use as means of maintaining peace and national security.

46. For a related argument, see Philip D. Stewart, Margaret G. Hermann, and Charles F. Hermann, "Modelling the 1973 Soviet Decision to Support Egypt," *American Political Science Review* 83, no. 1 (March 1989): 35–59.

47. Jervis, *Perception and Misperception*, chap. 3; Rogers, "Crisis Bargaining Codes and Crisis Management"; Snyder and Diesing, *Conflict among Nations*, 297–310.

48. Douglas W. Blum, "The Soviet Foreign Policy Belief System: Beliefs, Politics, and Foreign Policy Outcomes," *International Studies Quarterly* 37, no. 4 (December 1993): 373–94. Also see George's discussion of "philosophical beliefs" in "The 'Operational Code.'"

49. Blum, "Soviet Foreign Policy Belief System."

Hard-liners' intentions and their images of the adversary vary,[50] and this affects the way they respond to opponents' bargaining behavior. An "opportunist" sees a mirror image opponent, an irresolute state that, if tested incrementally, will retreat. The opportunist's goals are limited to what he or she can obtain without serious conflict, and opportunists are deterred when they meet firm resistance. Of the many decision makers examined in this study, Delcassé best fits this mold. Although a hard-liner advocating expansion when he was colonial secretary, he attempted to use the Fashoda crisis to secure concessions from the British. He gradually learned, however, that the British were not willing to compromise and that he would have to back down.

Decision makers who I call "defensive deterrers," in contrast, have different images of themselves and their opponents. Their own intentions are primarily defensive, and they behave aggressively out of a belief that coercion is the only means of preserving the national interest. Policy makers who hold such beliefs are difficult, if not impossible, to deter, and they rarely or never learn from their opponent's behavior. Palmerston provides the clearest example. His firm advocacy of coercive tactics was based on his belief that the use of force was the only means of preserving Britain's security.[51] The defensive deterrer's image of the opponent is sometimes not so benign. At times, adversaries are aggressive, expansionist, and possessed of unlimited, interdependent goals. In a word, they must be forcefully resisted. Palmerston attributed such intentions to the Russian czar when he proclaimed, "From moderation to moderation he might finish, if one let him have his way, by invading the entire world."[52] At other times, however, the defensive deterrer may see a more opportunistic, less resolute opponent, such as the one in Palmerston's May 1853 assessment of Russia: "[t]he policy and practice of the Russian Government has always been to push its encroachments as fast and as far as the apathy or want of firmness of other Governments would allow it to go, but always to stop and retire when it was met with decided resistance, and then to wait for the next favourable opportunity to make another spring on its intended victim."[53]

Unlike their hawkish colleagues, soft-liners are less concerned with

---

50. For a related discussion, see Snyder's distinction between "aggressive realists" and "defensive realists" in *Myths of Empire*, 11–12.

51. See the discussion of Palmerston's strategic beliefs in Snyder, *Myths of Empire*, esp. 174–80.

52. Quoted in Ann Pottinger Saab, *The Origins of the Crimean Alliance* (Charlottesville: University Press of Virginia, 1977), 8.

53. Evelyn Ashley, *The Life and Correspondence of Henry John Temple, Viscount Palmerston*, 2 vols. (London: Richard Bentley & Son, 1879), 2:273.

national power than with the peace and stability of the international system. They advocate accommodation and compromise. The dove's image of the opponent is largely that described by cooperation theory—a state that pursues limited, specific, independent, and legitimate goals. Accommodating these demands is therefore the most effective means of resolving conflict.

Soft-liners' faith in the efficacy of force as an instrument of diplomacy may vary dramatically, however, depending on the rigidity of their beliefs. At one extreme, "unconditional compromisers" may view themselves as too weak to coerce the opponent and will nearly always advocate accommodation. Unconditionally conciliatory bargainers maintain that answering coercion always leads to escalation and war, and they rarely or never adjust their images in response to an opponent's behavior. Prime Minister Aberdeen's belief in the good intentions of Czar Nicholas I on the eve of the Crimean War never faltered, for example, despite coercive Russian behavior.

In contrast, the "contingent compromiser" prefers accommodation to confrontation but believes in the limited use of force when necessary. He ceases to cooperate if early offers prove unsuccessful in eliciting concessions from the other state.[54] The dovish British prime minister during the Fashoda conflict provides the best example. In a series of foreign policy crises in the late nineteenth century, Salisbury demonstrated his ability to learn from his opponent's behavior, resorting to coercion when he felt it necessary to protect Britain's vital interests.

While the structure of decision-making authority in a unitary, autonomous state determines that the chief executive is responsible for decision making in a crisis, the content and rigidity of the leader's beliefs explain how the state responds to its opponent's bargaining behavior. The initially coercive strategy prescribed by deterrence theory is based on an assumption that the adversary is a hard-line opportunist who infers from early coercion that his opponent is resolved to stand firm and from early concessions that the adversary is weak willed. Such a strategy fails against defensive deterrers, as well as against contingent cooperators.[55] For very different reasons, each infers from early coercion that the adversary is hostile.

The initially conciliatory strategy prescribed by cooperation theory, in contrast, is premised on the assumption that the opponent is a contin-

---

54. Unconditional compromisers are irrational bargainers, according to Snyder and Diesing's scheme, while contingent compromisers are rational soft-liners. See *Conflict among Nations*, 333–39.

55. Nearly any strategy would succeed against an unconditional soft-liner, such as Aberdeen.

gent cooperator who infers from early concessions that his or her adversary is reasonable and trustworthy. While it succeeds against soft-liners, an initially nice strategy fails against a hard-line opponent, who takes early concessions as a sign of weakness and irresolution.

In the Crimean War crisis, British strategy influenced Russian policy by interacting with the beliefs of the chief executive, Czar Nicholas I. Because he possessed sole jurisdiction over foreign policy, subject to the recommendations of his foreign minister and other advisors but not to legislative control, Nicholas I was unencumbered by domestic constraints. While domestic rivalries existed, the autocratic state allowed Nicholas I to listen to debates among his advisors or not as he chose.[56] His initial hard-line (defensive deterrer) beliefs were confirmed by the early British response. Indeed, London's restraint gave Nicholas I "cause to hope that we shall be able to advance in the way I laid down for myself."[57] By the time British warnings penetrated his hawkish worldview, the crisis had progressed too far.

Ironically, the organization of decision-making authority in the United States in the 1950s bears a greater resemblance on the issue of executive autonomy to czarist Russia than to the other democracies in this study. Because the U.S. Constitution specifically delegates remarkably few foreign policy powers to either Congress or the president, that document has been described as an "invitation to struggle" over foreign policy.[58] The unitary structure and the relative autonomy of foreign policy-making power reflected in the creation of the "imperial presidency"[59] was thus the product of tradition and consensus as much as constitutional mandate. Prior to the Berlin crisis and until the U.S. war in Vietnam, Congress largely surrendered its ambiguous responsibility for general foreign policy and especially acquiesced in presidential initiative during international crises. Although presidents frequently informed the congressional leadership of their intentions, there was rarely a need for a president to seek prior congressional approval for his actions.[60] Within

---

56. On domestic dissent, see Harold N. Ingle, *Nesselrode and the Russian Rapprochement with Britain, 1836–1844* (Berkeley: University of California Press, 1976), esp. 26–27.

57. Vernon John Puryear, *England, Russia, and the Straits Question 1844–1856* (Hamden, CT: Archon Books, 1931; reprint, 1965), 233.

58. Edward S. Corwin, *The President: Office and Powers 1787–1957* (New York: New York University Press, 1957), 171; Crabb and Holt, *Invitation to Struggle*.

59. Arthur M. Schlesinger, Jr., *The Imperial Presidency* (Boston: Houghton Mifflin, 1973).

60. Frans R. Bax describes 1953–66 as "the period of congressional acquiescence." See "The Legislative-Executive Relationship in Foreign Policy: New Partnership or New Competition?" *Orbis* 20 (winter 1977): 881–904.

the executive branch, foreign policy authority was and remains concentrated in the office of the president. Though he was no czar, the American president of the 1950s and before was largely unencumbered in his foreign policy role by the political pressures that often characterized the domestic policy-making process.[61]

Domestic rivalries played a far greater role in the United States than in Russia. As I demonstrate in chapter 5, there were considerable differences within the Eisenhower and Kennedy administrations. Because of other obvious differences between American and Russian societies, these factions had a much larger impact on the American presidents than on the Russian czar. Nevertheless, because the structure of the American state was that of a relatively unitary and autonomous executive, U.S. policy consistently reflected the preferences of the president. Indeed, even though U.S. leaders were democratically elected and the state was weak relative to its own society in overall terms, the United States was a strong state in crisis decision making.

In the Berlin crisis, the United States responded accommodatively to Soviet restraint in the months following the November 1958 ultimatum. While there was significant disagreement between hard-line and soft-line elements of the U.S. government, early U.S. policy reflected Eisenhower's relatively moderate tactical beliefs. The major shift in policy occurred only in 1961, when Kennedy assumed office. This shift to a more coercive strategy resulted primarily from a change of leadership, not from a change in domestic incentives facing the U.S. leadership.

Though the U.S. and Russian political systems differed in virtually every other respect, on the crucial variables—the organization of executive authority and the degree of executive autonomy from a national legislature—they were similar enough to suggest a comparison. A nuanced cognitive approach that examines actors' intentions and their images of the adversary best explains decision making in these two unitary, autonomous states. The bargaining process is primarily cognitive; elites learn. The adversary's strategy interacts with a chief executive's beliefs to determine the outcome of a crisis.

A Diffuse, Nonautonomous Executive:
The British Cases

Domestic political factors have the greatest influence on crisis bargaining when the foreign policy executive is composed of a number of different offices that share responsibility for foreign policy making and when

61. On the strength of the U.S. executive, especially vis-à-vis the British prime minister, see Waltz, *Foreign Policy and Democratic Politics*.

the legislature performs a significant oversight function. In a type IV (diffuse, nonautonomous) state, an adversary's strategy influences both the domestic incentives facing policy makers and the distribution of power among foreign policy elites. In short, both propositions of bureaucratic politics theory apply: national leaders' preferences are shaped by domestic pressures, and the state's policy response is the result of internal bargaining. While national policy reflects the distribution of power among elites, national leaders' preferences reflect the pressures of legislative and public opinion.

Preexisting beliefs about international politics remain an important source of individuals' policy preferences in any type of state, but institutional structures within a type IV state shape the way policy makers define their preferences and the resources they are able to muster in support of their preferred policies. Unable to act alone in the nation's name, individual policy makers must be cognizant of their domestic opponents, who may appeal directly to the people. Interest groups, political parties, the media, and public opinion enter the policy-making process because the foreign policy executive is responsible to a national legislature and, even if indirectly, to the public.

Because many executive offices participate in foreign policy making, even the most powerful leaders in a type IV state must build a coalition in support of their preferred policy. While existing bureaucratic explanations note the importance of compromise and coalition formation, they cannot predict how the content of an opponent's strategy affects this coalition-building process. To do so, we must again consider the preferences of the members of the foreign policy executive.

Whether the government is headed by soft-liners or hard-liners determines whether a state responds accommodatively or coercively to the bargaining behavior of another state.[62] A wise strategy aims to shift the distribution of power within the opposing government in order to bring the most moderate leaders into power and secure a cooperative resolution of the conflict. Regardless of the type of government or the political

62. The following discussion and hypotheses are based on Jack Snyder, "International Leverage on Soviet Domestic Change," *World Politics* 42, no. 1 (October 1989): 1–30, in which the author argues that a hostile international environment promotes militaristic, imperialist, or protectionist domestic coalitions and undermines liberal, free-trade regimes; and on Ronald Rogowski, *Commerce and Coalitions* (Princeton: Princeton University Press, 1989), in which the author argues that an increase in free trade leads owners of locally abundant factors to become more politically assertive. In addition, see Charles Glaser, *Analyzing Strategic Nuclear Policy* (Princeton: Princeton University Press, 1990), 81–82; Glaser, "Political Consequences of Military Strategy"; Snyder, "The Gorbachev Revolution," esp. 130–31; and Snyder and Diesing, *Conflict among Nations*, 522.

ideology of a type IV state, initially coercive strategies undermine the faction directing policy—whether hard-line or soft-line—and support the opposing faction. Conversely, an initially conciliatory strategy strengthens the influence of the ruling coalition—whether hard-line or soft-line—and undercuts the opposition's arguments. In short, the appropriate strategy to pursue in order to empower relative moderates and encourage compromise depends on the nature of the ruling coalition.

At the time of the Crimean and Fashoda crises, the British cabinet made all major foreign policy decisions. This process involved many different executive offices and officeholders. Both Aberdeen and Salisbury headed coalition governments in which policy reflected the balance of political power within the cabinet. In neither crisis did the executive enjoy significant autonomy from the legislative branch, since the government's tenure depended on the maintenance of majority support within Parliament. Individual decision makers in both periods faced strong domestic incentives, and coalition politics prevailed. Russian coercion undermined the conciliatory Aberdeen government in Britain in 1853–54 and shifted the domestic balance of power in favor of coercion. Delcassé's uncompromising colonial policy similarly weakened the softline Salisbury and prevented compromise over Fashoda nearly fifty years later. The British prime minister alone could not dictate foreign policy in either case.

As the two nineteenth-century British cases demonstrate, a nuanced coalition approach that considers the preferences of foreign policy elites and the balance of power among them best explains decision making in diffuse, nonautonomous states. The institutions of the state shape the way national leaders formulate their preferences by allowing societal actors a voice in the process. State structure also determines that policy will be the outcome of domestic bargaining and coalition building. The opponent's bargaining strategy interacts with this internal process to produce the policy response and, ultimately, the outcome of the conflict.

Diffuse, Autonomous Elites: The Soviet Union
Decision making within type III (diffuse, autonomous) states resembles that within type IV states: an internal process of coalition building and compromise produces national policy during a crisis. A state's bargaining strategy influences the distribution of power between advocates of coercion and accommodation in the opposing state. Initial coercion undermines a government's support, while initial concessions reinforce the arguments of the ruling coalition.

Type III decision making differs in one fundamental respect from the process within a diffuse, nonautonomous state. Where the executive branch, no matter how diffuse, enjoys significant autonomy from a national legislature, societal constraints do not enter the decision-making process. Members of the foreign policy elite may appeal to various bureaucratic or institutional constituencies if they oppose the government's policy, but a direct appeal to the people or to interest groups, should they even exist, would be ineffective. No representative element of the government exists to channel public opinion or private interests into the policy-making process during a crisis.

In the Soviet Union, a type III state, the general secretary of the Communist Party headed a large, highly centralized bureaucracy but also shared foreign policy authority with the other members of the Presidium and the Secretariat. Harry Gelman and others have referred to the upper echelons of party leadership in the Soviet Union as a kind of "oligarchy." As in any state with a diffuse foreign policy executive, different members of this elite possessed greater or lesser power depending on personal prestige or institutional resources, but the structure of the state allowed them to participate in foreign policy making. As Gelman concludes, the Politburo was a "battleground" among the oligarchs for control of the national bureaucracy.[63] Such a diffuse executive structure necessitated coalition building. While the Soviet state resembled nineteenth-century Britain in this regard, unlike the British cabinet the Soviet oligarchy enjoyed significant autonomy from a largely symbolic representative body. Khrushchev had to guard his flank against elite opposition, but he did not face the kind of public and media opposition that the two British governments had faced.

As in a type IV state, the key determinant of the success or failure of an opponent's bargaining strategy in influencing the policy response of a type III state is the orientation of the regime—whether the government is dominated by hard-liners or soft-liners. An initially coercive strategy erodes the credibility of those in power and bolsters that of the opposition. The bargaining behavior of the United States influenced Soviet policy and the outcome of the crisis by influencing the distribution of power in Moscow. Early U.S. restraint reinforced the relatively moderate arguments of the general secretary, but the later shift to coercive diplomacy exacerbated Khrushchev's domestic opposition, provoking an increasingly coercive Soviet response.

Coalition politics prevail in a state where the foreign policy executive encompasses a multitude of different offices. On the issue of crisis

---

63. Gelman, *The Brezhnev Politburo*, chaps. 2–3. While Gelman's focus is on the Brezhnev era, his general view of the structure of the Soviet state is confirmed by the other works cited in note 36 in this chapter.

decision making, Khrushchev's position differed from that of nineteenth-century British leaders only in that he faced little or no societal pressures, since the Soviet Union lacked an effective national legislature.

A Unitary, Nonautonomous Executive:
The Third Republic
Although the unitary nature of executive decision making precludes the need for large-scale coalition building in a unitary, nonautonomous (type II) state, the chief executive cannot ignore the domestic imperative created by the executive-legislative relationship. Thus, while state structure dictates that a single executive formulates foreign policy, it also means that private interests will penetrate the state apparatus via the representative element of government. The chief executive's policy preferences in a type II state like the Third French Republic therefore reflect not only his or her preexisting beliefs, as cognitive psychology predicts, but also the pressures exerted by political parties, interest groups, public opinion, and the legislature.

Like the British cases, the Third Republic in France was a parliamentary democracy in which the executive was responsible to the lawmaking body. However, the minister of foreign affairs typically enjoyed a large degree of freedom in foreign policy. Governments under the Third Republic often were very weak and dependent on elite coalition building to make domestic policy and, indeed, to keep the government in office. However, there was little or no need for coalition building in the area of foreign policy; all French foreign ministers possessed remarkable, if not complete, autonomy from the rest of the cabinet. Additionally, the *Quai d'Orsay* enjoyed some small measure of stability in a period of governmental instability: the seventy different French governments formed during the Third Republic included only thirty-seven different foreign ministers.[64]

As in Khrushchev's type III Soviet state, crisis decision making in type II states, such as France under the Third Republic, is a hybrid case. Because he ruled within a diffuse state structure, Khrushchev faced domestic political (but not societal) pressures and the need to build a coalition in support of his policy. An adversary's bargaining strategy influences a type II state differently: the opponent's policy affects a state with a national legislature but a unitary foreign policy executive by influencing the domestic incentives of the chief executive. An initially

---

64. Frederick L. Schuman, *War and Diplomacy in the French Republic* (Chicago: University of Chicago Press, 1931), 29. Also see Mark B. Hayne, "The *Quai d'Orsay* and the Formation of French Foreign Policy in Historical Context," in Robert Aldrich and John Connell, eds., *France in World Politics* (London: Routledge, 1989).

coercive strategy undermines a type II leader, although it does so by increasing the societal pressures to compromise, not by shifting the distribution of power within a ruling coalition as happens in types III and IV states. In type II states, only one tenet of bureaucratic politics theory applies: national leaders are driven by domestic political imperatives.

As foreign minister, Delcassé held the foreign policy reins in the Fashoda crisis. British strategy influenced French actions and the outcome of the conflict through its impact on the foreign minister's preferences. Delcassé knew from the outset of the conflict that Fashoda was within the British colonial sphere and that eventually he would have to withdraw the French mission. In short, Delcassé was a hard-line opportunist who thought he could extract concessions from the British in exchange for Colonel Marchand's withdrawal from Fashoda. Britain's coercive bargaining stance convinced the French foreign minister that he would have to lower his expectations and back down.

Yet Delcassé was not free from domestic pressures. Although public opinion in France did not support war, as it did in Britain, there was a small but vocal and well-organized colonialist minority with a strong base in Parliament that advocated continued resistance and made it increasingly difficult to retreat without gaining at least procedural concessions. Delcassé's fears for the survival of the French government led him to postpone the inevitable concessions to the British while he mollified French colonialists. This policy reflected the domestic constraints under which he labored. While the French foreign minister could not afford to ignore parliamentary and public opinion because of the executive-legislative relationship, the unitary structure of the executive minimized the need for Delcassé to seek the support of a majority of the cabinet.

Two institutional components of the state determine the avenues through which foreign policy is made in all four types of states. The structure of executive decision making and the degree of legislative oversight together determine the usefulness of cognitive and bureaucratic hypotheses in explaining the evolution and outcome of international crises. In all cases, however, it remains necessary to know the strategic beliefs of the key decision makers in order to predict the relationship between bargaining behavior and crisis outcome. Figure 2 summarizes my hypotheses on the bargaining process.

Methodology

In this book, I examine five potentially competing explanations for the success or failure of different sequences of bargaining tactics in resolving international crises: systemic, cognitive, motivated bias, bureaucratic

Type I: unitary, autonomous	⟶	single chief executive; nuanced cognitive approach
Type II: unitary, nonautonomous	⟶	single chief executive subject to societal constraints
Type III: diffuse, autonomous	⟶	elite coalition building
Type IV: diffuse, nonautonomous	⟶	coalition building subject to societal pressures; nuanced bureaucratic approach

Fig. 2. Summary of hypotheses

politics, and my own theory about the impact of state structure on the decision-making process. In chapters 3 through 5, these five explanations are pitted against each other in three case studies of international crisis.

The Variables

The five theories proposed seek to explain the relationship between one state's bargaining strategy and the outcome of a crisis. The key measure of the independent variable, bargaining strategy, is whether the initial move is primarily coercive or conciliatory. For the purposes of this study, "coercion" means using armed strength or the threat to inflict unacceptable damage on the adversary, while "accommodation" refers to a policy aimed at conciliating through the use of concessions.[65] The initial move is the crucial variable because a successful strategy of reciprocity can be initially coercive or conciliatory. Thereafter, it responds in kind to the opponent's moves.

This study has two closely related dependent variables—the particular policy chosen by the state in response to an adversary's actions and the outcome of the conflict. Ultimately, the reason to study the interaction between two states' bargaining behaviors is to be able to explain the outcome of the crisis. However, there is no simple correlation between one side's bargaining strategy and the outcome of the conflict, since the outcome depends on the interaction of both sides' strategies. We should view each crisis as a series of interactions between two states, where the outcome is the final policy response—whether war, compromise, diplo-

---

65. For a list of coercive bargaining moves, see Snyder and Diesing, *Conflict among Nations*, 199–203. On accommodation, or "reassurance," see Lebow and Stein, "Beyond Deterrence"; and Stein, "Deterrence and Reassurance."

matic defeat, or victory. Each of the five theories explains both a state's policy response and the conditions under which different strategies ultimately succeed or fail in resolving crises.

Each explanation proposes different intervening variables that are measured prior to the outbreak of the crisis. The structure of the conflict is measured by examining the balance of capabilities and relative interests of the states at the outset and the ways, if any, in which each changes throughout the crisis as a result of state action. I determine the beliefs of the key decision makers within each state prior to the outbreak of the crisis by examining private and public statements in earlier foreign policy conflicts, preferably with the same state. Like testing a cognitive approach, testing decisional conflict theory requires detailed analysis of decision-makers' perceptions of the opponent throughout the conflict. Finally, within each case study I also determine the structure of decision-making authority prior to, and independent of, a state's behavior during the crisis and the outcome of the conflict. This is achieved by examining constitutional principles, norms, traditions, and government practices in previous foreign policy crises.

Case Selection

I examine three cases of international crises from the nineteenth and twentieth centuries, each involving two major powers. The cases were chosen using two criteria. First, bargaining behavior had to be contingent. For example, I did not consider cases where one party was bent on war from the outset or pursued a unilaterally coercive or conciliatory strategy. Bargaining can rarely influence outcome if one side is committed to war from the start.

Second, those cases selected vary on both the bargaining strategy employed by each side and the ultimate outcome of the conflict. Three cases were chosen, one that escalated to war (Crimea) and two that were resolved short of war. Of the latter two, one ended in mutual compromise (Berlin) and the other in capitulation of one side (Fashoda).

Testing Methods and Findings

Three cases provide many more than three tests of the competing explanations. First, because there are frequently several key decision makers within each state, it is possible to test the various theories on different individuals within the same or different states in the same case. Second, because a crisis consists of a series of interactions between two sides, not just one state's bargaining moves and another's response, each case permits several successive tests of the competing hypotheses. Third, it is possible to test the usefulness of the different approaches across a range of states with different domestic structures.

These tests reveal that international structural or systemic approaches provide only the broadest explanations of the outcome of international crises; international structure tells us nothing about *how* states resolve conflict. A systemic explanation is the most convincing in the Fashoda conflict, but in the Crimea and Berlin cases it provides indeterminate predictions. Although the distribution of bargaining power provides the backdrop for internal and external bargaining during international crises, even the Fashoda case makes clear that states' preferences and intentions are extremely difficult to decipher independent of a state's prestrategic interests.

Motivated bias explanations are the least compelling. The clearest negative evidence comes from British decision making in the Crimean case. Despite the coercive nature of early Russian behavior and the near inevitability of war due to increasingly hostile British public opinion, British leaders recognized Russian efforts to cooperate and some even wished to accept the offers. Although the Cabinet refused the concessions, most members did so consciously and deliberately. The Berlin case produced more ambiguous results. On the one hand, Khrushchev continued to view U.S. leaders as "realists" who wished to cooperate, even while he shifted to a coercive strategy to bolster his weak domestic position. This behavior contradicts motivational psychology's prediction that Khrushchev would overestimate U.S. hostility and believe that escalation was inevitable. On the other hand, Khrushchev may have overestimated his ability to secure American concessions; that is, he may have engaged in wishful thinking.

Alone, neither cognitive psychology nor bureaucratic politics theory can explain the outcome of international crises. Almost without exception, decision makers interpret the actions of others according to their preexisting beliefs, and their initial policy preferences derive largely from their beliefs about the adversary and the nature of international politics. In a case like czarist Russia, the story ends there. In other cases, such as the Soviet Union and Britain, decision makers face pressing domestic incentives, and coalition politics determines the outcome of the conflict.

The tests demonstrate that a state's domestic structures create a set of governing conditions or hypotheses: they define both the incentives facing individual leaders and the process through which national policy is forged. External bargaining strategies interact with the policy-making process, as it is shaped by the organization of decision-making responsibility, to produce the policy response and ultimately the outcome of the conflict. When a chief foreign policy executive enjoys significant autonomy from both the legislative body and other executive offices, cognitive processes explain the outcome. When decision-making authority is dispersed within the executive branch and the executive's overall autonomy from the representative element of the state is limited, coalition politics prevails and actors adjust their preferences throughout the conflict according to the domestic costs and benefits of alternative courses of action.

3

The Crimean War Crisis, 1852–54

The Crimean War has been called "the only perfectly useless modern war that has been waged," "the outcome of a series of misjudgments, misunderstandings and blunders, of stupidity, pride and obstinacy rather than of ill will. More than any great war of modern times, it took place by accident."[1] The diplomatic crisis that preceded the war provides an excellent opportunity to test my theory on the domestic politics of crisis bargaining. This conflict shows the intersection of two bargaining strategies: the initial coercion prescribed by deterrence theory and adopted by Russia, and the initial conciliation prescribed by cooperation theory and employed by Britain.

Historians and observers of the conflict tend to fall into one of two camps, depending on their view of the utility of these two bargaining strategies. Some analysts blame the war on Britain, whose early conciliation "misled the tsar": "Mistaking [British] timidity for acquiescence, if not actual friendliness, the Tsar stumbled head-on into the more resolute will of the English press and public in 1853 and 1854."[2] Others blame the outbreak of war on Russia, whose "diplomacy followed a hard line into an isolated position and unnecessarily created disputes and friction where there should have been none."[3]

This chapter assesses these claims by tracing the impact of each state's bargaining strategy on the perceptions, domestic political situation, and behavior of decision makers in the other state. It argues that these perspectives, whether based on deterrence and cooperation theory

---

1. Sir Robert Morier, quoted in J. A. R. Marriot, *The Eastern Question* (Oxford University Press, 1940), 249; M. S. Anderson, *The Eastern Question 1774–1923: A Study in International Relations* (London: Macmillan, 1966), 132.

2. Saab, *Origins of the Crimean Alliance*, 16; Lawrence Edward Breeze, "British Opinion of Russian Foreign Policy 1841–1871" (Ph.D. diss., University of Missouri, 1960), 131.

3. Charles Emerson Walker, "The Role of Karl Nesselrode in the Formulation and Implementation of Russian Foreign Policy, 1850–1856" (Ph.D. diss., West Virginia University, 1973), 309. On this argument, also see Paul W. Schroeder, *Austria, Great Britain, and the Crimean War: The Destruction of the European Concert* (Ithaca: Cornell University Press, 1972).

or on differing historiographical claims, are too simplistic to explain the process and outcome of the Crimean case. British and Russian policy responses were a function of the nature of the two adversaries—their state structures and the strategic beliefs of their foreign policy elite. In Russia, a type I (unitary, autonomous) state, foreign policy decisions occurred by autocratic fiat. Britain's initial restraint confirmed Czar Nicholas I's preexisting belief that Britain would not resist Russian actions in Constantinople. In contrast, England was a type IV (diffuse, nonautonomous) state in which policy was the product of collective decision making by a cabinet severely constrained by the principle of parliamentary sovereignty. Russian coercion undermined the arguments of the more moderate members of the government, such as Prime Minister Aberdeen and Foreign Secretary Clarendon, and reinforced those of hard-liners like Palmerston and Russell.

Following a brief history of the origins of the conflict, I begin with a review of existing explanations of the Crimean crisis, since my argument about state structure uses some of these approaches as building blocks. The third section of this chapter analyzes the structure of foreign policy authority and the foreign policy orientation of the British and Russian governments, while the remainder of the chapter provides a detailed, chronological account of crisis diplomacy.

The Origins of the Conflict

The conflict over the Holy Places that precipitated the Crimean War was the latest phase in an ongoing struggle between a small Catholic population, protected by France, and thirteen million Greek Orthodox subjects, one-third of the population of the Ottoman Empire, defended by Russia. In the late seventeenth century the sultan issued a *firman* or royal decree granting the Catholics a dominant position in certain churches, a position that was codified in a Franco-Turkish Treaty in 1740. In 1774, however, the *Sublime Porte* (the Ottoman government) also concluded a treaty with Russia granting Greek Orthodox Christians certain rights within the Ottoman Empire and allowing Russia to make representations on their behalf concerning a new church. It was this 1774 Treaty of Kutchuk-Kainardji that led Russian leaders to believe they possessed "a protective right on behalf of the Greek religion in all the Ottoman States, and usage ha[d] extended this protection over the Greeks themselves in their relations with the *Porte* as with foreigners."[4]

---

4. Nesselrode, 1825, quoted in Walker, "Role of Karl Nesselrode," 100. In fact, the treaty referred to a specific church and did not imply any of the guarantees that Russia

By the early nineteenth century, the Ottoman Empire showed signs of strain that might threaten the European balance. In 1825 and 1829, Russian committees recommended restraint, deciding that the benefits of maintaining the Ottoman Empire outweighed the costs of doing so. Although preserving Turkey was Russia's paramount interest, the committee recognized that the fall of the Ottoman Empire might not be preventable.[5] Under the 1833 Treaty of Unkiar Skelessi, Turkey became a Russian ally and was promised full military support in return for an agreement to close the Dardanelles and Bosphorus straits in time of war.

Following the first major Eastern crisis in 1838–39, Czar Nicholas I and his foreign minister, Nesselrode, visited London in 1844 to discuss the crumbling Ottoman Empire. These visits culminated in a series of notes between Russia and Britain, known as the Nesselrode Memorandum, in which both nations agreed to maintain the status quo as long as possible and to open discussions if the empire's fall appeared imminent.[6] This is how things remained until May 1850, when France initiated the demands that ultimately led to the Crimean War.

The 1852 Turkish decision to grant French demands for rights in the Holy Places was the immediate catalyst for the Crimean War crisis. After some vacillation, the *Porte* issued a *firman* to the Catholics nullifying the rights to the Holy Places that had been previously granted to the Greek Orthodox Church. Russian attempts to regain these rights and secure them for the future met stiff British resistance because they threatened the existing balance of power in the region.

Alternative Explanations

International Structure

A structural explanation for the outbreak of the Crimean War has a compelling logic: while Britain and Russia both preferred to preserve the status quo in the East, the slow disintegration of the Ottoman Empire made this impossible. Russia's major goal was to maintain influence

---

eventually sought. For the relevant texts see Great Britain, *Parliamentary Papers, Accounts and Papers, Eastern Papers*, 31 January–12 August 1854, vol. 71, pt. 1, 27–28 (hereinafter *Eastern Papers*).

5. Nicholas discussed the fall and disposition of the Ottoman Empire as early as 1833 and again in 1840. See G. H. Bolsover, "Nicholas I and the Partition of Turkey," *Slavonic and East European Review* 27 (1948): 115–45; and Constantin de Grunwald, *Tsar Nicholas I*, trans. Brigit Patmore (London: Douglas Saunders with Macgibbon & Kee, 1954), 195.

6. For the text of the Nesselrode Memorandum see *Eastern Papers*, vol. 71, pt. 6, 2–4.

in the Ottoman Empire, an area of strategic, commercial, and emotional significance to Russia as the "key to her house."[7] Nicholas I and Nesselrode sought to redress Orthodox (and hence Russian) grievances over the Holy Places and to obtain future guarantees. The British government also sought to protect Britain's economic and strategic interests in the Near East and to prevent a threat to the European balance of power by preventing Russia from dominating the Ottoman Empire. Aberdeen summed up British preferences best when he said, "I believe that [the Ottoman Empire's] preservation, at this moment, is a European necessity. I would, however, endeavour rather to preserve it by peace than by war."[8] British and Russian interests were similar, as Harold Temperley notes, because "Constantinople was the first strategic position in the world, and no Great Power could allow another to possess it. If the sword and shield dropped from the nerveless hands of the Sultan, someone must pick them up."[9]

At first glance, this approach seems to provide a persuasive explanation of the origins of the Crimean War: Russian and British interests in the Ottoman Empire were incompatible. Each power sought to control the Dardanelles Straits or to prevent the other from doing so. To the extent that their interests were compatible and both states agreed on the need to preserve the status quo in the Ottoman Empire, early Russian coercive tactics undermined the potential for cooperation. A second look shows this explanation to be insufficient.

While Russian interests prior to and during the Crimean conflict were formulated by the czar, reconstructing British interests requires understanding the domestic political situation in London. First, different policy makers held different conceptions of what constituted British interests. Most would have agreed with Palmerston's general sentiment when he hailed the sultan as "an ancient ally and old friend and as an important element in the balance of power in Europe."[10] Agreement ended there, however. As I discuss below, British policy makers differed in their perceptions of the relative importance of preventing Russian influence in Constantinople and maintaining European peace. The na-

7. G. H. Bolsover, "Aspects of Russian Foreign Policy, 1815–1914," in Richard Pares and A. J. P. Taylor, eds., *Essays Presented to Sir Lewis Namier* (London: Macmillan, 1956), 340–43.

8. Quoted in Sir Arthur Gordon, *The Earl of Aberdeen* (London: Sampson, Low, Marston, 1893), 237.

9. *England and the Near East: The Crimea* (Hamden, CT: Archon Books, 1964), 4.

10. Quoted in Charles Webster, *The Foreign Policy of Palmerston 1830–1841: Britain, the Liberal Movement, and the Eastern Question*, 2 vols. (London: G. Bell, 1951), 1:279.

ture of cabinet government meant that the national interest was the aggregation of individual policy makers' preferences. Second, several key British decision makers recognized the Russian desire to cooperate and would have continued to advocate a conciliatory stance were it not for the inflamed state of British public opinion; that is, Russian demands were not incompatible with British interests independent of the effects of Russian bargaining tactics on domestic politics in London.

Neither of these points suggests that a structural approach is incorrect. Rather, these arguments reinforce the need to look at the domestic sources of states' preferences. Only because Russia was a unitary, autonomous state can we talk about Nicholas I's preferences and Russian interests interchangeably. British preferences, in contrast, reflected the composite, nonautonomous nature of the British cabinet system.

Motivated Bias

Existing applications of motivational psychology to crisis decision making predict that domestically vulnerable national leaders will overestimate the hostility of their opponent and pursue overly confrontational policies, and that they will overestimate the likelihood that their own strategy has succeeded. The Aberdeen government was a fragile coalition that was increasingly threatened from within its own ranks. As the crisis progressed, hostile press and public opinion deluged the cabinet. Compromise with the Russians, following the early Russian tactics of intimidation, would have been hard for any government, but it was extremely difficult for Aberdeen's.

While motivational psychology accurately predicts the British shift to coercion in the second stage of the conflict, it misspecifies the process by which this change occurred. The foreign secretary, Clarendon, provided the swing vote for coercion when he sided with Palmerston and Russell against Aberdeen. While Clarendon was motivated by domestic political considerations, he continued to perceive Russia as he always had—as a mostly benign power that sought to protect the rights of the Russian Orthodox Church in Constantinople. Russian coercive tactics increased the domestic pressures facing the British foreign secretary, but they did not cause him to overestimate the hostility of the opponent or to deceive himself into believing that British threats would succeed.

Cognitive and Bureaucratic Explanations

International structural explanations cannot explain the bargaining process and motivated psychology inaccurately describes that process, but cognitive and bureaucratic approaches each succeed in explaining part of the picture. My argument integrates and builds on these two explanations. In the Russian case, a cognitive approach accurately describes the process of crisis bargaining. Czar Nicholas I interpreted initial British moderation as indicating that his strategy was successful and as confirmation of his belief that Britain would not oppose Russia. In Britain, coalition politics prevailed: the initially coercive Russian strategy affected the incentives and resources of the key players, thereby influencing the content of British policy. In short, both a cognitive and a coalition politics approach explain part of the crisis bargaining process before the Crimean War.

State Structure and the Decision-Making Process in London and St. Petersburg

The key to explaining the difference in the decision-making processes within the two states lies in the institutions of the state, specifically the organization of foreign policy authority. The organization of the executive and the executive's autonomy from a national legislature together explain the process by which bargaining occurs, while the strategic beliefs of national leaders explain state behavior. This section briefly examines those structures and the beliefs of key decision makers, before the rest of the chapter investigates the influence of both factors on the bargaining process during the Crimean crisis.

Britain

The period in British politics between the 1832 and 1867 reforms has been called "the age of equipoise,"[11] an era in which the extension of the franchise had weakened the authority of the Crown, cabinet, and House of Lords, relative to Parliament, without yet developing a disciplined party system. The result, by one account, was "a political structure which gave too little power to the executive, too much to the private member; too much to interest and too little to principle."[12] Collective authority for foreign policy resided in a cabinet that enjoyed little autonomy from legislative oversight.

The British cabinet's very survival required the maintenance of

---

11. W. L. Burn, *The Age of Equipoise: A Study of the Mid-Victorian Generation* (London: Allen & Unwin, 1964).

12. Norman Gash, *Politics in the Age of Peel: A Study in the Technique of Parliamentary Representation 1830–1850* (London: Longman Greens, 1953), xxi.

majority support within Parliament. If it were defeated on a vote of confidence or, more likely, on a major policy decision, the cabinet could choose either to resign as a whole or to dissolve Parliament and call elections. It generally chose the former option. Since the Crown had to grant permission for a dissolution of Parliament, ministers usually considered this option a dangerous weapon of last resort.[13]

The Reform Act of 1832 increased popular participation and parliamentary influence at a time when the country had not yet developed a strong party system that might have allowed greater control of decision making. In short, the Reform Act helped define the organization of foreign policy authority in Britain: the cabinet as executive enjoyed little autonomy from the national legislature.[14] Legislative reform also indirectly affected the organization of the executive branch itself, resulting in a series of weak, short-lived, coalition governments. While executive authority for foreign policy decisions rested squarely in the cabinet, the organization of this arm of the government also reflected the changing nature of Victorian society and politics.

Under the constitutional principle of collective responsibility, well established by 1815, no single cabinet member, not even the prime minister, had the authority to make decisions for the government.[15] Although cabinet decision making, by definition, was a collective enterprise, Aberdeen's weak position within his own cabinet further exacerbated the fractured nature of decision making during the Crimean crisis. Aberdeen was a Peelite, a free trade Tory or Conservative, but Palmerston, Russell, and Clarendon were all Whigs or Liberals. While the Peelites commanded only 30 of the 662 seats in the House of Commons, the Whigs held 130, the protectionist Tories or Derbyites 292, the Radicals 160, and the Irish Brigade 50.[16] A policy decision, whether domestic

---

13. During the period from 1832 to 1868 a defeated government chose to dissolve parliament five times but chose resignation on eight occasions. See H. J. Hanham, ed., *The Nineteenth-Century Constitution 1815–1914: Documents and Commentary* (Cambridge: Cambridge University Press, 1969), 110–11; and Mackintosh, *British Cabinet*, 90.

14. The Second Reform of 1867 was soon to herald a new, mass-participation, two-party system. Yet in 1852 cabinet ministers were unable to rely on the primitive party structure to curb the enthusiasm or command the loyalty of members of Parliament. This period has, in fact, been referred to as "the heyday of the private member." See Hanham, *Nineteenth-Century Constitution*, 106.

15. Arthur Berriedale Keith, *The British Cabinet System, 1830–1938* (London: Stevens & Sons, 1939), 120–28; Hanham, *Nineteenth-Century Constitution*, 76.

16. Earl of Malmesbury, *Memoirs of an Ex-Minister* (London: Longmans, Green, 1885), 286–87. Also see J. B. Conacher, *The Aberdeen Coalition 1852–1855: A Study in Mid-Nineteenth-Century Party Politics* (Cambridge: Cambridge University Press, 1969), 35.

or foreign, could only be reached by coalition, and the composition of coalitions varied from issue to issue.

In addition to the problems he faced as the leader of a coalition government, Aberdeen was not a popular politician. His poor public-speaking skills, his lack of a popular base, and the fact that John Russell was waiting in the wings to succeed him as prime minister deprived Aberdeen of the power of his more popular colleagues, especially Palmerston, to threaten resignation as a means of securing support for his policies. As Muriel E. Chamberlain sums up the prime minister's position, "At best Aberdeen could only negotiate with his own cabinet. He could not command it."[17]

In sum, while many of Aberdeen's problems were unique to his government, most resulted from structural characteristics of the British system. The constitutional doctrines of parliamentary sovereignty and collective responsibility created a government in which executive authority for foreign policy during a crisis was dispersed among the ministers of the major departments and in which the cabinet enjoyed little autonomy from Parliament.

The Inner Cabinet

Because of the diffuse, nonautonomous structure of the state, foreign policy responsibility devolved to the cabinet, the key members of which were the prime minister, Aberdeen; the home secretary, Palmerston; the foreign secretary, Clarendon; and the leader of the House of Commons, Russell. The strategic beliefs of those four individuals, and the balance of power among them, determined the efficacy of Russian policy.

The foreign policy orientation of the British government at the outset of the crisis was largely set by the moderate prime minister, Lord Aberdeen, who a biographer once described as "the most devoted lover of peace who has governed the country since the Revolution."[18] Throughout his career, Aberdeen consistently preferred conciliation to coercion as a diplomatic tool. When he succeeded Palmerston as foreign minister in 1840, Aberdeen altered British policy significantly, championing conciliation of both France and the United States.

Aberdeen did not believe that the Ottoman Empire was critical to the European balance of power or that failure to act in that region would be detrimental to British interests elsewhere. In 1829, he wrote to his brother that the Ottoman Empire might soon crumble:

---

17. *Lord Aberdeen: A Political Biography* (London: Longman, 1983), 478. It was generally understood when the government was formed that Russell would succeed Aberdeen within a short time.

18. Gordon, *Earl of Aberdeen*, 219.

We may still attempt to avert the period of its final dissolution, and may possibly for a time succeed; but whenever this feeble and precarious dominion shall cease, we ought not to occupy ourselves in vain efforts to restore its existence. Our object ought rather to be to find the means of supplying its place in a manner the most beneficial to the interests of civilization and peace.

That manner was the defense of Greece: "I now look to establish a solid power in Greece, with which we may form a natural connection; and which, if necessary we may cordially support in the future."[19]

Aberdeen was more cautious in his estimation of Russian intentions than his otherwise dovish beliefs would suggest. He responded slowly to Russian overtures in 1840, because he was skeptical of the designs of the czar, who he regarded as an unreliable eccentric. Nesselrode, the Russian foreign minister, was an old friend, however.[20] As a conservative, Aberdeen even looked to Russia in the revolutions of 1848 as Britain's "anchor of safety in the west," praising the czar's "moderation and prudence" in not intervening, but hoping that, "when the proper time arrives," Nicholas I would intervene on behalf of the Austrian monarchy: "He will maintain the cause of justice, consistency, and good faith."[21]

Aberdeen's nemesis within the cabinet was the hawkish Palmerston, a defensive deterrer with a hostile image of Russia and a well-known proclivity for coercive foreign policy tactics. The home secretary held a highly conflictual image of the international system as a world in which interests were tightly interconnected. Palmerston advised against conciliation:

Foreign nations, as was to be expected, take our preferred love of peace even beyond the letter when they see the sincerity of our professions so abundantly proved by submission to everybody with whom we have any dealings. . . . Foreign governments will take the Hint, and will extort from us one after the other a great number of concessions which with a little firmness we never need have made; and some fine day, led on and encouraged by our want of proper spirit, they will drive us to the wall on some point on which they will have gone too far to recede. . . . the country will find out, though too late, that much previous disadvantage and humiliation might

---

19. Quoted in Chamberlain, *Lord Aberdeen*, 223, 222, respectively.
20. Chamberlain, *Lord Aberdeen*, 304, 380.
21. Quoted in Chamberlain, *Lord Aberdeen*, 402.

have been escaped by making the same stand at the first steps which we shall then have made at the last. . . .[22]

Palmerston firmly believed that coercion was the preferred means of preventing challenges to Britain's resolve.

Palmerston's image of the opponent was similarly hawkish; the home secretary saw czarist Russia as a "paper tiger," an unrelentingly expansionist adversary that would back down at the slightest hint of resistance.[23] While he believed that the czar's "greedy and indefatigable ambition of conquest is the great danger with which Europe at present is threatened," Palmerston also assumed that "Russia has advanced specially because nobody observed, watched and understood what she was doing. Expose her plans, and you half defeat them."[24] Nicholas I would push only where he saw weakness: "If Turkey is weak, Russia will on every suitable occasion encroach upon her rights and independence."[25]

The other two key leaders, Clarendon and Russell, stood somewhere between the extremes represented by Palmerston and Aberdeen. Foreign Secretary Clarendon leaned more consistently toward the dovish prime minister.[26] He, too, repeatedly opposed Palmerston's coercive stance toward the French, consistently advocating a more conciliatory posture.[27] In the Eastern crisis of 1840, Clarendon objected to Palmerston's policy of allying with Russia and Turkey against the French, strenuously protesting the issuance of an ultimatum to France.[28]

Like Aberdeen, Clarendon saw little need to defend interests not considered vital to England's security. He wrote to Palmerston on 14

22. Quoted in Philip Guedalla, *Palmerston, 1784–1865* (New York: G. P. Putnam's Sons, 1927), 261. Also see Palmerston to Russell, 29 September 1840, in G. P. Gooch, ed., *The Later Correspondence of Lord John Russell 1840–1878*, 2 vols. (London: Longman, Green & Co., 1925), 1:22–23.

23. Snyder, *Myths of Empire*, 5–6, 174–76.

24. Palmerston to Lamb, 6 May 1834, and Palmerston to Melbourne, October 1935, quoted in Kenneth Bourne, *Palmerston: The Early Years 1784–1841* (New York: Macmillan, 1982), 559, 561.

25. Palmerston, quoted in Temperley, *England and the Near East*, 270.

26. My depiction of Clarendon as a conciliatory bargainer is at odds with Schroeder's description of him as an "impressionable character" who vacillated. See *Austria, Great Britain, and the Crimean War*, 32, and passim.

27. Clarendon was considered the head of the "French party" in the British cabinet, even objecting to the Quadruple Alliance as an affront to France. See John Prest, *Lord John Russell* (Columbia: University of South Carolina Press, 1972), 166; and Webster, *Foreign Policy of Palmerston*, 2:665, 675.

28. Temperley, *England and the Near East*, 487–88; George Villiers, *A Vanished Victorian: Being the Life of George Villiers Fourth Earl of Clarendon 1800–1870* (London: Eyre & Spottiswoode, 1938), 134–37.

March 1840, "[I]t would indeed be lamentable if, for objects with which in reality we have little to do, the curse of war were entailed upon us at a moment when we are so ill able to bear it that it would almost amount to national ruin."[29] Unlike Aberdeen, however, Clarendon seems not to have had a well-developed image of Russia prior to the Crimean War crisis.

John Russell's strong rhetoric in the Crimean conflict earned him a reputation as a hawk. While he had occasionally towed Palmerston's line before that, on the eve of the Crimean crisis Russell had little foreign policy experience.[30] What beliefs he had publicly expressed were more moderate and mixed than Russell's subsequent behavior would suggest. In 1840, in the first test of his approach to international politics, Russell stood with Palmerston on the opium question, revealing a faith in the effectiveness of coercion.[31] Russell again sided with Palmerston against Clarendon in the 1840 Eastern crisis, and according to Palmerston, Russell's was the deciding vote for a coercive response. During this crisis, however, Russell also revealed his hesitation to use force and ultimately changed his mind. In the end, he threatened resignation if the cabinet did not go along with his revised proposal that France be invited to act with the other European powers to preserve peace in the Ottoman Empire.[32]

Russell exhibited his tendency toward moderation on other occasions as well. In 1840, Palmerston thought Russell panicked over the U.S.-Canada border dispute when Russell advocated a settlement.[33] The difference between the two men is perhaps best measured by their respective stands on the Ireland issue in the mid-1840s. As John Prest explains, "Palmerston thought there would soon be an end to the trouble if a priest were hanged every time a landlord was shot." In contrast, Russell's "immediate reaction was that the evils of Ireland could not be eradicated by coercion or they would have disappeared long ago."[34] In

---

29. Memorandum from Clarendon to Palmerston, quoted in Kenneth Bourne, *The Foreign Policy of Victorian England 1830–1902* (Oxford: Clarendon Press, 1970), 241.

30. Known in his early career as "Lord John Reformer," Russell had occupied himself with domestic reform and with the ever present Ireland problem. See Prest, *Lord John Russell*.

31. Russell to Melbourne, 6 November 1839, quoted in Prest, *Lord John Russell*, 165.

32. See Gooch, *Later Correspondence of Lord John Russell*, 1:4; Prest, *Lord John Russell*, 166–68; Stuart J. Reid, *Lord John Russell* (London: Sampson Low, Marston, 1895), 120; and Villiers, *Vanished Victorian*, 136–37.

33. Palmerston to Russell, 19 January 1841, quoted in Prest, *Lord John Russell*, 165.

34. Clarendon introduced a bill in which individual localities would be forced to pay for their crimes: "the lord lieutenant was to be given a discretionary power to impose

addition, Russell did not share Palmerston's distrust of Russia and its ruler. Following the 1848 revolutions Russell commented that he "admired as much as anyone the noble conduct of the Emperor of Russia in withdrawing his forces from Hungary when the object for which he had ordered them there had been accomplished."[35]

In sum, the orientation of the Aberdeen government at the outset of the Crimean crisis was set by its conciliatory prime minister and, to a lesser extent, by his foreign minister, Clarendon, but their outlook was balanced by the hawkish Palmerston and, to a lesser extent, by Russell. As the crisis progressed, Russian policy undermined Aberdeen's and Clarendon's pleas for peace and reinforced the domestic appeal of Palmerston's and Russell's confrontational stance.

Russia

The government of nineteenth-century Russia provides a perfect contrast to that of Victorian England. While some domestic opposition existed, Nicholas I ruled as an absolute monarch who enjoyed complete autonomy both from any legislative body and from his own ministers. Indeed, his rule reflected an official state ideology that ordained a belief in the divine authority of the czar.

"Official nationality," government doctrine since 1833, allowed no opposition to its three main tenets: orthodoxy, autocracy, and nationality.[36] This creed dictated belief in the Orthodox religion, one Russian fatherland, and the absolute authority of the czar. The czar derived his power directly from God, according to the catechism of official nationality: "[T]he Emperor of all the Russians is an autocrat monarch, whose power is unlimited. God himself orders all to obey his supreme will, not only from fear, but from conviction."[37]

The structure of the czarist state reflected its underlying doctrine; the czar sat atop a government distinct in this study for its intensely hierarchical structure. Nicholas I shared authority neither with a national legislature nor with the ministers of his government.[38] The two

heavier fines for the murder of a good landlord than for the murder of a bad one." See Prest, *Lord John Russell*, 273.

35. Quoted in Breeze, "British Opinion of Russian Foreign Policy," 109.

36. Ivan Golovine, *Russia under the Autocrat, Nicholas the First*, 2 vols. (London: Henry Colburn, 1846; reprint, New York: Praeger, 1970); Ingle, *Nesselrode and the Russian Rapprochement*, 34; Nicholas V. Riasanovsky, *Nicholas I and Official Nationality in Russia, 1825–1855* (Berkeley: University of California Press, 1959), chap. 3.

37. Quoted in Golovine, *Russia under the Autocrat*, 1:170. Also see Riasanovsky, *Nicholas I and Official Nationality*, 97.

38. The following draws heavily on Golovine, *Russia under the Autocrat*, 2:113–30.

agencies of the government that logically might have shared executive authority for foreign policy making exercised none in fact. The Council of the Empire handled all internal and external policy matters, but the czar appointed its members and presided as president of the general assembly of the Council. The Committee of the Ministers, which was composed of all the ministers of the government as well as the heads of the departments within the Council of the Empire and other individuals designated by the czar, exercised no executive authority.

Although official nationality was state ideology throughout Nicholas I's reign, significant disagreement in foreign policy outlook existed between the "German Party" (*nemetskaia partiia*) and the "Russian Party" (*russkaia partiia*). The foreign minister, Nesselrode, was considered the head of the German, or Foreign, Party, to which much of his ministry belonged.[39] While Nesselrode and others sometimes disagreed with the czar, however, Nicholas I accepted the advice of his foreign minister when it suited him, but he favored the advice of other ministers or trusted friends outside the government when he chose. Nesselrode described himself as "a modest tool of the emperor's designs, and an instrument of his political plans."[40] Nesselrode's experience was no worse than those of his predecessors. An earlier foreign minister, Gorchakov, commented, "In Russia, there are only two people who know the policy of the Russian cabinet: the emperor who makes it and myself who prepares and executes it." An 1837 report on the foreign ministry portrayed it as "merely the faithful executor of the intentions" of the czar: "Its every action . . . was carried out under the orders and direction of the tsars themselves."[41]

Though domestic rivalries did exist, in short, the czar's authority was absolute. Such "parties" as existed were not formally instituted or sanctioned, and once Nicholas I made a decision or issued an order, he abided no dissent. Because Czar Nicholas I was the quintessential unitary, autonomous leader, his beliefs explain the failure of British conciliation.

Nicholas I

Nicholas I's beliefs are not easily categorized. At the outset of the Crimean War crisis, the czar was in many ways a classic hard-liner. His militarization of the Russian regime and his propensity to use force were

---

39. On Nesselrode's beliefs, see Ingle, *Nesselrode and the Russian Rapprochement*, 50, 122–23. On the Russian or National Party, see Ingle, *Nesselrode and the Russian Rapprochement*, 26–27.

40. Quoted in Riasanovsky, *Nicholas I and Official Nationality*, 45.

41. Quoted in Bolsover, "Aspects of Russian Foreign Policy," 323, 322.

well known.[42] He was a hard-line "defensive deterrer" who advocated a tough stance as the best means of preserving Russian interests in a threatening international environment. While he did not seek to provoke the British, Nicholas I sought to counter British naval strength with Russian strength: in the 1830s, he oversaw a large-scale buildup of the Russian navy.[43] Furthermore, since at least 1833, the czar had worried out loud about the threat posed by what he took to be the imminent collapse of the Ottoman Empire. Although he preferred to maintain the empire, decisive action would need to be taken if it actually began to crumble.

Despite long-term suspicions of England, though, the czar's image of the adversary was far more benign than one would expect from such a hawk. He was not optimistic about the possibilities for long-term cooperation with Britain. As Nesselrode commented in 1841, the czar tended to view "the present relationship between the European powers as one coalition against the other."[44] His friendly relations with Aberdeen, however, reassured him that he could trust Britain not to intervene in the Ottoman Empire. The 1844 conversations and subsequent agreement between the two nations convinced the czar that he could count on British friendship once Aberdeen took office.[45] Far from the image most hard-liners hold of their opponents as either expansionist or opportunistic, Nicholas I viewed Britain under Aberdeen's stewardship as a benign, even trusted, ally that would not oppose Russian interests in Constantinople.

While the unitary, autonomous nature of foreign policy authority in Russia determined the process by which crisis decision making occurred during the Crimean conflict, the hard-line views of the czar determined that British conciliation would not be an effective tactic: British bargaining reinforced Nicholas I's beliefs, thereby contributing to the escalation of the conflict. The following section chronicles the interaction of British and Russian strategies with the opponent's domestic political context.

---

42. See Riasanovsky, *Nicholas I and Official Nationality*, 43; and Ingle, *Nesselrode and the Russian Rapprochement*, 27–28.

43. Ingle, *Nesselrode and the Russian Rapprochement*, 96–98.

44. Nesselrode to Meyendorff, 10 November 1841, quoted in Ingle, *Nesselrode and the Russian Rapprochement*, 145.

45. Charles Frederick Vitzhum von Ecstäedt, *St. Petersburg and London in the Years 1852–1864*, ed. Henry Reeve, trans. Edward Fairfax Taylor, 2 vols. (London: Longman, Greens, 1887), 1:29, 33. Nicholas I's ambassador in London, Brunnow, had similarly reported, on the occasion of Aberdeen's assumption of power, "What he [Aberdeen] says is solid, true, and carries the seal of integrity." Quoted in Chamberlain, *Lord Aberdeen*, 304.

The Crimean Crisis

The Crimean conflict can be divided into four stages: (1) the Seymour conversations and the early Menshikov mission, December 1852 to 5 May 1853; (2) the second phase of the Menshikov mission, 6 May to 22 May 1853; (3) a period of European diplomacy from June to October 1853; and (4) the Russo-Turkish war from October 1853 to March 1854. The European powers entered the military conflict in March.

Seymour Conversations and the Menshikov Mission: December 1852 to 5 May 1853

Despite the best efforts of his foreign minister to restrain the czar, Russia adopted a highly coercive stance in the early stage of the crisis. The Russians sent a menacing diplomatic mission to Constantinople. At the same time, the czar engaged in cryptic conversations with the British about what he saw as a bleak future for the Ottoman Empire. In contrast, British leaders exercised considerable restraint in the early part of the crisis and urged the Turks to yield to Russian demands. British restraint confirmed Nicholas I's beliefs in the efficacy of force and in the willingness of Britain to compromise. British perceptions of Russian intentions varied, although by the end of the first stage, two members of the cabinet—Russell and Clarendon—began to advocate a more coercive response than they had originally. In Clarendon's case, this shift reflected a recognition of the way Russian strategy had altered domestic incentives by undermining the credibility of a conciliatory response.

Russia
Sometime in December 1852 or January 1853 the czar produced a memorandum considering his options in responding to the French challenge and Turkish concessions. Among the policies he considered were negotiation, intimidation, and force (including a declaration of war), Russian occupation of the semiautonomous Turkish principalities of Moldavia and Wallachia, and a surprise attack on Constantinople. Russian objectives in choosing among the options were to secure reparations for the past and guarantees for the future in the Holy Places.[46] His first response was the mobilization of two army corps on the Turkish border and the preparation of forts and flotillas on the Black Sea. As Nicholas I stated, "I wished to avoid war, in the East as in the West and, so as not to be

---

46. For the text of Nicholas's memo see M. S. Anderson, *Great Powers and the Near East 1774–1923* (London: Edward Arnold, 1970), 68–69.

obliged to undergo it, . . . I felt the necessity of speaking to those wretched Turks with firmness."[47]

In December 1852, Nesselrode counseled Nicholas I to try to preserve the Ottoman Empire, not to talk of its partition. The foreign minister argued that Britain and Austria would urge France and Turkey to compromise if Russia reassured them of "the purity of her intentions" and the "nature of her grievances."[48] At the same time, however, Nesselrode suggested that a mission be sent to the *Porte* to restore Russian rights, saying, "Fear threw it [the *Porte*] into the arms of the French; it is likewise fear that must bring it back to us."[49]

Despite Nesselrode's warnings, the czar had already decided to engage in conversations with Seymour, the British ambassador to St. Petersburg, on the future of Turkey. In his 1 January report, Nesselrode again opposed approaching Britain about partitioning the Ottoman Empire and suggested the diplomatic mission. Nicholas I was not swayed. He thought it encouraging that the new prime minister had made the hawkish Palmerston home secretary, rather than foreign secretary. The czar also trusted Seymour and found it significant that he had not been dismissed even though he had failed to carry out Palmerston's directives on an earlier question.[50]

The first of what became known as the Seymour conversations occurred in January. Nicholas I expressed concern to the British ambassador about the increasingly unstable situation in Turkey: "[W]e have on our hands a sick man—a very sick man; it will be, I tell you frankly, a great misfortune if, one of these days, he should slip away from us, especially before all necessary arrangements were made." If the dissolution of the Ottoman Empire "should occur unexpectedly, and before

---

47. Cited in Temperley, *England and the Near East*, 303–4. There is some dispute over whether Nesselrode knew of the mobilization orders. In his memoirs, Vitzhum von Eckstäedt, who was in St. Petersburg at the time, claims that Nesselrode did not know, although he also claims that Nesselrode was unaware of the impending Menshikov Mission, an undertaking it is generally assumed that Nesselrode suggested. See *St. Petersburg and London*, 1:38. Walker claims not only that Nesselrode knew about the mobilization orders but that he deliberately deceived the British into thinking he did not. See "Role of Karl Nesselrode," esp. 108.

48. Quoted in Bolsover, "Nicholas I," 137–38.

49. Cited in John Sheldon Curtiss, *Russia's Crimean War* (Durham: Duke University Press, 1979), 63.

50. Brison D. Gooch, "A Century of Historiography on the Origins of the Crimean War," *American Historical Review* 62 (October 1956): 33–58, reprinted as Publications in the Humanities, no. 25 (Cambridge: MIT Press, n.d.), 56. In contrast, both Temperley and Walker argue that Nicholas decided to begin the Seymour conversations before he knew Aberdeen was to be prime minister. See Temperley, *England and the Near East*, 270–71; and Walker, "Role of Karl Nesselrode," 104.

some ulterior system has been sketched," European war would result.[51] The czar went on to say that, although he had no intention of occupying Constantinople, circumstances might force him to do so temporarily. These conversations continued the next month, when, on 20 February, Nicholas I approached Seymour at a party. The final conversation occurred the next day, with the czar concluding that "[t]he Turkish Empire is a thing to be tolerated, not to be reconstructed; in such a cause I protest to you I will not allow a pistol to be fired."[52]

Nesselrode quickly clarified the meaning of the czar's statements. The foreign minister agreed that the existence of the Ottoman Empire was certainly precarious, but he argued that Russians should "concern ourselves above all with prolonging it as long as possible—nations have more vitality than they are usually credited with." He also told Seymour that, while Nicholas I was too preoccupied with the consequences of the fall of the empire, Nesselrode's own views were shared by all the czar's closest advisors.[53]

Nicholas I did not feel the same need to reassure the British and apparently inferred from this first exchange to occur since the conflict erupted that Britain supported Russia against France. The czar's chief aim was to preserve the Ottoman Empire, although his means of doing so were sometimes less than tactful, and he believed Britain would acquiesce in his preservation attempts. He left the Seymour conversations with the belief that an Anglo-French alliance against Russia was impossible.[54]

Nesselrode suggested a diplomatic mission to Constantinople as a means of restraining Nicholas I.[55] While he felt that Russia needed to frighten the Turks into backing down, Nesselrode was conscious from the start of the need to reassure Europe, and especially Britain, of Russia's benign intentions. He advocated for the mission Count Orlov, a trusted official who had recently become chief of the secret police of the empire, or Count Kisselev, minister of the imperial domain and former

51. Seymour to Russell, 11 January 1853, *Eastern Papers*, vol. 71, pt. 5, 2; Seymour to Russell, 22 January 1853, *Eastern Papers*, vol. 71, pt. 5, 4.

52. Seymour to Russell, 22 January, 21 February, and 22 February 1853, *Eastern Papers*, vol. 71, pt. 5, 4, 8, 11.

53. Walker, "Role of Karl Nesselrode," 115. The quotation is cited in Bolsover, "Nicholas I," 141.

54. See Bolsover, "Nicholas I," 140–41; Curtiss, *Russia's Crimean War*, chap. 4; and *Eastern Papers*, vol. 71; pt. 5, 3–6.

55. Walker, "Role of Karl Nesselrode," 101–3. David Wetzel is alone in suggesting that Nesselrode opposed the Menshikov Mission because he thought it would estrange Europe. See *The Crimean War: A Diplomatic History* (New York: Columbia University Press for East European Monographs, 1985), 52.

ambassador to Paris. Instead, Nicholas I chose Prince Alexander Menshikov, the former minister of the navy, because he felt Menshikov's brusque manner would allow him to be more aggressive with the Turks.[56]

Menshikov arrived in Constantinople on 28 February. His instructions were designed to meet two major Russian goals: to obtain satisfactory arrangements on the Holy Places and to secure guarantees for the future. He also was authorized to extend to Turkey a treaty of defensive alliance against France and to confirm any rumors of Russian military preparations.[57] Nesselrode and, on his instructions, the Russian ambassador in London did not tell the British cabinet about Menshikov's order to secure a treaty with the Turks, because of fear of opposition. At the same time, with the exception of the issue of the *sened* guaranteeing future rights, Nesselrode felt confident that Aberdeen would be moderate and trusting and would comply with the Russian objectives.[58]

From the outset, there was no mistaking the intent of the mission. On the day after Menshikov's arrival on a war vessel, another warship arrived carrying the commander of the Black Sea fleet and several other military officers. Menshikov paid a visit to the Turkish grand vizier on 2 March. The Russian diplomat had been instructed to refuse to deal with Fuad Effendi, the Turkish foreign minister, who the Russians blamed for the brewing crisis. Contrary to diplomatic custom, Menshikov was dressed in a frock coat and hat, not his uniform, and he walked by the open door of the foreign minister, who was waiting to receive him. Fuad immediately resigned over the insult and was replaced by Rifaat Pasha. Menshikov did not formally present Russia's demand for full implementation of the 1852 *firman* until 16 March. This note contained a hint of the demands that would follow, saying that any agreement could "no longer be confined to barren and unsatisfactory promises which may be broken at a future period."[59]

Britain
British perceptions of initial Russian actions were benign. When Seymour informed London of the Russian mobilization, he explicitly con-

---

56. H. E. Howard, "Brunnow's Reports on Aberdeen, 1853," *Cambridge Historical Journal* 4 (1932–34), 317; Walker, "Role of Karl Nesselrode," 123. Had Orlov been assigned the mission, the outcome might have been different, since he opposed any Russian designs in the Near East and had pressed for withdrawal. Wetzel, *Crimean War*, 51.

57. See Curtiss, *Russia's Crimean War*, 85–88; Temperley, *England and the Near East*, 306–7; and Walker, "Role of Karl Nesselrode," 123–35.

58. On possible Russian deception, see Howard, "Brunnow's Reports on Aberdeen," 317–20. On Nesselrode's perceptions of Britain, see Walker, "Role of Karl Nesselrode," 133–34.

59. *Eastern Papers*, vol. 71, pt. 1, 149.

nected it to a French threat to send an expedition to Syria and attributed no hostile intentions to the Russians.[60] The British ambassador in Paris also shared the belief that the outbreak of the crisis "was the fault of France."[61] It is not surprising, then, that none of the major decision makers in London was alarmed by early Russian policy. Even the Seymour conversations did not alarm them. Those perceptions began to shift, if only slightly, with the arrival of Menshikov in Constantinople and his brusque presentation of Russian demands.

In his initial reaction, Russell expressed some concern that the independence of the *Porte* not be compromised, but he argued that Britain was not interested in the merits of the dispute over the Holy Places. Since France had been wrong in initiating the conflict, it should make the first concessions. Russell rejected an overture from France seeking alliance with Britain, stating that the British government was "persuaded that the Emperor of Russia will not enter willingly, and certainly not without the consent of England, into any schemes for the subversion of the Ottoman power. Her Majesty's Government has reasons quite satisfactory to it for this persuasion."[62]

Clarendon blamed "the restless ambition and energy of France,"[63] while the most soft-line of British policy makers, Aberdeen, did not hesitate to condemn the Turks. Early in 1853 he told Brunnow, the Russian ambassador to London, "I hate the Turks for I regard their government as the most repressive in the world. One of the most difficult duties of my political life has been to lend my support to the maintenance of the Ottoman Empire."[64] Privately, Aberdeen commented to Russell that "the affair of the Holy Places certainly looks much better; and if [the French ambassador] Lavalette should really leave Constantinople, as is now intended, there will probably not be much difficulty in coming to a settlement. . . ."[65] British policy makers recognized both

60. *Eastern Papers*, vol. 71, pt. 1, 56. Also see Puryear, *England, Russia, and the Straits Question*, 206–7.

61. Cited in A. J. P. Taylor, *The Struggle for Mastery in Europe 1848–1918* (London: Oxford University Press, 1954), 53. Also see Cowley to Russell, 9 February 1853, in Gooch, *Later Correspondence of Lord John Russell*, 2:147.

62. Russell to Cowley, 29 January 1853, quoted in Puryear, *England, Russia, and the Straits Question*, 220–21. Also see Puryear, 216; Russell to Cowley, 29 December 1852, Public Records Office (hereinafter PRO) 30/22/10F, 186–87; Russell to Seymour, 25 January 1853, Foreign Office (hereinafter FO) 181/295, no. 18; and Russell to Seymour, 28 January 1853, FO 181/296, no. 57.

63. Quoted in Taylor, *Struggle for Mastery in Europe*, 53.

64. Quoted in Walker, "Role of Karl Nesselrode," 141.

65. Aberdeen to Russell, 28 January 1853, PRO 30/22/10G, 274.

legitimate Russian interests in the region and French and Turkish encroachments against them.

Neither did the early Seymour conversations alarm the British, despite Nicholas I's repeated comments on the imminent fall of the Ottoman Empire and his suggestions for its partition.[66] Seymour's own reactions to the czar's comments reflect a progression from early trust in Nicholas I to anxiety by late February. On 12 January, he reported to Russell that

> [a]lthough the Emperor walks about in a helmet, sleeps on a camp-bed, and occasionally talks gunpowder, he is not more keen on war than his neighbours. He occasionally takes a precipitate step; but as reflection arrives, reason and Count Nesselrode make themselves heard. He is not sorry to be able to recede if he can do so without a loss of dignity. He cannot, however, give up his pretensions as to the Holy Places; his case is too clear, and the question is one which is very interesting to the feelings of the Church of which he is in some measure the head.[67]

By 22 January, he was still not alarmed, reporting that "I am bound to say, that if words, tone and manner offer any criterion by which intentions are to be judged, the Emperor is prepared to act with perfect fairness and openness towards Her Majesty's Government."[68]

As the talks continued, however, these perceptions began to shift. On 9 February, Seymour summed up Nicholas I's overtures in a letter to Russell:

> I, Nicholas, by the grace of God and so forth, not willing to incur the risk of war and desirous not to compromise my character for magnanimity, will never seize upon Turkey; but I will destroy her independence. I will reduce her to vassalage and make her existence a burden to her and that by a process which is perfectly familiar to us, as it is the same which was employed with so much success against Poland. The danger is that England and France will foregather for the purpose of preventing this consummation. I will

---

66. Temperley goes as far as to suggest that the conversations produced good feelings between Britain and Russia. See *England and the Near East*, 278, 312–13. He also argues, however, that the first British suspicions were those voiced by Russell on 29 April, an assertion that is disputed in this chapter but one that is also made in Wetzel, *Crimean War*, 48.

67. Gooch, *Later Correspondence of Lord John Russell*, 2:145.

68. Seymour to Russell, 22 January 1853, *Eastern Papers*, vol. 71, pt. 5, 5.

therefore show a decided preference for one of these powers and will do my best to disunite them.[69]

Although he still credited Nicholas I with moderation, Seymour told London that the 20 February conversation offered "matters for most anxious reflection."[70]

Still, there was little response in London to the Seymour conversations, and what response there was seemed positive or indifferent. On 9 February, then Foreign Secretary Russell acknowledged "the moderation, the frankness, and the friendly disposition of His Imperial Majesty" in protecting the Greek Church, a task "prescribed by duty and sanctioned by treaty."[71]

Menshikov's presentation of his demands on 16 March had a greater impact. Following this action, Turkey appealed to Britain and France for assistance, and the French responded on 19 March by sending a fleet to Salamis in Greece. At a 20 March meeting, in which the inner cabinet decided not to join the French, Russell and Palmerston favored immediate action, but Aberdeen and Clarendon were able to dissuade them.[72] This emerging split was to remain in place throughout the crisis.

Clarendon still distrusted the Turks, trusted the czar, and failed to see any dire ramifications to British inaction. On 1 March, Clarendon—now foreign secretary—said he felt it was better that the Turks "should eat dirt than that we should be in trouble on their account."[73] The French should not try to draw the British fleet into "this mischief in the East": "They cannot drag us into a question with which we have nothing to do."[74] The foreign secretary expressed his continued confidence in the good intentions of the czar:

> The Emperor has over and over again given us his assurances *as a Gentleman* that he desired to maintain the independence and integrity of the Ottoman Empire and that whenever his policy and views underwent a change he would give us distinct notice of it. I will therefore no more disbelieve him nor think him false or treacherous

69. Seymour to Russell, 9 February 1853, quoted in Temperley, *England and the Near East*, 275.

70. *Eastern Papers*, vol. 71, pt. 5, 8–12.

71. Russell to Seymour, 9 February 1853, FO 181/296; A. W. Ward and G. P. Gooch, eds., *The Cambridge History of British Foreign Policy 1783–1919*, 3 vols. (New York: Macmillan, 1923), 2:340.

72. Herbert Maxwell, *The Life and Letters of George William Frederick, Fourth Earl of Clarendon*, 2 vols. (London: Edward Arnold, 1913), 2:3.

73. Clarendon to Cowley, 1 March 1853, FO 519/169, 10.

74. Clarendon to Cowley, 22 March 1853, FO 519/169, 108.

than I would any other Gentleman who had thus voluntarily expressed himself.[75]

Clarendon continued to trust the czar's assurances and quietly reproached the French for acting prematurely.[76]

Aberdeen was again quick to condemn the Turks. Expressing his fear of escalation, he counseled that extreme care be taken in preparing instructions for the returning ambassador to Constantinople, Lord Stratford:

> "The assurances of prompt and effective aid on the approach of danger," given by us to the Porte, would, in all probability, produce war. These barbarians hate us all, and would be delighted to take their chance of some advantage, by embroiling us with the other powers of Christendom. It may be necessary to give them a moral support, and to endeavour to prolong their existence; but we ought to regard as the greatest misfortune any engagement which compelled us to take up arms for the Turks.[77]

Agreeing with Clarendon, Aberdeen proclaimed, "Whether right or wrong, we advise the Turks to yield."[78]

Russell's views were beginning to resemble Palmerston's hard-line stance. In a 20 March letter to Clarendon, Russell stated, "The Emperor of Russia is clearly bent on accomplishing the destruction of Turkey, *and he must be resisted*"; "[t]he vast preparations at Sevastopol show a foregone purpose, and that purpose is, I fear, to extinguish the Turkish Empire. . . ." At the same time, however, he still believed that the Turks should have accepted Menshikov's terms.[79] Russell maintained this hawkish position throughout the crisis. As the conflict progressed, however, it became clear that at least part of this shift was due to domestic pressures in Britain. Russian strategy was beginning to erode the credibility of conciliatory arguments.

Russia
Early British indifference and even support did not go unnoticed in St. Petersburg. In early February, in the margins of a memorandum from

75. Clarendon to Cowley, 21 March 1853, FO 519/169, 89–90.

76. *Eastern Papers*, vol. 71, pt. 1, 93–95; Maxwell, *Life and Letters of Clarendon*, 2:6–7.

77. Quoted in Spencer Walpole, *The Life of Lord John Russell*, 2 vols. (New York: Haskell House, 1969), 2:178.

78. Quoted in Puryear, *England, Russia, and the Straits Question*, 232.

79. Quoted in Walpole, *Life of Lord John Russell*, 2:181; Chamberlain, *Lord Aberdeen*, 481.

Lord Russell that pledged that Britain had no desire to hold Constantinople, Nicholas I wrote, "I am very appreciative for I see [in all this] the guarantee against the future which I fear."[80] Later that month, Brunnow reported to Nesselrode Aberdeen's general dislike of the Turks and the prime minister's comment that Britain would force the Turks to yield. He also noted (inaccurately) that British public opinion was not much in favor of supporting the Ottoman Empire.[81] When Nicholas I read Brunnow's dispatch, he reportedly responded, "To my mind this is the most remarkable dispatch of all; it explains the unexpected success of our first steps, and gives me cause to hope that we shall be able to advance in the way I laid down for myself."[82] Perceiving British support, or at least the impossibility of Anglo-French joint opposition, the czar proceeded with his tactics of intimidation in Constantinople.

On 22 March, Menshikov delivered to the new Turkish foreign minister a second note, which demanded immediate negotiations and presented a Russian draft convention. He met with Rifaat Pasha four days later and required that, before he would disclose the nature of his mission and his government's complete demands, Rifaat should promise that the *Porte* would not disclose the details to the British or French. The Turk refused.

Meanwhile, reassuring news from London continued. On 20 April, Brunnow apparently showed Aberdeen a copy of Menshikov's instructions, including those concerning the *sened* for future guarantees, to strengthen the prime minister's position at home. The Russian ambassador reported to St. Petersburg that Aberdeen acquiesced. Based on these reports, H. E. Howard concludes that

> Aberdeen accepted everything. He agreed not to inform his colleagues of the details which Brunnow had given him; but he felt confident—and so did Brunnow—that he could persuade them to support Russia. The ambassador was more cautious in his talks to Clarendon. . . . But Aberdeen certainly knew of the nature of the Russian designs long before his colleagues, and approved.[83]

By late April, Russia had reached agreement with Turkey on the immediate issue of the Holy Places, and a *firman*, similar to the one that had been issued and evaded in 1852, was issued by the *Porte* on 3 May.

80. Quoted in Temperley, *England and the Near East*, 275.
81. Howard, "Brunnow's Reports on Aberdeen," 319.
82. Cited in Puryear, *England, Russia, and the Straits Question*, 233.
83. Howard, "Brunnow's Reports on Aberdeen," 320. There is no support for this assertion in the British documents.

Two days later, Menshikov replied that the Turkish proclamation met Russian demands regarding the Holy Places, thereby settling that issue, but that it provided no guarantee for the future. Russia still wanted a formal treaty, and Menshikov presented an ultimatum requesting a reply within five days. Russian demands included maintenance of the status quo concerning the rights, privileges, and immunities of the Orthodox Church, as well as agreement to grant the Greeks any future rights secured by other Christians.[84]

Britain

The French fleet sailed for Salamis on 22 March despite the British refusal to join the action. From then on, London increasingly faced a choice between France, the European balance, and the survival of the Ottoman Empire, on the one hand, and its friendship with Russia, on the other. Domestic concerns soon precluded the option of appeasing Russia.

In early April Stratford Canning returned to Constantinople. The ambassador was well known for his dislike of Russia, a reputation that had caused Nicholas I to refuse to receive him as ambassador to St. Petersburg in 1833. Stratford's instructions upon returning, which had been begun by Russell and completed by Clarendon based on the ambassador's own memorandum, discussed Nicholas I's "magnanimous and wise" "moderation" and ordered Stratford to bear in mind "the superior claims of Russia both as respects the Treaty obligations of Turkey, and the loss of moral influence that the Emperor would sustain throughout His dominions if, as the Ecclesiastical Head of his Church, He were to yield any privileges it has hitherto enjoyed, to the Latin Church of which the Emperor of the French claims to be the Protector."[85] Stratford apparently interpreted his instructions a little differently. Within days of his arrival, he wrote to his wife, "If the Russians are in the wrong, as I believe they are, my business is to make the wrong appear, and to stand by the Porte, or rather make the P[orte] stand by me."[86]

Very soon after reaching Constantinople, Stratford forwarded to London the Russian "secret" demands for "a complete and undisturbed maintenance of the *status quo* in future by some form of written engagement," to "preclude all further pretensions on the side of France, and

---

84. *Eastern Papers*, vol. 71, pt. 1, 185–86.

85. Quoted in Harold Temperley and Lillian M. Penson, eds., *Foundations of British Foreign Policy from Pitt (1792) to Salisbury (1902)* (Cambridge: The University Press, 1938), 140, 143. Also see Temperley, *England and the Near East*, 314–15.

86. Quoted in Norman Rich, *Why the Crimean War? A Cautionary Tale* (Hanover: University Press of New England, 1985), 48.

make the Porte directly responsible to Russia for any future innovation respecting the holy places." Although Stratford himself characterized the demands as "fair and reasonable enough" and "even desirable," he opposed them, arguing that the demands amounted to a virtual Russian protectorate. He advised the Turks to separate the question of the Holy Places from that of future guarantees in negotiations with the Russians.[87]

Despite Brunnow's claim that he had shown Aberdeen his orders, many of the statements and later recollections of British policy makers suggest that they did not understand the full extent of Russian demands until late April, when Stratford's memos began to arrive. The duke of Argyll, a member of the Aberdeen cabinet, recalled, "It was not till the 26th of April, 1853, that we received a despatch from Lord Stratford which at last left no doubt that Russia was deliberately deceiving us, and that Menschikoff, in the teeth of all assurances, had some secret demands to make on the Porte in the exclusive interests of his own Government."[88]

This course of events had little impact on Aberdeen's view of Russian intentions. He continued to trust Nicholas I and appears to have paid little attention to Brunnow's presentation of 20 April, preferring to believe that Russia did not want a protectorate in the Ottoman Empire. Before Russian demands for future guarantees became clear, even Palmerston gave Nicholas I the benefit of the doubt: "The Emperor of Russia is ambitious and grasping, but he is a gentleman and I should be slow to disbelieve his positive denial of such things as those in question." Clarendon, too, believed through late April that "[w]e did quite right in showing confidence in the pledged word of the Emperor of Russia."[89]

Clarendon began to worry, however, about the future of the current British government, which had been defeated in Parliament on several recent questions and which faced an increasingly hostile press and public: "Things look very ill and though to myself personally it would be very agreeable to be again out of office yet I cannot contemplate without alarm the confusion that would follow the eviction of Lord Aberdeen's Ministry and the almost impossibility of finding another that would command the support of the Public."[90] In response, the tone of Clarendon's statements changed perceptibly. He worried that "our trusty and beloved Nicholas has not been quite honest or disinterested, for while adhering to the religious questions that were to be the sole objects of Prince Menshikov's mission he has sought to divide the Turkish Empire

87. *Eastern Papers*, vol. 71, pt. 1, 125, 127–29.

88. George Douglas Campbell, eighth duke of Argyll, *Autobiography and Memoirs*, 2 vols., ed. the dowager duchess of Argyll (London: John Murray, 1906), 1:444.

89. Both statements are quoted in Temperley, *England and the Near East*, 270, 313.

90. Clarendon to Cowley, 15 April 1853, FO 519/169, 216–18.

with the Sultan by making himself the Protector of the Greeks."[91] Despite his fear that "there may in the near while be trouble and anxiety," Clarendon nevertheless clung to his belief that "nothing can be more pacific or friendly than the assurances of the Emperor of Russia."[92] The foreign secretary continued to interpret Russian actions according to his prior beliefs. Although Russian coercion led him to fear the domestic consequences of continued conciliation, he was not motivated by domestic pressures to overestimate Russian hostility.

Russell, whose perceptions had already begun to shift closer to those of Palmerston, seemed convinced of the aggressive intentions of the czar. On 29 April he commented, "It is clear to me that the Russian Government has been trying to deceive us, and to bind Turkey to a treaty of submission to the Russian yoke."[93] Russia's coercive diplomacy, in short, only solidified Russell's emerging hard-line stance.

Menshikov Mission II: 6 May to 22 May 1853

In the second phase of the Crimean conflict—from the presentation of Menshikov's demand for future guarantees to the time he quit Constantinople—both Russian and British bargaining tactics began to shift. Nicholas I continued to interpret British inaction as indicating acquiescence and to blame the Turks for the escalating crisis, but Menshikov made a number of diplomatic concessions in his final days in Constantinople. It was not enough, however. The nature of Russian demands only reinforced the arguments of hard-liners in London and, by arousing the British press and public, undercut the position of a key dove, Lord Clarendon. British policy then began to harden.

Russia
Russian moderation—although still backed by the threat to sever diplomatic relations—characterized the second phase of the Menshikov mission. The British decision not to send the fleet had been interpreted in St. Petersburg as support for the Russian cause. Nesselrode reportedly commented to the Austrian government in early April that this action demonstrated continued British confidence in Russia. Similarly, he told the Bavarian minister, Count Otto von Bray-Steinberg, that recent British behavior had been everything Russia desired.[94]

On 10 May, the Turks rejected the Russian ultimatum as a violation

91. Clarendon to Cowley, 29 April 1853, FO 519/169, 255–56.
92. Clarendon to Cowley, 3 May 1853, FO 519/169, 281–82.
93. Gooch, *Later Correspondence of Lord John Russell*, 2:147.
94. Cited in Walker, "Role of Karl Nesselrode," 169.

of their sovereignty. Menshikov did not sever relations, however, as he had originally been instructed. Instead, he made the first of several concessions. Menshikov was tempted to agree to the 10 May Turkish note but was convinced by other members of his delegation to persist. On the tenth, he wrote to Reshid Pasha, who was then out of office, asking him to act as an intermediary with the sultan. Menshikov repeated his demands on the next day, but this time he avoided the words *sened, treaty,* or *convention* and called only for "an act emanating from the sovereign will of the Sultan, a free but solemn engagement."[95] This was a substantial concession, since an earlier such act, the 1852 *firman,* had been revoked. Menshikov repeated his threat to break relations with the Turks within three days if compliance was not forthcoming.

The apparent victim of an elaborate plot, Menshikov encouraged changes that inadvertently shifted the Turkish ministry in favor of the anti-Russian party. Ann Pottinger Saab, who has carefully analyzed the Turkish side of the crisis, argues that Rifaat and Mehemet Ali were about to accept Menshikov's demands in the form of a note when they were dismissed in the shuffle.[96] This new Council of Ministers met on 13 May and opposed conciliation. Two days later, Reshid Pasha, the new foreign secretary, informed Menshikov of the decision and appealed for an extension of the ultimatum until 17 May.

Menshikov again conceded and extended the deadline, but the Grand Council rejected the offer. When Reshid called on the Russian diplomat with the news, Menshikov repeated his concession, offering to let the sultan issue a diplomatic note instead of a formal declaration or treaty. When the Turks rejected this offer too, he broke off diplomatic relations with the Ottoman Empire and left Constantinople on 21 May. Although he has been severely criticized for his actions, Menshikov had followed the coercive strategy laid out for him by his superiors and had engaged in significant concessions in the later part of his mission. One analyst of the crisis concludes that Menshikov had "scaled down Russia's demands so appreciably that it is impossible to find in the demands themselves any threat to the sovereignty and independence of the sultan."[97] The Turks nevertheless rejected them and banked on European support.

Following Menshikov's departure, the czar issued preliminary orders for the occupation of the Turkish principalities of Moldavia and

95. Quoted in Saab, *Origins of the Crimean Alliance,* 39.
96. *Origins of the Crimean Alliance,* 40. Also see Puryear, *England, Russia, and the Straits Question,* 262; and Temperley, *England and the Near East,* 323–25.
97. Rich, *Why the Crimean War?* 56.

Wallachia, threatening to occupy these territories until he received satisfaction from the Turks. Nesselrode opposed the occupation and requested that Seymour ask Nicholas I to refrain from undertaking it, but the foreign minister believed neither France nor Britain would view the move as a violation of the Straits convention or would react by sending their fleets into the Straits.[98] On 31 May, Russia issued an ultimatum to the Turks that reiterated Menshikov's final demands; either the Turkish government had to accept the 20 May note without modifications within eight days or Russian troops would cross the border of the Ottoman Empire. The Turks rejected the offer, and in early July Russian troops began to cross the Pruth River.

Russian leaders largely blamed Stratford Canning for the failure of the Menshikov mission and the subsequent need for the occupation. Nicholas I and Nesselrode felt Stratford had interfered in the negotiations in Constantinople, opposed Russian demands, and encouraged Turkish resistance.[99] The official Russian account of the origins and conduct of the war, published almost thirty years later, also places much of the blame on Stratford. His actions, according to the account, were "openly hostile to us; and to him belongs the sad celebrity of having prevented the success of our pacific efforts, and of having rendered war inevitable."[100] Nicholas I did not believe that Stratford's views were shared in London. In late May he wrote, "I still want to believe that Canning has acted on his own and against his government's instructions."[101]

Nicholas I seems to have genuinely believed he was not challenging the status quo in the Ottoman Empire and that, instead, he merely wished to preserve it. In conversations with Seymour, Nesselrode argued that the demands of 5 May and thereafter changed nothing and that the Russians claimed no new rights. He also argued that the French had long

98. Walker, "Role of Karl Nesselrode," 197, 223. Before announcing the note publicly to the country, Nesselrode softened the language of the manifesto explaining the occupation orders. See Walker, 222.

99. For example, see Nesselrode to Brunnow, 1 June 1853, *Eastern Papers*, vol. 71, pt. 1, 241–45.

100. *Diplomatic Study on the Crimean War (1852 to 1856)*, 2 vols., Russian Official Publication (London: W. H. Allen, 1882), 1:181, 183. Authorship of the work is generally attributed to Baron Jomini of the Russian Foreign Office.

101. Cited in Walker, "Role of Karl Nesselrode," 195. The secondary sources contain a wide range of arguments about Stratford's role in the escalation of the crisis. For example, Puryear, in *England, Russia, and the Straits Question* (esp. 264, 268, 289), and Rich, in *Why the Crimean War?* (esp. 9, 75–78), argue that the ambassador encouraged Turkish resistance leading to the failure of the mission, while Temperley, in *England and the Near East*, claims that Stratford acted responsibly and was not to blame for the escalation.

exercised such rights regarding Roman Catholics in Turkey as Russia now sought concerning Greek Orthodox Christians.[102] Although early British moderation reinforced Nicholas I's perceptions of the legitimacy of his demands, it did not lead the czar to infer that the British were weak. Russia never raised its demands following initial British restraint.

Britain

In late May, following reports of Russian mobilization, the British cabinet authorized Stratford to call up the fleet at Malta to any place he considered it necessary to protect Turkey. Rather than being a response to Russian action, however, Clarendon stated that this move was undertaken as "the least measure" that would "satisfy public opinion and save the government from shame hereafter."[103] He still believed in Nicholas I's "word of honour" and blamed Menshikov for exceeding his instructions,[104] but the position of the soft-liners within the government was weakening. By early June, the Tory newspapers were demanding the impeachment of both Aberdeen and Clarendon for aiding Menshikov in his mission.[105]

During the first week in June, the cabinet met and decided to send the fleet to Besika Bay.[106] During the meeting, Russell, Clarendon, and Palmerston agreed on the need for prompt action. Only Aberdeen opposed the action. Clarendon was clearly on Palmerston's side by this point and argued the need for a dramatic move.[107] The British fleet arrived in Besika Bay on 13 June and was joined by the French fleet on the following day. However, the cabinet agreed in mid-June that, if Russia invaded the principalities, Britain would advise the *Porte* not to declare war and would order Stratford not to call the British fleet to Constantinople.[108]

British perceptions hardened following the failure of the Menshikov mission. Aberdeen appeared wounded by Menshikov's final demands, saying they were "unreasonable and ought to be resisted. But I cannot yet believe that it will be necessary to do so by war if the Emperor

102. *Eastern Papers*, vol. 71, pt. 1, 212, 276–77, 296–97. Also see Nesselrode's memo to Brunnow, 1 June 1853, in Curtiss, *Russia's Crimean War*, 143–44.

103. Quoted in Conacher, *Aberdeen Coalition*, 151.

104. Clarendon to Cowley, 13 May 1853, FO 519/169, 303–4.

105. Conacher, *Aberdeen Coalition*, 155.

106. This move was apparently not a response to the Russian occupation, since news of the occupation plans only reached London on 5 June. See Conacher, *Aberdeen Coalition*, 153.

107. Chamberlain, *Lord Aberdeen*, 482. See also Rich, *Why the Crimean War?* 62–63.

108. Aberdeen to Russell, 21 June 1853, PRO 30/22/11A, 104–5.

should hitherto have been acting in good faith; if his whole conduct should have been a cheat the case is altered."[109] At the same time, Aberdeen agreed with Brunnow's assessment of the situation. In a memo to Aberdeen on 22 May, the Russian ambassador recounted all his conversations with Russell and Clarendon, asking Aberdeen if he objected to anything. The prime minister returned the memo and attested to its accuracy.[110] Aberdeen was the quintessential "irrational bargainer"; despite Menshikov's departure from Constantinople, the prime minister resisted changing his beliefs.

Palmerston and Russell remained bellicose and attributed aggressive intentions to the Russians. In response to Menshikov's departure, Russell complained that if *"[e]very privilege* of the Greek Orthodox (not of all Christians) is to be made a matter of engagement with Russia, it is intolerable. It is the way of the bear before he kills his victim!"[111] Palmerston's beliefs in the expansionist aims of the Russians were reinforced by Menshikov's coercive tactics, and he advocated firm resistance. On 22 May, he wrote to Clarendon:

> The policy and practice of the Russian Government has always been to push forward its encroachments as fast and as far as the apathy or want of firmness of other Governments would allow it to go, but always to stop and retire when it was met with decided resistance, and then to wait for the next favourable opportunity to make another spring on its unintended victim.[112]

He, too, was a strong advocate of sending the fleet to Besika Bay: "I feel strongly that if we allow a long delay to intervene, circumstances may arise which make us the laughing stock of Europe."[113]

Clarendon's statements and policy prescriptions fell somewhere between the extremes represented by Aberdeen, on the one hand, and Russell and Palmerston, on the other. According to Clarendon, Menshikov's final note reiterating Russian demands for future guarantees put Russia *"in the wrong*, and there we must endeavour to keep her."[114] Clarendon held that Menshikov's demands had given "a new and most unpleasant character to the question that has for so long kept Europe in

---

109. Quoted in Conacher, *Aberdeen Coalition*, 151.
110. Chamberlain, *Lord Aberdeen*, 481.
111. Quoted in Temperley, *England and the Near East*, 335.
112. Ashley, *Life and Correspondence of Palmerston*, 2:273.
113. Quoted in Conacher, *Aberdeen Coalition*, 152.
114. Quoted in Schroeder, *Austria, Great Britain, and the Crimean War*, 33.

excitement."[115] Clarendon too now advocated firm action. He instructed Seymour to inform the Russian government that Britain supported the sultan and ought not to have advised him to accept Menshikov's demands. He also supported sending the fleet and authorizing Stratford to summon the fleet if necessary, saying he wished they had done it earlier.[116] At the same time, however, he still expressed disdain for "all these disputes about nothing and this miserable rivalry for useless influence."[117]

The Russian occupation of the principalities only exacerbated the situation. Palmerston considered the occupation an unjust aggression, and he advocated a firm response, suggesting that "the excessive forbearance with which England and France ha[d] acted" had led to Russian aggression.

> . . . the result might have been foreseen. It is in the nature of men whose influence over events and whose power over others are founded on intimidation, and kept up by arrogant assumptions and pretensions, to mistake forbearance for irresolution, and to look upon inaction and hesitation as symptoms of fear, and forerunners of submission. . . . [I]f when Menshikoff began to threaten, the two squadrons had been sent to the neighbourhood of the Dardanelles, and if the Russian Government had been plainly told that the moment a Russian soldier set foot on Turkish territory, or as soon as a Russian ship-of-war approached with hostile intentions the Turkish coast, the combined squadrons would move up to the Bosphorus, and, if necessary, operate in the Black Sea, there can be little doubt that the Russian Government would have paused in its course, and things would not have come to the pass at which they have now arrived. But the Russian Government has been led on step by step by the apparent timidity of the Government of England. . . .[118]

This belief was reinforced by the news from Constantinople, where Stratford blamed the policy of negotiation and a "hesitating, uncalculating course" for the escalation of the conflict.[119]

---

115. Clarendon to Cowley, 25 June 1853, FO 519/169, 387–88.

116. *Eastern Papers*, vol. 71, pt. 1, 204; Chamberlain, *Lord Aberdeen*, 481–82.

117. Quoted in F. A. Wellesley, *The Paris Embassy during the Second Empire* (London: Thornton Butterworth, 1928), 26.

118. Ashley, *Life and Correspondence of Palmerston*, 2:278. Also see Gooch, *Later Correspondence of Lord John Russell*, 2:150–51; and Walpole, *Life of Lord John Russell*, 2:182–83.

119. *Eastern Papers*, vol. 71, pt. 1, 371.

Although increasingly frustrated and disappointed that the situation was "drifting fast toward war," Aberdeen remained concerned that Britain not engage in provocative behavior.[120] As late as July, he still felt the crisis could be resolved and opposed Palmerston's suggestion to send the fleet further—into the Bosphorus Straits or the Black Sea.[121]

While Clarendon's policy preferences placed him squarely in the Palmerston-Russell camp by the time of the occupation, he recognized the czar's difficult position and the need "to spare his dignity as much as possible."[122] The foreign secretary feared the czar would be driven to coercion "by the notion that all Europe would consider him disgraced by concession and by the formidable party of orthodox religionists which now exercises so much influence in Russia by its fanaticism and its nationality."[123] Clarendon did not think Nicholas I had expanded his goals in the Ottoman Empire. Rather, the foreign secretary believed that Britain needed only to "construct the bridge of retreat," to extend "a friendly hand to help [Nicholas I] out of his difficulties."[124] Yet domestic politics in Britain would allow no such thing. As Clarendon recognized, "Our pacific policy is at variance with public opinion so it cannot long be persisted in."[125] Although he was by now highly motivated by domestic pressures, the foreign secretary did not misperceive Russian intentions or overestimate the ability of British threats to influence the czar. His original beliefs and his estimations of Russian intentions remained unchanged, and he believed conciliation was the most effective policy. Nevertheless, he altered his policy preferences in response to domestic political incentives.

European Diplomacy: June to October 1853

Diplomatic efforts to resolve the crisis intensified. Between June and December 1853, eleven different diplomatic solutions were attempted with varying degrees of success.[126] These proposals originated in London, Vienna, St. Petersburg, Paris, and Constantinople, sometimes simultaneously, and the details of the different plans fueled further conflict.

---

120. Maxwell, *Life and Letters of Clarendon*, 2:15.

121. Conacher, *Aberdeen Coalition*, 160; Gordon, *Earl of Aberdeen*, 225–26.

122. Quoted in Temperley, *England and the Near East*, 344.

123. Clarendon to Cowley, 17 June 1853, FO 519/169, 439–40. Also see Clarendon to Cowley, 10 June 1853, FO 519/169, 420–21.

124. Clarendon to Cowley, 5, 6, and 9 July 1853, FO 519/169, 515, 537, 566.

125. Quoted in Temperley, *England and the Near East*, 344.

126. Stanley Lane-Poole, *The Life of the Right Honourable Stratford Canning*, 2 vols. (London: Longmans, Green, 1888), 2:278–80.

On 16 June, Britain and France urged Austria to convene a conference at Vienna, and both nations began to draft proposals for the conference's consideration. On 8 July, in response to a Russian appeal for mediation, the French submitted a draft proposal to the czar. Meanwhile, the British cabinet approved its own proposal drafted by Clarendon. While the Russians had no serious disagreement with the British proposal, it was soon superseded by the French one. In Russell's words, the plan was that "[t]he Emperor [of Russia] should be allowed to choose the French or the English project as he likes best: and whichever he chooses must be imposed on the Turks."[127] This never happened.

Count Buol, the Austrian foreign minister, summoned the ambassadors of the four neutral powers to the Vienna conference on 24 July. A week later, the conference adopted the Vienna Note, the French proposal with some modifications, as the exclusive basis for negotiations. The note acknowledged that "the Emperors of Russia at all times evinced their active solicitude for the religious and orthodox Greek Church," and that the sultan has at times "spontaneously granted" the Greek Church certain privileges and immunities. The sultan had to agree "to preserve from all prejudice either now or hereafter, the enjoyment of the spiritual privileges which have been granted by Her Majesty's august ancestors to the Orthodox Eastern Church, and which are maintained and confirmed by him. . . ." He could not alter the status quo in the Holy Places without the prior consent of the French and the Russians.[128] The czar immediately accepted the note on the condition that the Turks also accept it without modification.

The Vienna Note might have succeeded, were it not for the fact that a parallel effort was simultaneously underway in Constantinople. On 16 July, representatives of the four European powers met at the British embassy to consider a solution to the conflict, and several days later Stratford submitted a note to the *Porte*. The Grand Council opted for a stronger version that came to be known as the Turkish Ultimatum or Constantinople Note. This note protested the Russian ultimatum and occupation of the principalities and confirmed only the spiritual privileges of non-Moslem subjects of the *Porte*. The Turkish Ultimatum reached Vienna on 29 July, but Buol declined to send it on to St. Petersburg, substituting the Vienna Note instead. Almost a month later, the Turks rejected the European effort and suggested several amendments. Most important, they wanted to delete from the note the stipulation that

---

127. Quoted in Walpole, *Life of Lord John Russell*, 2:183–84.
128. *Eastern Papers*, vol. 71, pt. 2, 26–27, 81.

the Greeks would share in all rights granted to other Christians within the Ottoman Empire.[129]

Throughout six months of sometimes feverish diplomacy, Russia consistently demonstrated its willingness to cooperate. British leaders recognized Russian attempts to compromise, but the conflict had progressed too far. Public outrage in Britain and Turkish opposition, both of which had been hardened by Russian coercion, placed limits on the Aberdeen ministry. Soft-liners' strategic arguments had been severely eroded by Russia's coercive tactics, and the balance had already begun to shift against the moderate members of the cabinet. The situation worsened when, following the Turks' rejection of the Vienna Note, Nicholas I refused to accept the proposed modifications and Nesselrode reinterpreted the original note as favorable to Russian interests. Britain then abandoned the Vienna Note. It is difficult to argue that this action was taken in response to the Russian action, however, since attitudes in London had already shifted. More likely, Russia's interpretation of the Vienna Note was used as a rationalization for an action the British had already decided was necessary—unqualified support of the Ottoman Empire against the Russians.

Britain

Whether through Stratford's deception or communication delays, the dual track of the summer's negotiations worsened the situation. Indeed, Stratford's exact role in the development of the conflict remains a mystery. He neither placed the French proposal before the Turks nor informed them of the Vienna negotiations, insisting only that if his own plan were "found incapable of execution, the Convention may subsequently be brought forward." While recognizing that the Turkish plan represented a harsh ultimatum to the Russians, he reported that the *Porte* would hear of nothing else.[130] In London, Aberdeen and Clarendon were suspicious of Stratford's inaction on the Vienna plan, and Aberdeen prepared the queen for the ambassador's possible dismissal. According to the British ambassador to Paris, the news from Constantinople suggested that, while Stratford was obeying his instructions, "he lets it be seen at the same time that his private opinion is at variance with his official language."[131]

Among the members of the inner cabinet, there was a general

---

129. See *Eastern Papers*, vol. 71, pt. 2, 69–70, 78–79, 81.

130. For the quote see *Eastern Papers*, vol. 71, pt. 2, 52; see also Lane-Poole, *Life of Canning*, 2:286–90.

131. Cowley to Clarendon, 29 August 1853, Maxwell, *Life and Letters of Clarendon*, 2:16–19, quote at 18. Also see Walpole, *Life of Lord John Russell*, 2:185.

consensus that the Vienna Note should be the basis for negotiation, that Nicholas I had compromised by accepting the note immediately, and that he should not be asked to accept the Turkish changes. "[A]fter what the Emperor has already done," Aberdeen argued, "I doubt if he will accept them. At all events, after his prompt acceptance of our Note and his ready agreement to the alteration made by the English Government in the interest of the Porte, it is clear we have no right to ask him." The czar's position would, according to Aberdeen, be substantially improved if he would publicly announce his immediate withdrawal from the principalities upon Turkish acceptance of the Vienna Note: "This, I believe to be his intention; but this is what the course now adopted by the Turks will make it impossible for him to do."[132]

Clarendon found nothing in the note that might offend the "dignity or the independence of the Sultan"; he suggested that the Turks had made the modifications "under the conviction that they could not be complied with," and that they were now "determined not to have any settlement." According to Clarendon, the czar was in any event "perfectly free to reject" them.[133] Rather than blame Nicholas I, the foreign secretary blamed his own ambassador in Constantinople, for whom Clarendon believed "[t]he humiliation of Russia has become a necessity of his nature."[134] He firmly believed Stratford wanted war.[135]

Even Russell thought the Turks were being treacherous, although his views shifted throughout the course of negotiations over the proposed modifications. Initially, he argued that the Turks should be forced to yield. While still thinking the Turks "immense fools," he later expressed his hope that Nicholas I would concede and accept the changes. He clearly recognized Russia's "last compliance," and he argued that Britain should "not abet [the Turks] in their obstinacy." He fretted, however, that "this Eastern question has got us into as entangled a position as can well be."[136] By early September, before the "violent interpretation" that is usually blamed for negative British images of the Russians (discussed in the following sections on Russia and Britain), Russell had changed his view of the situation. Without any recent

132. Aberdeen to Russell, 26 August 1853, PRO 30/22/11A, 195–98; Aberdeen to Russell, 30 August 1853, PRO 30/22/11A, 205–6.

133. See, respectively, Gooch, *Later Correspondence of Lord John Russell*, 2:152; Clarendon to Russell, 27 August 1853, PRO 30/22/11A, 201–2; Gooch, 2:151–52; and *Eastern Papers*, vol. 71, pt. 2, 95, 86.

134. Clarendon to Cowley, 23 July 1853, FO 519/169, 605.

135. Clarendon to Cowley, 19 August 1853, FO 519/169, 716–20.

136. Quoted in Walpole, *Life of Lord John Russell*, 184–86; Russell to Clarendon, 20 August 1853, PRO 30/22/11A, 185.

change in Russian behavior, he had begun to question Russian intentions and to suggest that Britain stand by the Turks:

> When the Sultan, astonished at [the Russian] demand, asked his Allies for advice they said he was the best judge of his own honour and dignity. All he now asks is to make some amendments, to save his honour and dignity, in a Note presented to him by these four powers. Such being the case we surely cannot again present to him the same Note unamended, with whatever explanations we may accompany it. . . . If the Emperor of Russia rejects both the amended note of the Conference and the Turkish Note of the 23rd of July, we must conclude that he is bent on War, and prepare our measures accordingly.[137]

Much of the explanation for the shift in British response to the proposed modifications can be found in domestic public opinion. Although Nicholas I's willingness to compromise was recognized in London, it was ignored because of the public outcry. In addition to the general furor that had grown throughout the crisis, by August there was an increasing sense that war was inevitable. This pressured decision makers directly, and by the time of the proposed Turkish modifications, it was also wreaking havoc in British financial markets.[138] Throughout the summer, parliamentary debate on foreign policy became increasingly heated. By the last night of the session on 16 August, when a severely anti-Russian speech was delivered, only one member of Parliament defended the policy of the Aberdeen government.[139] The position of soft-liners within the cabinet was increasingly precarious.

Russia
Nicholas I and Nesselrode responded with surprising restraint to the Turkish demands for modification of the Vienna Note. On 7 September, Nesselrode sent a moderate but firm response to Vienna, saying that Russia would allow no modifications and that it was the responsibility of the four powers to obtain Turkish compliance. The Russians blamed Stratford for the *Porte's* rejection of the note, which they felt met the demands concerning the Holy Places and future guarantees. In a rever-

---

137. Russell memorandum, 3 September 1853, PRO 30/22/11A. Also see Conacher, *Aberdeen Coalition*, 177–78.

138. Lytton Strachey and Roger Fulford, eds., *The Greville Memoirs, 1814–1860*, 8 vols. (London: Macmillan, 1938), 6:437.

139. Conacher, *Aberdeen Coalition*, 166–74.

sal of their usual roles, Nicholas I was inclined to accept the amendments, but Nesselrode persuaded him to reject them.[140]

Meanwhile, on 7 September, Nesselrode sent a dispatch to his ambassadors in the field explaining why Russia could not accept the proposed modifications to the Vienna Note. This document interpreted the original note as favorable to Russian interests. News of the dispatch, which subsequently became known as the "violent interpretation," reached London on 16 September.[141] British leaders seized on this dispatch to justify an increasingly hostile policy.

Britain

Before the violent interpretation became known in London, the British and French ambassadors in Constantinople called up four small steamships, but Stratford resisted French efforts to call the whole fleet. Soon after news of Nesselrode's dispatch reached London and Paris, the French suggested a joint naval action, and the British agreed. On 23 September, the British and French authorized their fleets to pass through the Dardanelles to Constantinople, in violation of the 1841 treaty.[142]

The public response to the violent interpretation was swift and severe. The *Daily News* denounced the Vienna Note, saying it had been offered to help the Russians; and it was suggested in the London press that the Aberdeen government was in Russian pay. Even the *Times*, which had been sympathetic to the Aberdeen cabinet, suggested that Turkey had been justified in rejecting the original Vienna Note.[143] On 20 September 1853, an observer noted, "Day after day the Radical and Tory papers, animated by very different sentiments and motives, pour forth the most virulent abuse of the Emperor of Russia, of Austria, and of this Government, especially of Aberdeen."[144]

---

140. Nesselrode may have argued against compromise because "the little Minister" had been widely criticized at home. German and Protestant by birth, Nesselrode was the target of many attacks during an era of official nationality. See Riasanovsky, *Nicholas I and Official Nationality*, 145; Grunwald, *Tsar Nicholas I*, 181; and Walker, "Role of Karl Nesselrode," 231–33.

141. There is conflicting evidence on whether the violent interpretation was inadvertently leaked or deliberately given to the press. For the two views see Schroeder, *Austria, Great Britain, and the Crimean War*, 69; and Taylor, *Struggle for Mastery in Europe*, 55–56 n. 1.

142. This decision was apparently taken in response to rioting in that city. See Conacher, *Aberdeen Coalition*, 188.

143. Kingsley Martin, *The Triumph of Lord Palmerston: A Study of Public Opinion in England before the Crimean War* (London: Hutchinson & Co., 1963), 128–37.

144. Strachey and Fulford, *Greville Memoirs*, 6:450.

Palmerston continued to view Russian intentions as hostile and to advocate firm resistance, commenting on 1 November that "Russia must, by fair means or foul, be brought to give up her pretensions and withdraw her aggression."[145] Russell's distrust of Russia and desire to support the Turks only intensified. Upon hearing the news that Russia had refused the Turkish modifications, he commented, "If that is the case, the question must be decided by war, and if we do not stop the Russians on the Danube, we shall have to stop them on the Indus."[146] On 17 September he threatened to resign rather than force the unmodified Vienna Note on the *Porte*.[147]

Clarendon's and Aberdeen's public statements reflected shock at the apparent Russian intrigue. Their underlying views were little changed, however, again suggesting that they were driven by conscious considerations of domestic pressures and not by motivated misperception. Aberdeen thought that Nicholas I's rejection of the proposed amendments was understandable and more favorable a position than might have been expected, "for the Emperor adhered to the Vienna Note, from which he might have freed himself if he pleased, according to the terms of his former acceptance."[148]

Clarendon's policy preferences were hawkish and driven largely by domestic incentives. Although he maintained that the construction put on the Vienna Note by Nesselrode was grounds for suspicions, at the end of September Clarendon argued that the czar could not be expected to submit to any more humiliation.[149] At the same time, the foreign secretary was also aware of the growing public furor against Russia. Clarendon knew the czar would like a way to back down with honor, but he argued, "We cannot press the Turks too hard about the Note because public opinion would be against it, and secondly, because they would fight it out single-handed." He advocated sending the British fleet, saying, "With reference to public feeling in England, we could not well do less, and if any Russian attack were made upon Turkey that our fleet might have

---

145. Ashley, *Life and Correspondence of Palmerston*, 285.

146. Quoted in Conacher, *Aberdeen Coalition*, 182.

147. Walpole, *Life of Lord John Russell*, 2:190. Also see Maxwell, *Life and Letters of Clarendon*, 2:22–23; and Herbert C. F. Bell, *Lord Palmerston*, 2 vols. (Hamden, CT: Archon Books, 1966), 2:87–88.

148. Aberdeen to Russell, 26 September 1853, PRO 30/22/11A, 225–28. In that memo, Aberdeen also blamed Stratford, claiming that even if the four European powers adopted the modifications as their interpretation of the Vienna Note, "I fear it is still more doubtful whether Lord Stratford will allow the Turks to accept it."

149. *Eastern Papers*, vol. 71, pt. 2, 110–11; Schroeder, *Austria, Great Britain, and the Crimean War*, 87. Clarendon also blamed Stratford, who he believed was "bent on war." See Clarendon to Cowley, November 1853, FO 519/169, 1172.

prevented, we never should have heard the end of it."[150] On 23 September, Clarendon went so far as to remark that Russia had done Britain "a good turn" by issuing the violent interpretation.[151] Paul Schroeder's conclusion appears accurate: Clarendon had decided to reject the Vienna Note before the violent interpretation surfaced, but he used Nesselrode's dispatch as a rationalization.[152]

The official British response to the violent interpretation was to abandon the Vienna Note as the basis for negotiations and to suggest that the four powers adopt the Turkish modifications as their interpretation of the original note. This was necessary because the Russian dispatch showed that they "placed a different interpretation upon the original note, and thus, to a great extent, justified the fears of the *Porte* as to the pretensions which Russia would hereafter found upon it."[153] In reality, Russian coercion had so undermined the strategic arguments of the doves that they could no longer advocate compromise.

Russia

Despite growing concern about British unwillingness to compromise, Nicholas I undertook his largest concessions yet. During the last week of September, Nesselrode and the czar went to Olmütz to meet with British, French, Prussian, and Austrian representatives. The Russians again assured their colleagues that they desired no new rights and were willing "to meet every legitimate wish" of the European powers, implicitly refuting the violent interpretation. At Nicholas I's request Buol drew up a new proposal, known as the Buol Project or Olmütz Proposal, which built on the failed Vienna Note. In it, the czar offered to withdraw from the principalities as soon as the Vienna Note was signed.[154]

Meanwhile, events in Constantinople were overtaking European diplomatic efforts. On 4 October, the Turkish Grand Council officially declared war and gave Russia fifteen days to evacuate the principalities before hostilities would commence. The Russian commander in the principalities who had received the Turkish ultimatum replied on the eighteenth that he had no authority to respond. The Turks took this as a negative reply and initiated hostilities on 23 October.

Not only was the Russian response to the declaration of war to

---

150. Quoted respectively in Martin, *Triumph of Lord Palmerston*, 126–27; and Maxwell, *Life and Letters of Clarendon*, 2:26.

151. Clarendon to Cowley, 23 September 1853, FO 519/169, 883.

152. *Austria, Great Britain, and the Crimean War*, 65.

153. *Eastern Papers*, vol. 71, pt. 2, 217.

154. See Curtiss, *Russia's Crimean War*, 197; Rich, *Why the Crimean War?* 84–85; *Eastern Papers*, vol. 71, pt. 2, 128–29.

maintain a defensive posture, but the czar continued to pursue a negotiated settlement. On 17 October, Nesselrode indicated that Russia
would accept a settlement based on the Buol Project and a direct
Russo-Turkish understanding but that Turkey had to make the first
move. In response, Buol convened another conference of ambassadors
and drafted a new proposal, according to which Constantinople would
send a representative to negotiate with Russia in a neutral place.[155]
Because they felt the proposal favored Russia, however, Britain and
France refused to support it.

Britain
Despite a Turkish declaration of war, a peaceful settlement still appeared possible. Russia repeatedly offered concessions and continued to
act with restraint toward Constantinople. Of the major decision makers,
however, only Aberdeen advocated restraint. On 3 October, he wrote to
the queen, "Last night despatches were received from Olmütz, which
gave an account of a very strong declaration on the part of the Emperor
of Russia, of his desire to obtain nothing in Turkey beyond the actual
status quo in religious matters." The next day, Aberdeen said he would
resign rather than be a party to war with Russia "on such grounds as the
present."[156] He was, however, in an increasingly tenuous position at
home in relation to both his own cabinet and his parliamentary support.
His threat to resign carried little weight, since Russell's recent threat to
resign had revived the issue of his succession.[157]

The rest of the cabinet opposed the Olmütz proposal, but Clarendon at least did not question Nicholas I's intentions. The foreign secretary recognized the nature of the czar's offers at Olmütz, commenting
that Nicholas I "did eat dirt and went far to neutralize the dispatch of
objections to the modifications." Clarendon even felt that the czar
might offer further concessions: "Nicholas seems now prepared to eat a
great deal of dirt and to swallow modifications and other things he
would not look at four months ago but I suppose there must be a
limit."[158] The foreign secretary argued that Buol's abandonment of the
Vienna Note and failure to protest the decision to send the fleets to the

155. *Eastern Papers*, vol. 71, pt. 2, 187–88.
156. Quoted respectively in Conacher, *Aberdeen Coalition*, 192; and Chamberlain, *Lord Aberdeen*, 486.
157. Chamberlain, *Lord Aberdeen*, 478. Also see Maxwell, *Life and Letters of Clarendon*, 2:30–31.
158. Quoted in Schroeder, *Austria, Great Britain, and the Crimean War*, 102. Seymour agreed that the Olmütz proposal was "a notable specimen of what can be done in the
way of backing" down. See Schroeder, 79.

Straits meant that Russia had given him instructions "to agree to whatever we propose."[159]

Clarendon nevertheless provided the swing vote, with Palmerston and Russell, against accepting the Olmütz proposals. His reason was less suspicion of Russian intentions than fear of Turkish refusal and of the "false and embarrassing" position in which it would put the British cabinet, particularly in the face of domestic public opinion. On 5 October, Clarendon wrote, "The public seems to think that there is nothing to do but to declare war against Russia, just when she is yielding the point in dispute."[160] As with the Vienna Note, if the *Porte* rejected the Buol Project, Britain would have no obvious complaint against Nicholas I.[161] In early November, Clarendon wrote to Aberdeen, "We are now in an anomalous and painful position, and, although I shall admit it to no one but yourself, I have arrived at the conviction that it might have been avoided by firmer language, and a more decided course five months ago."[162]

The British cabinet rejected Russian concessions as failing to repudiate the violent interpretation and, on 8 October, ordered the fleets to proceed immediately to Constantinople. A week later, the government authorized the fleets to pass through the Bosphorus and enter the Black Sea if Russia attacked the Turks. Clarendon attempted one more diplomatic settlement in late October. The new note incorporated the Turkish objections to the Vienna Note but also met many of the Russian demands. It was rejected as too pro-Turkish by Buol, however, who suggested a collective note that omitted any reference to concessions by the Greek Church of privileges granted to other religions.[163]

The Russo-Turkish War: October 1853 to March 1854

Once Russia and Turkey were at war, events quickly overtook diplomacy. While Russia initially fought a defensive war and Britain

---

159. Quoted in Schroeder, *Austria, Great Britain, and the Crimean War*, 97.

160. Quoted in Martin, *Triumph of Lord Palmerston*, 140. On Clarendon's fears that public opinion was driving the cabinet to war, see also Clarendon to Cowley, 4 October 1853, FO 519/169, 931–32.

161. See Curtiss, *Russia's Crimean War*, 195–96; and Schroeder, *Austria, Great Britain, and the Crimean War*, 63–73, 79–81. The British ambassador to Paris, Cowley, drew similar conclusions: "I must say that I never expected to get as much out of the Czar"; "[t]he real difficulty for us appears to be to avoid getting again into *the fix* out of which we have just escaped—that is finding ourselves advocating Russia against Turkey." Schroeder, *Austria, Great Britain, and the Crimean War*, 79.

162. Quoted in Conacher, *Aberdeen Coalition*, 207–8.

163. *Eastern Papers*, vol. 61, pt. 2, 186.

proceeded with its diplomatic initiatives, the conflict soon escalated. In the end, as Clarendon conceded, public opinion forced him to abandon any attempt at compromise.

Russia

The British shift from early accommodation to an uncompromising stance on the Eastern question puzzled Russian leaders. Following London's failure to force the Vienna Note or the Olmütz Proposal on the Turks, the czar and his foreign minister finally questioned British intentions. They no longer only blamed Stratford or thought him unrepresentative of the British cabinet; they now held the Aberdeen ministry as a whole responsible for the escalation of the crisis. In a 27 October conversation with Seymour, Nesselrode expressed his belief "that if England insisted as she ought to have done at Constantinople, the Porte would long ago have given way, and the Vienna note would have been signed; that England, in fact, was solely to blame for the complications of the moment, and for those disastrous consequences to which they were likely to lead."[164] Despite this growing mistrust, Nicholas I did not escalate the conflict. He did not want war, but he had been placed in a position from which retreat would mean humiliation.

Britain

Given their recognition both of Russian concessions and of their own precarious position, the British continued to pursue a negotiated settlement. After Britain refused to support Buol's project and the Turks rejected it as favoring the Russians, a new European initiative was undertaken. A combined British-French proposal was sent to Vienna, and the conference of ambassadors recommenced on 3 December to consider the proposal. Two days later, the conference adopted a Collective Note, which invited the *Porte* to set forth its own proposals and set conditions for a settlement in the form of a list of assurances to be given by both parties.[165]

The dovish prime minister continued to be sympathetic to the czar's position and thought Nicholas I's intentions remained limited and reasonable. On 15 November, Aberdeen commented, "I have no doubt that the Emperor himself desires peace; and the difficulties of his present position are quite sufficient to make him reasonable. But I know that

---

164. *Eastern Papers*, vol. 71, pt. 2, 213.
165. Conacher, *Aberdeen Coalition*, 213; Schroeder, *Austria, Great Britain, and the Crimean War*, 106–11. For the text of the Collective Note see *Eastern Papers*, vol. 71, pt. 2, 297–98.

he cannot submit to personal degradation. . . ." He also recognized Nicholas I's restraint: "The Emperor of Russia had most unjustifiably invaded the Principalities, but he had not declared war, and did not require an inch of territory."[166]

These diplomatic efforts were soon overcome by the events of the Russo-Turkish war. On 30 November, the Russian pattern of fighting a defensive war changed dramatically. In the Battle of Sinope the Russian navy went on the offensive, destroying the Turkish fleet and the city of Sinope and killing thousands of Turks. The news of the "massacre" did not reach London until 12 December, after the Collective Note had already been sent. The reaction of the public and press was swift and vicious. Sir James Graham commented, "The attack on Sinope has produced an immense effect on the public mind both in France and in England. It is difficult to put any restraint on the national desire to avenge what is regarded as a contempt and defiance of our flags."[167]

Within a few days of hearing the news of Sinope, Palmerston resigned from the government, ostensibly in opposition to a franchise reform bill. It was widely assumed, however, that the real reason for his departure was the Aberdeen government's failure to take a firm stand against Russia. The *Morning Post* even reported that the home secretary had resigned because of the "un-English" foreign policy of the Aberdeen government.[168] Palmerston's resignation was sorely felt by his colleagues; support for the government within Parliament declined sharply.[169] Both the news of Sinope and Palmerston's resignation led to public attacks on Prince Albert, who reportedly brought about the secretary's departure through his unconstitutional interference in foreign policy. These attacks reached a climax in January 1854, and it was even rumored that the prince

166. *The Correspondence of Lord Aberdeen and Princess Lieven, 1832–1854*, ed. E. Jones Parry, 3d ser., 62 vols. (London: Royal Historical Society, 1938–39), 62:653; Gordon, *Earl of Aberdeen*, 238.

167. Charles Stuart Parker, *Life and Letters of Sir James Graham*, 2 vols. (London: John Murray, 1907), 2:226. On the press reaction to Sinope, see Breeze, "British Opinion of Russian Foreign Policy," 156–57. Contrary to Graham's statement, this public outcry was not echoed in Paris, where the business and political elites were enraged by the massacre, but where the mass public reacted very little. See Lynn M. Case, *French Opinion on War and Diplomacy during the Second Empire* (Philadelphia: University of Pennsylvania Press, 1954), 16–18. The French ambassador's response reflected this public reaction; Castelbajac reportedly congratulated the czar on his victory at Sinope, since it would mean a quick end to the war. See Vitzhum von Eckstäedt, *St. Petersburg and London*, 1:9.

168. Martin, *Triumph of Lord Palmerston*, 148.

169. Russell to Clarendon, 15 December 1853, PRO 30/22/11B, 235–36; Aberdeen to Russell, 20 December 1853, PRO 30/22/11B, 271–74.

had been impeached for high treason.[170] Both Lord Lansdowne and Russell also reportedly threatened resignation around this time.[171]

Russian action at Sinope destroyed the last chance for a peaceful settlement, although it did not result immediately in war, only in the abandonment of the Collective Note. In London, news of the attack was taken as evidence of Russian aggressive intentions and deceit, although not of imminent war. Stratford reported from Constantinople, "[i]t appears that the Turks were the first to fire; this does not prevent the Russians from having been the aggressors." Clarendon laid responsibility for the action directly on St. Petersburg, where decision makers knew of British and French instructions to their fleets: "[I]t was not the Turkish squadron alone that was deliberately attacked in the harbour of Sinope."[172] Nevertheless, Clarendon made it clear that it was public opinion driving the nation to war:

> . . . if this last attempt at negotiation fails and the war goes on till the spring the impatience of the people will become uncontrollable. Palmerston might then put himself at the head of the war and antireform Party (which is one and the same) and turn out the Government for the purpose of *not making* peace without some *previous war* with Russia. This would not be disliked now in England; before Easter arrives it would be very popular. . . .[173]

According to Clarendon, even if the British government wanted to "backslide," it "should not be allowed to do so" by the public.[174]

Aberdeen remained pacific, arguing until the end that war was not inevitable.[175] While British leaders did not seek war, domestic pressure made it increasingly likely. In December, Russell summed up British hesitancy about war when he wrote, "I do not blame the Russians; they are fighting for Empire, [and] they do it boldly—But we must not

170. Arthur Christopher Benson and Viscount Esher, eds., *The Letters of Queen Victoria*, 3 vols. (London: John Murray, 1907), 3:3; Walpole, *Life of Lord John Russell*, 2:202–3.

171. Taylor, *Struggle for Mastery in Europe*, 58; Walpole, *Life of Lord John Russell*, 2:200.

172. Clarendon to Seymour, 27 December 1853, *Eastern Papers*, vol. 71, pt. 2, 322.

173. Clarendon to Cowley, 16 December 1853, FO 519/169, 1380–81. Also see Clarendon to Cowley, 27 December 1853, FO 519/169, 1434–35, 1453–54; and Clarendon to Cowley, 10 January 1854, FO 519/170, 47.

174. Clarendon to Cowley, 2 February 1854, FO 519/169, 163–64.

175. The prime minister even stood before the House of Lords to defend Nicholas I several weeks after the start of the British war with Russia. See Chamberlain, *Lord Aberdeen*, 531.

be conniving parties to the subjugation of Turkey, either morally or physically."[176]

In response to the public outcry generated by the Sinope massacre, the British Cabinet decided on 22 December, in Palmerston's absence, to send the fleet to join the French in the Black Sea and to inform the Russians that any Russian ship caught out of harbor would be seized or sunk. The Allied fleets arrived in early January 1854, and on the eighth the British warship *Retribution* entered Sevastopol harbor. The British commander notified Admiral Menshikov of his orders to protect Turkish ships and territory and to restrict Russian vessels to their ports.[177] Public opinion was now largely determining the British response.

Russia

Nicholas I was outraged by the British action but did not declare war. Throughout the next month, some sporadic but unsuccessful efforts were made to resolve the crisis short of war. The shift in the czar's perception of Britain, from a friendly ally that was cooperating with Russian efforts to restore the status quo to an uncompromising adversary that had ignored Russian efforts to compromise, was complete.

In January 1854, Nicholas I stepped up his attacks on Nesselrode who, he argued, was too moderate and had convinced him to offer concessions at Olmütz. And, of course, he blamed the British. In response to the presence of the British fleet in Sevastopol, Nicholas I raged, "This is too much. . . . I can no longer tolerate this English arrogance. The honour of Russia is compromised, English forces are to war; let the responsibility for it weigh on her before God who knows I wanted peace."[178] But he did not declare war against the British or even consider the British action a declaration of war against Russia, reasoning that if Turkish ships were also confined to port, there was not yet any reason for war.

At the same time, Nicholas I sent Count Orlov to Vienna to seek assurances of Austrian and Prussian neutrality in any conflict and to attempt one more diplomatic resolution. The Vienna conference produced another protocol, the terms of which had little or no chance for success.[179] On 29 January, Louis Napoleon sent a letter to the czar proposing that Russia evacuate the principalities in exchange for the British and French squadrons' departure from the Black Sea. Russia was then

---

176. Quoted in Conacher, *Aberdeen Coalition*, 239.

177. Walker, "Role of Karl Nesselrode," 255.

178. Quoted in Walker, "Role of Karl Nesselrode," 258.

179. Only Aberdeen was reassured by Orlov's mission. See Conacher, *Aberdeen Coalition*, 247–48.

to negotiate a treaty directly with Turkey and submit it to a four-power conference. If Russia refused this offer, Britain and France would declare war.

Nicholas I responded by questioning Napoleon's motives in sending the letter, but he stated that he was willing to negotiate with the Turks. It was too late, however, since Britain refused to restrict Turkish ships to port as requested by the Russians, and on 4 and 5 February, the Russian ambassadors left London and Paris. Although they severed diplomatic relations with the British and French, the Russians still did not declare war. This action they left to the French and British, who declared war on 27 and 28 March 1854, respectively.

Conclusions

One is left with the eerie, tragic sense that Russia and Britain slowly, but very deliberately, marched to war in 1854, that shortsighted and inept diplomats wanted peace but could never quite find their way there. In large part, this was because neither side understood how its policy interacted with the domestic political situation in the opposing states. In St. Petersburg, Czar Nicholas I interpreted the initially conciliatory British response as confirmation of his belief in the efficacy of force and in the willingness of Britain to compromise on the issue of the Holy Places. He was surprised to learn late in the crisis that Britain was unwilling to relinquish its interests in the Ottoman Empire. Russian bargaining strategy influenced British policy in a fundamentally different manner: the Menshikov mission and the invasion of the Turkish principalities undermined the arguments of the soft-liners within the British cabinet and reinforced those of the more hawkish elements, making compromise impossible. The difference in the two nations' decision-making processes resulted from radically different state structures. The unitary, autonomous nature of the Russian state meant that the czar was responsible for foreign policy, while the diffuse, nonautonomous nature of the British state meant that decision makers were subject to domestic pressures and that the content of British policy reflected the collective nature of decision making.

Two alternative approaches—international structural theories and motivational psychology—do not fare well in the Crimean case. Structural theories predict that the Crimean crisis would end in war, but they cannot account for the origins of British and Russian interests or explain how one state's strategy influences another state's response. The overestimation of an opponent's hostility and of the efficacy of one's own tactics that motivational psychology predicts did not transpire. In the end, British leaders shifted to coercive tactics and the crisis escalated to war, not because their images of Russian intentions had dramatically changed, or because they mistakenly believed that threats would succeed, but because domestic pressures in Britain precluded further compromise. It is theoretically possible that Nicholas I engaged in wishful thinking by initially believing that Britain would compromise, but the czar certainly was not motivated by domestic vulnerability.

The argument of this chapter does not displace cognitive or bureaucratic explanations of crisis decision making. Rather, it integrates and builds on them by adding the variable of state structure. The facts of the case bear out the major prediction of cognitive psychology, that people interpret the events of a crisis according to their preexisting beliefs. In the Russian case, this explains the bargaining process and the outcome of the conflict. Nicholas I initially interpreted the situation according to his preexisting beliefs about the willingness of Britain to compromise. It took strong negative evidence, which did not arrive until too late, to convince the czar that Britain would resist. In a state like Britain, however, where executive authority is diffuse and dependent on the legislature, a cognitive approach does not explain the decision-making process.

A bureaucratic politics approach best captures the bargaining process in London on the eve of the Crimean War. The British leaders' decisions reflected societal pressures and the imperatives of elite coalition formation. Initial Russian coercive tactics undermined the strategic arguments and policy prescriptions of the more dovish members of the government and strengthened those of the hard-line opposition. The moderate Clarendon provided the swing vote that led to the shift toward a more coercive British policy. Although his perceptions of Russian intentions were little changed, his incentives were structured by the volatile domestic situation in London. By the time Nicholas I shifted to conciliation, it was too late to compromise. Any voices of moderation within the British government had been silenced by the roar of public opinion. The state structure variable, then, determines the usefulness of existing cognitive and bureaucratic explanations for understanding the Crimean War crisis.

4

The Fashoda Crisis, 1898

Britain and France came dangerously close to war in 1898 over posses-
sion of an abandoned fort in the swamps of the Nile River. Conventional
wisdom about the Fashoda crisis reflects the logic of deterrence theory:
the initially coercive British strategy brought diplomatic victory because
the balance of power and interests favored London. British bargaining
behavior convinced the French to recognize the inferiority of their position and to accept a humiliating defeat. This strategy also explains the
subsequent, long-term improvement in Anglo-French relations, because
it resolved the underlying source of conflict.[1] Nevertheless, existing theories are insufficient. While the balance of capabilities favored London, it
is impossible to establish the primacy of British interests in the Sudan
without reference to domestic political factors.

The mostly unitary nature of the French foreign policy executive
meant that the foreign minister, Théophile Delcassé, enjoyed great freedom of action, but the nonautonomous nature of the executive-legislative
relationship meant that he was constrained by societal pressures. Delcassé's hard-line, opportunist beliefs led him to test the British at
Fashoda, but French public opinion opposed colonialist expansion. At
the same time, however, a small group of procolonial organizations and
members of the French Assembly sought compensation in East Africa for
the loss of Fashoda. Delcassé stalled for time while he tried to secure
concessions to appease these private actors.

The British state of the 1890s is also best described as nonautonomous, but the British executive comprised multiple offices. As in the
Crimean case, the opponent's hard-line strategy eroded the credibility of
the moderate prime minister and garnered support for the strategic
arguments of his hawkish domestic opponents. In both France and Britain, in short, the political institutions of the state determined the bargaining process, while the foreign policy orientation of the government determined the state's policy response. A brief description of the origins of

---

1. See Charles Lockhart, "Conflict Actions and Outcomes: Long-Term Impacts,"
Journal of Conflict Resolution, 22 (December 1978): 565–98.

the conflict and of existing explanations for its outcome follows, after which I discuss the structure of foreign policy authority and the foreign policy orientations of the two governments. The remainder of the chapter then traces the chronological development of the crisis.

Origins of the Conflict

The clash at Fashoda was the culmination of years of Anglo-French rivalry in Africa. In the West, Paris and London quarrelled over territory in the Upper Niger region, while their conflict in the East focused on Egypt. Military intervention in Egypt in 1882 to preserve the pro-Western government had established British dominance in the region. London next began to advance claims to the Upper Nile region, based on the historic claims of Egypt to the Sudan, and to challenge the claims of an indigenous Mahdist state.[2] The French rejected British claims to the area, claiming that it was *res nullius*; all foreign authority, they argued, had disappeared with the British evacuation in 1885, following the fall of Khartoum to the Mahdists.[3]

Paris launched a series of expeditions to the region to challenge British rule.[4] Hearing of these expeditions, the British responded in April 1895 with a threat issued by the undersecretary of state for foreign affairs, Edward Grey. On the floor of the House of Commons, Grey declared that Britain would view any French expedition as "an unfriendly act."[5] The British further argued in 1897 that no "other European Power than Great Britain has any claim to occupy any part of the Valley of the Nile."[6] Far from being frightened off, the French dismissed the Grey Declaration and proceeded to launch several more expeditions to the Nile.[7] Only the expedition led by Captain Jean-Baptiste Marchand made it through to Fashoda, arriving there on 10 July.

---

2. See Morrison Beall Giffen, *Fashoda: The Incident and Its Diplomatic Setting* (Chicago: University of Chicago Press, 1930), 44, 49–57; Thomas M. Iiams, Jr., *Dreyfus, Diplomatists, and the Dual Alliance: Gabriel Hanotaux at the Quai d'Orsay (1894–1898)* (Paris and Geneva, 1962), 50–51; and Patricia Wright, *Conflict on the Nile: The Fashoda Incident of 1898* (London: Heinemann, 1972), 3–108.

3. See Giffen, *Fashoda*, 37–44.

4. On these missions, see G. N. Sanderson, *England, Europe, and the Upper Nile, 1882–1899* (Edinburgh: University Press, 1965), 140–52.

5. Sanderson, *England, Europe, and the Upper Nile*, 214.

6. Monson to Hanotaux, 10 December 1897, quoted in Salisbury to Cromer, no. 185, 2 August 1898, in G. P. Gooch and Harold Temperley, eds., *British Documents on the Origins of the War 1898–1914*, 11 vols. (London: His Majesty's Stationery Office, 1927), 1:160 (hereinafter *British Documents*).

7. On the French expeditions to Abyssinia, see William L. Langer, *The Diplomacy of Imperialism, 1890–1902*, 2d ed. (New York: Knopf, 1956), 540–46.

The British also stepped up their activity in the Sudan. In March 1896, the cabinet ordered the sirdar of the Egyptian army, General Herbert Kitchener, to advance up the Nile to Dongola, about 450 miles north of Fashoda, to recover Egyptian territory. In January 1898, the Salisbury government authorized Kitchener to advance further to Khartoum and to reconquer the Sudan. When he arrived at Fashoda on 19 September, however, he found the French expedition already encamped there.

Alternative Explanations

International Structure

Of the cases examined in this study, Fashoda provides the strongest support for a systemic explanation of crisis bargaining. The balance of interests and the distribution of power placed the two adversaries in a game of Bully in which each side preferred to win, but in which only Britain preferred war to cooperation in Africa. A British strategy of initial coercion resulted in diplomatic victory, according to a structural approach, because it clarified the situation to French decision makers. As one historian describes it, "[t]he situation of France . . . was one of complete helplessness. . . . The outcome of the conflict was a foregone conclusion."[8]

The balance of military capabilities favored Britain. On the ground at Fashoda, Kitchener's force outnumbered Marchand's group of six officers and 120 Senegalese soldiers by two hundred to one. In fact, the French force was too weak to defend itself against an attack by native dervishes.[9] Britain also held a preponderant advantage in overall forces, most notably in the naval forces necessary to obtain and maintain a colonial empire.[10]

---

8. Langer, *Diplomacy of Imperialism*, 563, 576. For similar arguments see Winfried Baumgart, *Imperialism: The Idea and Reality of British and French Colonial Expansion, 1880–1914* (New York: Oxford University Press, 1982), 68; J. A. S. Grenville, *Lord Salisbury and Foreign Policy: The Close of the Nineteenth Century* (London: University of London, 1964), 218; Sanderson, *England, Europe, and the Upper Nile*, 355–62; Snyder and Diesing, *Conflict among Nations*, esp. 123–24, 532; and Taylor, *Struggle for Mastery in Europe*, 380.

9. Rodd to Salisbury, 25 September 1898, no. 13, in Great Britain, *Parliamentary Papers, Egypt No. 2, Correspondence with the French Government Respecting the Valley of the Upper Nile*, vol. 112, 1898 (London, 1899), no. 1 (hereinafter *Correspondence*), 375; Colonel Wingate to Sir Arthur Bigge, 23 September 1898, in George Earle Buckle, ed., *The Letters of Queen Victoria*, 3d ser., 3 vols. (New York: Longmans, Green, 1932), 3:287.

10. See Arthur J. Marder, *The Anatomy of British Sea Power: A History of British Naval Policy in the Pre-Dreadnought Era, 1880–1905* (Hamden, CT: Archon Books, 1964), 321.

While the distribution of power favored London, it was not clear from the outset of the crisis that an inferior France would have to stand alone in a war with England. Prior to the conflict, even the British ambassador in Paris, Edmund Monson, argued that France would be supported by its Russian ally in any conflict with Britain. In July 1898, he wrote that "it would be extremely dangerous were we to base our policy in any controversy with France upon the assumption that we should be allowed to deal with her as our sole enemy."[11] Most important, the British navy doubted its ability to defeat a combined Russian-French force.[12]

Conventional wisdom further asserts the superiority of British interests in the Fashoda conflict. Egypt had been a British protectorate since 1882, and the British presence in the Sudan in 1898 resulted from renewed support for Egyptian claims to the Upper Nile. Because of the region's importance in protecting lines of communication to India, Britain's historical claims to the area, and recent activity there, British authorities preferred war to surrendering any territory along the Nile to the French.[13] According to this argument, Britain sought to preserve the status quo in Egypt or, at the least, to root claims to new territory in the existing division of Africa. French leaders questioned the legitimacy of British dominance, however, arguing that any such role had ended with London's defeat in 1885.

The very success of systemic theories in explaining the outcome of the Fashoda crisis suggests their shortcomings. While Britain possessed undisputed military superiority, a factor that clearly influenced the outcome of the crisis, it is impossible to establish the supremacy of British interests and the overall structure of the conflict independent of the prestrategic interests of the state. Reconstructing British and French interests, and the way each was affected by the other's behavior, requires an analysis of the domestic structure and foreign policy orientation of the regime. Such a focus raises two important issues.

First, the relative intensity of public opinion in the two countries was the primary reason British interest in Egypt exceeded French interest. Paris had forgone intervention in 1882, according to Delcassé, because of parliamentary opposition.[14] While there was a vocal, if small,

---

11. Monson to Salisbury, 4 July 1898, no. 184, *British Documents*, 1:159.

12. Robert Taylor, *Lord Salisbury* (New York: St. Martin's Press, 1975), 140, 142.

13. See Iiams, *Dreyfus, Diplomatists, and the Dual Alliance*, 58; Lebow, *Between Peace and War*, 320–26; Lockhart, *Bargaining in International Conflicts*, 22, 85; and Snyder and Diesing, *Conflict among Nations*, 123–24, 508, 524.

14. Christopher Andrew, *Théophile Delcassé and the Making of the Entente Cordiale* (London: Macmillan, 1968), 21–22.

part of the public that favored colonial expansion in Africa, even over British resistance, the overwhelming majority of the French people opposed it. The British ambassador to Paris, Monson, recognized this in his correspondence with London: "The Colonial group is very noisy, and has very able exponents in the press, . . . but I do not believe that the country at large either cares much about such matters or knows anything about them. . . . I do not mean to say that Frenchmen in general care very much about Egypt, or resent very much the position which Great Britain holds there."[15] When faced with external resistance to France's colonial policy, the French public withheld its support.

Second, different policy makers held different conceptions of the national interest. As they had differed over the value of preventing Russian influence in Constantinople in the Crimean War crisis, British leaders differed in their views of the relative value of Fashoda, specifically, and of colonies, generally. As I discuss later in this chapter, Salisbury placed a much higher value on rapprochement with France and on preserving European peace than did Chamberlain, who strongly advocated colonial expansion. Public opinion supported Chamberlain's view. However, the fact that societal factors entered the decision-making process and national policy reflected the aggregation of individual preferences has more to do with the structure of the state than with any objective notion of the national interest. Again, as in the Crimean case, this does not invalidate international structural theories. It merely suggests that, even in the best case, they are insufficient to explain crisis dynamics.

Motivated Bias

Motivational psychology predicts that a domestically vulnerable leader will misperceive or ignore coercive tactics, particularly in the highly threatening context of an international crisis. As the Fashoda case demonstrates, however, domestic weakness alone is insufficient to explain the evolution of a crisis, since the highly vulnerable Delcassé eventually realized Britain's unwillingness to compromise and backed down.

Domestic politics, but not motivated misperception, was the driving force behind British policy in the Fashoda crisis. Richard Ned Lebow hypothesizes that Salisbury engaged in coercive behavior to appear firm to his colleagues.[16] However, the prime minister was not motivated—

---

15. Monson to Salisbury, 4 August 1898, no. 186, *British Documents*, 1:161–62. For similar statements in the British press see Andrew, *Théophile Delcassé*, 50.
16. *Between Peace and War*, 322.

either by the weakness of his position, or by the vehemence of British public opinion—to overestimate French hostility and advocate confrontational policies; indeed, he believed threats might prove counterproductive. Until the end, he recognized the need for procedural concessions to help Delcassé out of his own domestic morass. Furthermore, Salisbury did not engage in wishful thinking; he recognized the domestic imperatives he faced, noting in early October, "No offer of territorial concession on our part would be endured by public opinion here."[17]

France presents a more ambiguous case for motivational psychology. Delcassé's domestic position was precarious given the Paris strikes and the public outcry over the Dreyfus Affair. But while this domestic situation made it difficult for the foreign minister to compromise, it did not make it impossible. In fact, the domestic situation compelled Delcassé to concede defeat in the end. The French public simply would not tolerate war with Britain over Fashoda.

Nevertheless, Delcassé's behavior early in the crisis is consistent with a motivated bias approach. Even given the coerciveness of Britain's early policy, Delcassé remained optimistic about his chances for obtaining concessions. In early October, he noted, "Each day that passes is a step towards a calmer atmosphere." He acknowledged that "the situation is still grave, but we are gaining time and time causes reflection." He further maintained, "There now seems to me some *détente* between England and ourselves."[18] While it is possible that British threats and French domestic volatility may have motivated Delcassé to believe his policy was succeeding, it is more likely that his optimism was a rational response to Salisbury's conciliatory statements.

While the evidence for the presence of motivated bias is ambiguous, that against it is not. Both British and French leaders were domestically weak, but this condition had different effects on the two governments. Delcassé compromised despite—and even because of—his extreme domestic weakness.

Cognitive and Bureaucratic Explanations

As in the Crimean case, cognitive and bureaucratic approaches each capture a part of the decision-making process. National leaders in both Britain and France viewed their opponent's behavior against a background of preexisting beliefs, but in both countries some elements of

---

17. Buckle, *Letters of Queen Victoria*, 3:290.
18. All three statements are quoted in Andrew, *Théophile Delcassé*, 100.

bureaucratic politics theory also apply. Delcassé was a hard-line opportunist who probed for weakness then retreated in the face of British resolve, but his behavior can be explained more simply by examining the domestic level of analysis. The majority of the French public and press opposed Delcassé's colonial policies and pressed for compromise with the British. Yet some domestic actors, especially the Colonial Party within the Chamber of Deputies, actively resisted compromise, leading Delcassé to stall for time—a policy that edged the conflict dangerously close to war. These actors only entered the decision-making process because of the structure of the French state.

In Britain, key members of the Cabinet interpreted French actions according to their different political beliefs, but coalition politics explains British policy. French strategy undermined Prime Minister Salisbury's conciliatory arguments and reinforced the hawkish views of the colonial secretary, Chamberlain. In both countries, the domestic structure of the state determined the process by which the crisis was resolved and, therefore, the usefulness of cognitive and bureaucratic political explanations. The following section describes those structures and the foreign policy orientation of the key actors.

State Structure and the Decision-Making Process in London and Paris

Britain

In the years between the Crimean War and the Fashoda crisis, the rise of political parties weakened, but did not eliminate, the principle of parliamentary sovereignty in British politics. Executive authority nevertheless continued to be collectively exercised by a stronger cabinet, and Britain remained a type IV—diffuse, nonautonomous—state.

Electoral reforms in 1867 and 1885 strengthened party cohesion, discipline, and influence.[19] A larger electorate and redistricting created a more direct link between voter and politician. As leaders appealed directly to the public, political parties became increasingly important means of curbing members of Parliament, whose role gradually declined to supporting one's party and its leaders. These reforms gave the

---

19. See Gary W. Cox, *The Efficient Secret: The Cabinet and the Development of Political Parties in Victorian England* (Cambridge: Cambridge University Press, 1987), 10–11; Mackintosh, *British Cabinet*, 161–62, 188; and Marvin Swartz, *The Politics of British Foreign Policy in the Era of Disraeli and Gladstone* (New York: St. Martin's Press, 1985), 3–4.

cabinet of the late nineteenth century greater freedom of action than earlier British cabinets had enjoyed.[20]

It is possible, however, to overstate the extent of this freedom. As John P. Mackintosh explains, what changed was the type of control Parliament was able to exercise, not the fact of its influence. Whereas the British cabinet of the early and middle decades of the century worried that Parliament would defeat its measures, the cabinet of the 1880s and beyond fretted that the attempt to push a specific piece of legislation through the House might irrevocably damage party cohesion.[21] In the later part of the century, the cabinet resigned less frequently following the failure of a vote of confidence and it dissolved Parliament more often, but more questions were considered votes of confidence.[22] A strong belief in popular sovereignty and the power of Parliament remained. As Mackintosh concludes, "The House of Commons still exercised a strong influence, but it did so more as an indicator of public opinion, a warning of what the electors might decide at the next election, than as an authority that might dethrone a Cabinet or reverse its policies."[23]

The second aspect of British government, the doctrine of collective responsibility, remained virtually unchanged in the late nineteenth century; executive authority for foreign policy was diffuse. Consensus within the cabinet was essential since, in theory, any member of the inner circle could veto a decision. Salisbury's 1895 complaint that the cabinet refused to accept his policy regarding the Ottoman Empire was echoed several years later when the prime minister was compelled to adopt Chamberlain's preferred West Africa policy on the eve of Fashoda.[24]

Salisbury's own weakness exaggerated the difficulties of cabinet politics. Like Aberdeen's, Salisbury's government was a coalition in which Liberals held five of the nineteen seats in the cabinet of a Conservative prime minister.[25] The parallels continue: the influence of the aging Salisbury had recently declined, further encouraging debate and dissent within the inner circle.[26] Nevertheless, the structure of the Brit-

---

20. See Cox, *Efficient Secret*, chap. 3; Hanham, *Nineteenth-Century Constitution*, 138–39, 224–27; Mackintosh, *British Cabinet*, 162–95; and Martin Pugh, *The Making of Modern British Politics 1867–1939* (New York: St. Martin's Press, 1982), chap. 1.

21. Mackintosh, *British Cabinet*, 204.

22. Cox, *Efficient Secret*, 80–84.

23. *British Cabinet*, 162.

24. On 1895, see Grenville, *Lord Salisbury and Foreign Policy*, 10. On Salisbury's later "forced retreat" on West Africa, see Taylor, *Lord Salisbury*, 173.

25. Ronald Robinson, John Gallagher, and Alice Denny, *Africa and the Victorians: The Official Mind of Imperialism* (London: Macmillan, 1974), 339.

26. Lebow, *Between Peace and War*, 303.

ish state would have given even a strong leader little room to maneuver. Executive authority remained diffuse and the degree of executive autonomy from the legislature, while improved, was not significant.

The Cabinet

The Salisbury government was a coalition of Conservatives and Liberal Unionists. In addition to his role as prime minister, Salisbury also served as his own foreign secretary. There were two other prominent Conservatives: Arthur Balfour, first lord of the treasury, and Michael Hicks Beach, chancellor of the exchequer. The three most influential Liberals in the cabinet—Chamberlain, Lansdowne, and Goschen—held the posts of colonial secretary, secretary for war, and first lord of the admiralty, respectively. The hard-line Chamberlain provided the major opposition to Salisbury's more moderate beliefs on foreign and colonial policy. Indeed, Salisbury was alone among the ministers in his advocacy of restraint in the Fashoda crisis.

The prime minister called himself "a reluctant imperialist."[27] He viewed the race for colonial possessions primarily as a means of influencing and preserving the European balance, and he was particularly suspicious of commitments that threatened British relations with France.[28] In the decades before the Fashoda conflict, Salisbury was often critical of the rush to divvy up the globe. He criticized those who "wished to go everywhere and take everything," and he bemoaned the tendency of imperialism to lead to "constant wars at distant points which bring us such large bills and such little credit and which it is afterwards their onerous task to justify."[29] He recognized the need to establish priorities; interests were not highly interdependent. In April 1860, Salisbury wrote that, unless British "diplomacy should become a systematic game at brag," a prospect he detested, the government had to "publicly renounce, as beyond our strength," certain commitments.[30]

Salisbury's beliefs about the use of force were consistent with his moderate views on imperialism. On the one hand, he called war "the final and supreme evil" and argued that "[a]ll the great triumphs of

---

27. Quoted in Taylor, *Lord Salisbury*, 171.

28. See Richard Jay, *Joseph Chamberlain: A Political Study* (Oxford: Clarendon Press, 1981), 211–15; and Taylor, *Lord Salisbury*, 67.

29. Quoted respectively in A. L. Kennedy, *Salisbury 1830–1903: Portrait of a Statesman* (London: John Murray, 1953; reprint, New York: Kraus, 1971), 206; and Taylor, *Lord Salisbury*, 13.

30. Salisbury, "The Budget and the Reform Bill," *Quarterly Review* 214 (April 1860), reprinted in Paul Smith, ed., *Lord Salisbury on Politics: A Selection from His Articles in the Quarterly Review, 1860–1883* (Cambridge: Cambridge University Press, 1972), 133.

civilization in the past have been in the substitution of judicial doctrine for the cold, cruel arbitration of war." On the other hand, Salisbury considered himself a realist. In October 1871, he argued forcefully, "We live in an age of blood and iron. . . . We must trust to our power of self-defence, and to no earthly aid."[31] Overall, though, Salisbury tied Britain's security to the stability of the international system. He was an opponent of peace-time alliances and often appealed for collective action by the European powers.[32]

His moderate and flexible beliefs influenced Salisbury's behavior in several foreign policy crises prior to Fashoda. In the Eastern crisis of 1877–78 and again in 1896–97, he was willing to abandon Britain's ally, Turkey: "[T]he only policy which it seems to me is left to us . . . [is] to strengthen our position on the Nile and to withdraw as much as possible from all responsibilities at Constantinople."[33] When Russia seized Port Arthur in 1898, he offered to "come to an understanding" with the Russians. Rather than partition China into British and Russian spheres, Salisbury concluded that "the only thing to be done is to object to the military occupation of Port Arthur in language sufficiently measured to allow Russia to find a way out."[34] About the conflict with the French in West Africa, he commented snidely in a 3 June 1898 letter to Chamberlain, "There is no loot to get except in Goldie's dreams."[35]

Salisbury's views on Egypt were complex, but they were consistent with his overall beliefs. He considered Egypt "a disastrous inheritance" and the Nile Valley a "malarious African desert" that was not worth war.[36] His ultimate goal was to restore stability to the country and withdraw. Indeed, the prime minister went so far on 21 March 1896 as to privately assure the French ambassador to London that Britain's success in crushing the dervishes in the Sudan would speed Britain's departure from Egypt.[37] Nevertheless, Salisbury felt England could not evacuate: "National or acquisitional feeling has been aroused; it has tasted the flesh pots and it will not let them go."[38]

The hawkish Chamberlain was the antithesis of the moderate Salis-

---

31. Quoted in Taylor, *Lord Salisbury*, 133, 42, respectively.

32. See Grenville, *Lord Salisbury and Foreign Policy*, 3, 83, 86; Smith, *Lord Salisbury on Politics*, 55; and Taylor, *Lord Salisbury*, 169.

33. Quoted in Grenville, *Lord Salisbury and Foreign Policy*, 94.

34. Quoted in Grenville, *Lord Salisbury and Foreign Policy*, 138, 144.

35. J. L. Garvin, *The Life of Joseph Chamberlain*, 6 vols. (London: Macmillan, 1934), 3:220.

36. For the quotes see, respectively, Taylor, *Lord Salisbury*, 137–38; and Salisbury to Monson, 19 October 1897, in Grenville, *Lord Salisbury and Foreign Policy*, 123.

37. Grenville, *Lord Salisbury and Foreign Policy*, 114.

38. Quoted in Taylor, *Lord Salisbury*, 138.

bury. The colonial secretary's well-known advocacy of imperialist expansion was rooted in his belief that colonies were necessary for Britain's economic survival.[39] He was more concerned with the interdependence of British commitments and more inclined to argue "in favour of showing our teeth"[40] than was the prime minister. Chamberlain challenged Salisbury's willingness to negotiate with the Russians over Port Arthur, for instance, instead advocating a more forceful response.[41] In West Africa, as well, Chamberlain was willing to risk war, because he feared the deleterious effects on British prestige of abandoning territory to the French: "I believe that a grant to another European nation of an *enclave* in British territory is unprecedented and would lead to the most serious complications in the future."[42] It was necessary to stand firm. Claiming that "the only hope of a peaceful arrangement was to convince the French, from the first, that they had tried our patience too far and that they must give way or take the consequences," Chamberlain argued that Britain needed to show "that we will not be trifled with. . . ."[43] When Salisbury proposed conceding territory in West Niger, a plan that in retrospect we know might have prevented the Fashoda crisis, Chamberlain complained that the prime minister was "prepared to give away everything and get nothing."[44] In Egypt, Chamberlain argued for "a more decided attitude with regard to the French." In January 1898, he compared the British position in East Africa with that in West Africa: "If we have rights and interests in any quarter of the world and are unprepared to defend them, it is certain that foreign nations will know how to take advantage of our weakness."[45]

When the Fashoda crisis broke, in sum, the British government was led by a conciliatory prime minister whose beliefs were moderate, but

---

39. See Chamberlain's comments quoted in Harry Browne, *Joseph Chamberlain, Radical and Imperialist* (London: Longman, 1974), 54; Peter Fraser, *Joseph Chamberlain: Radicalism and Empire, 1868–1914* (New York: A. S. Barnes, 1966), 166; Garvin, *Life of Joseph Chamberlain*, 2:465; and Robert V. Kubicek, *The Administration of Imperialism: Joseph Chamberlain at the Colonial Office* (Durham: Duke University Press, for the Duke University Commonwealth Studies Center, 1969), 11–12.

40. Quoted in Garvin, *Life of Joseph Chamberlain*, 1:538.

41. See Fraser, *Joseph Chamberlain*, 174; and Grenville, *Lord Salisbury and Foreign Policy*, 145–46.

42. Chamberlain to Salisbury, 1 December 1897, quoted in Garvin, *Life of Joseph Chamberlain*, 3:212.

43. Chamberlain to Lord Selbourne, 12 September 1897, and Chamberlain to Salisbury, 6 June 1897, quoted in Garvin, *Life of Joseph Chamberlain*, 3:204.

44. Chamberlain to Lord Selbourne, 1 December 1897, quoted in Garvin, *Life of Joseph Chamberlain*, 3:213.

45. Quoted in Garvin, *Life of Joseph Chamberlain*, 2:456 and 3:214.

not rigid. Despite Salisbury's preferences, the collective and nonautonomous structure of the nineteenth-century British state meant that coalition politics prevailed. The coercive French strategy undermined the credibility of Salisbury's strategic arguments and reinforced those of his hawkish opponent, Chamberlain.

France

The French Chamber of Deputies rivaled the British House of Commons in its ability to indirectly influence policy. France differed from Britain, however, in that the French foreign minister of the late nineteenth century possessed exceptional executive authority in the realm of foreign policy. In short, France was a type II state in which the organization of foreign policy authority was nonautonomous but mostly unitary.

Ultimate authority in the Third Republic rested in the legislative branch. Parliament exercised this authority through the cabinet, the "parliamentary executive," many of the members of which were also members of Parliament. As one observer described this executive-legislative relationship, "If [Parliament] does not advise, it orders. . . . Authority starts at the bottom. The government does not govern; it executes."[46]

The underdeveloped state of French political parties in the 1890s further contributed to the power of the deputies. While they did exist, parties lacked the cohesion and discipline to compel members to vote with them. Without a strong party system, the legislature acted as a transmission belt for private interests in the political process. The Chamber of Deputies "remained the forum through which these interests mediated their conflicts," while individual deputies "acted as the channel for the play of interests."[47]

One influential societal actor represented a wide range of colonialist organizations. The *Comité de l'Afrique* was founded in 1890 to protest the policy of the French foreign ministry toward Africa. The *Union Coloniale Française*, formed in 1893, was an association of the major French firms with commercial interests in French colonies. These two procolonialist groups influenced the policy-making process through the Chamber of Deputies. An interparty union of deputies who advocated colonial expansion in Africa, the *Groupe Colonial*, was formed in 1892 by the undersecretary of state for colonies, Eugéne Etienne. Although it

---

46. Quoted in Edward McChesney Sait, *Government and Politics of France* (Yonkers-on-Hudson, NY: World Book Company, 1920), 89. Also see Sait, 49.

47. R. D. Anderson, *France 1870–1914: Politics and Society* (London: Routledge & Kegan, 1977), chap. 4, quote at 87.

only had ninety-one members, with the backing of the *Comité* and the *Union Coloniale*, the *Groupe Colonial* exercised significant influence in the Chamber of Deputies. Together, these colonialist groups sought to build a great French empire in Africa.[48]

The influence of Parliament on foreign policy was indirect. Parliamentary debate was rare, because the 1875 Constitution granted the president a predominant role in this arena.[49] Nevertheless, the Chamber of Deputies exercised indirect influence—the ability to bring down a government—many times during the life of the Third Republic.

Executive power was vested in the cabinet, although French presidents lacked any institutional or constitutional basis of authority: "Actual executive power reside[d] in the ministry."[50] As in Britain, the ministers were collectively responsible to Parliament for the government's actions. Nevertheless, the minister of foreign affairs typically enjoyed a far larger degree of executive freedom in the foreign policy arena than did his colleagues in their respective areas of expertise. The foreign minister's independence derived in part from the governmental instability that defined the Third Republic. France had seventy different governments from 1871 to 1931, and on average a cabinet lived no more than ten months. If only by comparison, the management of the *Quai d'Orsay* was stable, changing hands only thirty-seven times in seventy different governments. This relative stability amid continual governmental turmoil gave the foreign minister a nearly free hand in shaping France's external relations, especially during an acute conflict.[51]

In short, the lines of authority in France in the late 1890s were not as clear as they were in some of the other states examined in this study. While the nature of parliamentary democracy dictated that the Chamber of Deputies could indirectly influence the content of foreign policy, even

48. See Andrew, *Théophile Delcassé*, 31–32, 49–52; C. M. Andrew and A. S. Kanya-Forstner, "The French 'Colonial Party': Its Composition, Aims, and Influence, 1885–1914," *Historical Journal* 14:1 (March 1971): 99–128; Baumgart, *Imperialism*, 78–79; and Roger Glenn Brown, *Fashoda Reconsidered: The Impact of Domestic Politics on French Policy in Africa 1893–1898* (Baltimore: Johns Hopkins Press, 1970), 19–24.

49. See Anderson, *France 1870–1914*, 82; Joseph Barthélemy, *The Government of France* (New York: Brentano's Publishers, n.d.), 112–13; and Hayne, "*Quai d'Orsay*," 195.

50. Schuman, *War and Diplomacy in the French Republic*, 13. On the role of the president see Hayne, "*Quai d'Orsay*"; and Sait, *Government and Politics of France*, 49–50, 54.

51. See Paul Gordon Lauren, *Diplomats and Bureaucrats: The First Institutional Responses to Twentieth-Century Diplomacy in France and Germany* (Stanford: Hoover Institution Press, 1976), 5–13; Sait, *Government and Politics of France*, 91; and Schuman, *War and Diplomacy in the French Republic*, 21, 28–30.

during a crisis, there were some constitutional limits on parliamentary input. Furthermore, although government by cabinet was, by definition, collective, foreign policy was an exception. The foreign minister possessed remarkable, but not complete, autonomy from the other members of the cabinet on foreign policy questions. At the outset of the Fashoda crisis, then, the organization of foreign policy authority was largely unitary but was nonautonomous.

Delcassé

Théophile Delcassé is this study's best example of a hard-line opportunist. An ardent champion of colonial expansion in the years before the Fashoda conflict, he repeatedly expressed his concern that French ambitions should not threaten good relations with Britain. While he believed coercion was the most effective means of convincing the English that they needed to cooperate with France, Delcassé was also an opportunist who probed his opponent's weakness and backed down when he met resistance.

Early in his career, while working as a journalist, Delcassé was a supporter and protégé of the colonialist Léon Gambetta. Delcassé's commitment was unquestioned; in 1892 he became a founding member of the *Groupe Colonial*. His support for colonialism was based on his belief that France needed secure markets to survive and prosper and, more important, that such possessions were a source of national prestige. In an 1891 speech, Delcassé asked, "[D]o you think that . . . we are able to abstain [from colonialism] without 'going under,' or without at least belittling ourselves?"[52]

He brought these same beliefs to his life in politics. First as undersecretary for colonies and later as minister of colonies, Delcassé was instrumental in launching the French expeditions to East Africa and in the attempt to unify French possessions in West Africa. As late as February 1898, Delcassé was eager to claim responsibility for the Marchand expedition in a speech to the Chamber of Deputies: "It is not I who am to blame . . . if from the banks of the Upper Ubangi the French flag has yet to be carried to the banks of the Nile, where it had been expected."[53]

Although his colonial ambitions were indisputable, Delcassé recognized the threat Germany posed to French interests in Europe and the

---

52. Quoted in Charles W. Porter, *The Career of Théophile Delcassé* (Philadelphia, 1936), 68.

53. Quoted in Andrew, *Théophile Delcassé*, 91. This contradicts the assertion by Langer, in *Diplomacy of Imperialism* (55), that there is no evidence that Delcassé supported the Nile expedition after 1894. On Delcassé's expansionist tendencies generally, see Langer, 27–52.

opportunity presented by improved relations with London. He considered Britain and France "two countries with everything to gain from a close association."[54] He believed the most effective means of achieving a cooperative relationship with London was to firmly demonstrate that British cooperation was necessary. In 1890, for example, Delcassé quoted Gambetta to attack the French government's weakness over Egypt: "The fact is that you have gratuitously made an important concession to England, who never makes gratuitous concessions herself."[55]

Delcassé's early thoughts on the Egyptian question reflected his hard-line, opportunistic beliefs—the need for colonies, the efficacy of coercion, and the willingness to make concessions rather than risk a break with England. He criticized what he saw as French weakness in not intervening in 1882 and he believed that France needed to stand firm on the issue, but he worried about the strain on Anglo-French relations. Delcassé therefore advocated an Egypt that was "[n]either French nor English but neutral": "Give Egypt to herself, and France will naturally, pacifically, recover the influence which tradition and a thousand scattered favors assure to her."[56] The relatively unitary and nonautonomous nature of foreign policy authority in the Third Republic meant that Delcassé's opportunism would have an important, but not determinate, influence on the outcome of the Fashoda conflict. The rest of this chapter details the interaction of British and French bargaining strategies with their opponent's domestic political environment.

The Fashoda Crisis

When General Kitchener arrived at Fashoda to find Colonel Marchand already entrenched, a full-scale diplomatic crisis erupted. I divide that crisis into three stages: (1) the initial confrontation from 19 September to 5 October 1898, (2) French compromise during the period from 5 October to 27 October, and (3) French capitulation from 27 October to 4 November.

Confrontation at Fashoda: 19 September to 5 October

As Kitchener approached Fashoda, the French attempted to ease the impending confrontation in two ways. First, not yet having received word that the French expedition had reached its destination, on 7 September Delcassé apparently ordered Marchand to stop short of Fashoda. Second,

---

54. Quoted in Andrew, *Théophile Delcassé*, 22.
55. Quoted in Porter, *Career of Théophile Delcassé*, 57.
56. Quoted in Porter, *Career of Théophile Delcassé*, 22, and 56, respectively. Also see Andrew, *Théophile Delcassé*. 21–22.

the foreign minister met with the British ambassador in Paris on the same day and warned him that the British mission might find Marchand at Fashoda. He also informed the ambassador that Marchand had been "distinctly told that he is nothing but an 'emissary of civilization.' "[57]

Meanwhile, Marchand had reached Fashoda, and on 18 September, Kitchener sent a letter to the French mission announcing his impending approach. Captain Marchand responded that he was under instructions to occupy Fashoda, that he had been attacked by Mahdist dervishes, and that he had sent for reinforcements against another attack, which, he said, the arrival of the British had prevented.[58] When Kitchener arrived at Fashoda that same day, although he was under instructions to fly both the British and Egyptian flags, he hoisted only the Egyptian flag, to prevent hostility with the French while he awaited further instructions from London.[59]

Throughout the first phase of the Fashoda crisis, Britain employed the initially coercive strategy prescribed by deterrence theory. Although Salisbury preferred a more conciliatory response, public opinion supported his colleagues' hard-line preferences. French strategy was equally as uncompromising, although for different reasons. Delcassé largely controlled French policy and his modus vivendi called for concessions from the British. So, too, did the avid colonialists who pressed him to hold out at Fashoda. While Salisbury appreciated Delcassé's delicate situation, the structure of the British state prevented compromise: British public opinion would allow no concessions, and none of Salisbury's colleagues would back a policy of compromise.

Britain

The initial British response to the French presence at Fashoda was to declare that the issue was not open to discussion. There seemed little worth discussing: the information coming into London portrayed a severely divided adversary and a small, insufficiently armed, and poorly supplied French force at Fashoda that would have been destroyed by the dervishes were it not for the fortuitous arrival of Kitchener's forces. The sirdar's initial communication with London described Marchand's position as being "as impossible as it is absurd" and French claims to be

---

57. Monson to Salisbury, no. 188, 8 September 1898, *British Documents*, 1:163–64. Also see Brown, *Fashoda Reconsidered*, 85.

58. Marchand to Kitchener, 19 September 1898, Inclosure B in no. 2, *Correspondence*, 895–96.

59. The British decision to fly two flags, which was made in July 1898, was intended to imply both British and Egyptian rights of conquest to all territories taken from the Mahdists. Salisbury to Cromer, 2 August 1898, no. 185, *British Documents*, 1:159–61.

occupying Fashoda as "more worthy of *Opera-Bouffe* than the outcome of the maturely considered plans of a great Government."[60] Reports from the British ambassador in Paris explained the situation: for domestic political reasons France probably could not afford to back down. In a particularly alarming telegram to Salisbury in late February 1898, Monson noted, "There are other intelligent observers, Frenchmen as well as foreigners, who are losing all hope that France can much longer escape an internal convulsion; a convulsion in which the Army will take a prominent part, and which will equally be followed by a foreign war."[61]

Despite his warnings about the precarious state of French politics, Monson recognized Delcassé's early restraint over Fashoda and attributed it to the moderate nature of French public opinion. In a 7 September meeting, Delcassé impressed Monson with his cordial language and manner, which the ambassador felt reflected

> . . . the deliberate judgement of the majority of his countrymen who had begun to recognise that there is nothing to be gained by blustering about Egypt, and that it will be more dignified for them to accept the inevitable. I do not mean to say that they are prepared to acquiesce without renewed remonstrance in the continuance of the British occupation, or that a great deal of abuse will not be showered upon us by the Parisian press. . . . The moderation of M. Delcassé's tone and manner inspires me with a certain amount of hope that, if the French are going to discuss this question at once, they will do so with calmness.[62]

The ambassador's reports only confirmed the widely held notion that the French would and should back down. The reports also would have confirmed Salisbury's belief in the necessity of restraint.

The prime minister apparently was attempting to water down the British response. For example, Geoffray, the French *chargé d'affaires* in London, noted that while the British press was generally violent, the *Daily Chronicle*—the mouthpiece of the British Foreign Office—was more conciliatory.[63] The next week, he also reported to Paris that the

---

60. Kitchener to Rodd (Cairo), 25 September 1898, no. 193, *British Documents*, 1:168; Sanderson, *England, Europe, and the Upper Nile*, 338.

61. Monson to Salisbury, 26 February 1898, no. 172, *British Documents*, 1:146.

62. Monson to Salisbury, 8 September 1898, no. 188, *British Documents*, 1:164.

63. See Geoffray to Delcassé, 12 September 1898, no. 348, in *Documents Diplomatiques Français (1871–1914)*, vol. 14, 4 January–30 December 1898 (Paris: Ministère des Affaires Etrangères, 1957), 543 (hereinafter, *DDF*); and Geoffray to Delcassé, 21 September 1898, no. 363, *DDF*, 568.

Salisbury government was probably behind what Geoffray took to be the moderation of the press. Noting that different papers seemed to be using language very similar to each other's and to Salisbury's, he argued that the government was probably responsible for this moderation.[64]

Despite the differences between Salisbury and his colleagues, there was widespread agreement within the cabinet about the general tone that a response should take: the French incursion on the Nile demanded firmness. On 7 September, Salisbury instructed Monson that if Delcassé again raised the subject of Fashoda, the ambassador should "point out to him that by the military events of last week, all the territories which were subject to the Khalifa passed by right of conquest to the British and Egyptian Governments. Her Majesty's Government do not consider that this right is open to discussion. . . ."[65]

British public opinion supported this action. As represented in the popular press, public opinion had been particularly hostile during the West Africa dispute and it only worsened as Kitchener advanced up the Nile. When the public learned that Kitchener had encountered Marchand at Fashoda, the attack reached a fevered pitch, especially among imperialist papers like the *Daily Mail*.[66] In short, while differences in outlook existed within the cabinet, there was no question how to respond to the French challenge at Fashoda; British interests and public feeling demanded nothing less than a tough response.

France

Following a brief period of restraint prior to Kitchener's arrival at Fashoda, Delcassé's strategy in the early phase of the conflict was uncompromising. Before Kitchener arrived at Fashoda, Delcassé argued to Georges Trouillot, the minister of colonies, that the situation had changed dramatically since the Marchand Mission began. Still not knowing that Marchand had reached his destination, on 7 September Delcassé reasoned that the British victory at Khartoum and England's limited rapprochement with Germany sufficiently altered the situation to warrant the Captain to stop his advance short of Fashoda.[67] On the same day, Delcassé warned Monson that Marchand might be at Fashoda but that he had been instructed not to provoke a conflict.[68] On 18 September, Delcassé nearly disowned the expedition, stating,

---

64. Geoffray to Delcassé, 29 September 1898, no. 392, *DDF*, 601–2.

65. Salisbury to Monson, 9 September 1898, no. 6, *Correspondence*, 871.

66. Langer, *Diplomacy of Imperialism*, 550, 552–53.

67. Andrew, *Théophile Delcassé*, 92.

68. Monson to Salisbury, 7 September 1898, no. 4, Monson to Salisbury, 8 September 1898, no. 7, *Correspondence*, 870–71.

"[T]here is no Marchand Mission."[69] Finally, on 28 September, Delcassé told Monson he believed "honest discussion" would produce an understanding. He then added, "I would rather have England for our ally than that other [Russia]."[70]

At the same time that Delcassé was intermittently attempting to conciliate the British, he faced serious domestic troubles that he thought Marchand's presence at Fashoda might alleviate. A major contributor to and indicator of domestic turmoil in France on the eve of the Fashoda crisis was the Dreyfus Affair.[71] In January and February 1898, inspired by an open letter charging an army conspiracy, thousands of Parisians took to the streets and gained international support for Dreyfus. In August 1898, the head of intelligence and counterintelligence for the army, Colonel Henry, was arrested and charged with forging documents to prove Dreyfus's guilt. The case is important for its affect on public opinion during the Fashoda crisis. By and large, Dreyfus supporters were "continentalists" who believed that French foreign policy should focus on Europe and the German threat. Anti-Dreyfusards tended to be colonialists. They also tended to be royalist, proclerical, and anti-Semitic. By September 1898, they were calling for the army to overthrow the Brisson government.

General public opinion reflected a similar split. Colonial groups, though small, were very vocal and well represented in the press, but public opinion was largely uninterested in Egypt and the Sudan.[72] The press was divided between right-wing journals and more moderate papers, some of which were considered to have strong ties to the *Quai d'Orsay*. Both groups of journals were calling for negotiations with the British in early September.[73] In fact, despite the political differences within the press, the papers were remarkably moderate until British reaction became severe. Then even the moderate papers responded to the assault in the British press, arguing that the British government "cannot but see that in following the lead of the chief English newspapers it will necessarily cause a complete change in the conciliatory attitude which [French] public opinion has manifested to the present."[74]

69. Monson to Salisbury, 18 September 1898, no. 191, *British Documents*, 1:165.

70. Quoted in Porter, *Career of Théophile Delcassé*, 135.

71. The following account draws on Brown, *Fashoda Reconsidered*; Guy Chapman, *The Dreyfus Case: A Reassessment* (Westport, CT: Greenwood Press, 1955; reprint, 1979); Iiams, *Dreyfus, Diplomatists, and the Dual Alliance*; and Douglas Johnson, *France and the Dreyfus Affair* (New York: Walker and Company, 1966).

72. See E. Malcolm Carroll, *French Public Opinion and Foreign Affairs 1870–1914* (New York: Century, 1931), 167–68.

73. Brown, *Fashoda Reconsidered*, 86. Also see Porter, *Career of Théophile Delcassé*, 115.

74. Carroll, *French Public Opinion and Foreign Affairs*, 173.

Delcassé believed that the French presence at Fashoda could be used to obtain concessions from the British that would bolster his government against its domestic critics. He told the cabinet on 3 October that, while it was pointless to try to keep Fashoda, Marchand's recall could be traded for territorial concessions.[75] The information coming in from London was mixed but may have encouraged Delcassé's idea that the British would grant such concessions. The telegrams from the French ambassador, Courcel, and especially the *chargé d'affaires*, Geoffray, noted both that the British press and public were violently opposed to any concessions on this issue and that Salisbury was more conciliatory. In August, Geoffray reported that it was public opinion and British nationalism that was pushing Salisbury—"the English statesman with whom negotiations were most likely to bring good results, and with whom one was most likely to find a common ground to satisfy all interested parties"—to act in Egypt.[76] Geoffray similarly warned about the jingoism of the English press: "Without worrying about the accuracy of the news which they put forth, no more than about the cogency of the arguments they invoke, they return daily to the question of French occupation of Fashoda, some of them with an unheard-of fury."[77] Yet Geoffray also noted from early in the crisis that Salisbury did not desire conflict with France. The prime minister, according to Geoffray, would seek a compromise with the French as a means of regaining support from his party and the British public.[78]

Despite Delcassé's recognition that France would ultimately have to back down and the relative indifference of the larger public to the underlying issue, French strategy in the first phase of the crisis was uncompromising. Delcassé based this policy on two arguments: (1) since the Nile Valley had not been effectively ruled by Egypt, France had the same legal rights of conquest at Fashoda that Britain claimed in the rest of the region; and (2) French public opinion, or at least some portion of it, would not tolerate a humiliating French defeat.[79]

On 10 September, Delcassé questioned the British declaration that all territories fell to England and Egypt by right of conquest, arguing that "[i]f Marchand is at Fashoda, his 'rights' are exactly the same as those of Kitchener at Khartoum."[80] He later told Monson that France

---

75. Brown, *Fashoda Reconsidered*, 92, 100–101.
76. Geoffray to Delcassé, 9 August 1898, no. 283, *DDF*, 441–42, quote at 441; Geoffray to Delcassé, 25 August 1898, no. 305, *DDF*, 478–79.
77. Geoffray to Delcassé, 21 September 1898, no. 363, *DDF*, 568.
78. Geoffray to Delcassé, 22 September 1898, no. 365, *DDF*, 572.
79. Grenville, *Lord Salisbury and Foreign Policy*, 226–27.
80. Quoted in Brown, *Fashoda Reconsidered*, 89.

had never recognized British claims in the Nile Valley and he argued that "[t]here could be no doubt that for a long time past the whole region of the Bahr-el-Ghazal had been out of the influence of Egypt."[81] On the twenty-eighth, Delcassé insisted on France's legal right to occupy Fashoda and the surrounding territories.[82] Two days later, Delcassé bluntly told the British ambassador that France would go to war rather than accept a humiliating defeat.[83]

Delcassé stalled for time. The Brisson government did not even discuss Fashoda at a formal cabinet meeting until 26 September, suggesting the extent of the foreign minister's autonomy. At that time, the cabinet decided to defer a decision until the government could get a report from Marchand on the seriousness of his situation.[84] This was not a simple matter, since the French could only communicate with Marchand via the British telegraph office at Cairo.

As a delaying tactic, the French foreign minister argued that domestic factors precluded him from backing down in the face of British demands. On 12 September, he complained, "What decisions can be taken when at any moment the cabinet could resign?" On the twenty-eighth, he pleaded with Monson "to take account of existing excitement in France, which is becoming dangerous and might in an instant break out into overt acts. . . . Do not ask me for the impossible; do not drive me into a corner." Finally, on 30 September he declared, "I am able to sacrifice material interests, but in my hands the national honor will remain intact. It is not from the minister before you that you can expect a capitulation."[85]

Delcassé directed French policy during the conflict. As the role of two other ministries make clear, however, he was not an entirely unitary executive actor. First, though they never materialized, fears of a military coup suggest the potential power of the secretary of war. Second, a split in the French cabinet resulted in an even more uncompromising policy than Delcassé exhibited in his communications with the British ambassador. Following the 26 September cabinet meeting, the minister of colonies, Trouillot, and the head of the colonial ministry's Africa bureau, Gustave Binger, undertook a more aggressively anti-British stand. In an attempt to increase pressure on the foreign ministry to take a tough line

81. Monson to Salisbury, 18 September 1898, no. 9, *Correspondence*, 872.
82. Monson to Salisbury, 28 September 1898, no. 198, *British Documents*, 1:171.
83. Brown, *Fashoda Reconsidered*, 99.
84. Brown, *Fashoda Reconsidered*, 97.
85. For the quotes see, respectively, Brown, *Fashoda Reconsidered*, 88; Monson to Salisbury, 28 September 1898, no. 198, *British Documents*, 1:171; and Brown, *Fashoda Reconsidered*, 99.

on Fashoda, a reporter from the right-wing journal *Le Gaulois* was called to the colonial ministry, without the clearance of the ministry of foreign affairs, and briefed on the encounter between Marchand and Kitchener. This resulted in the publication of a strongly anti-British article on the twenty-eighth and reflected the underlying tension between the *Pavillon de Flore* and the *Quai d'Orsay*.[86] Although Delcassé maintained general control over French policy, the nature of government by cabinet precluded total control. Nevertheless, that Trouillot and Binger sought to influence French policy by manipulating public opinion suggests the limits of their executive power.

Britain

Reports coming into London confirmed Delcassé's warnings about the precarious position of his government. The British ambassador to Paris reinforced this impression that Delcassé could not afford to concede. Following a 30 September meeting with the foreign minister, Monson reported to Salisbury that Delcassé was not bluffing; "he thoroughly meant what he said."

> Delcassé has judged quite correctly as to the utter impossibility of the French Government conceding the recall of M. Marchand. Such a step would involve, I am convinced, the immediate fall of the Cabinet, and would be disavowed by their successors. The irritation of the Army and of a large portion of the public over the Dreyfus "affair," renders the situation of the Government more than usually delicate; and any symptom of weakness on the Fashoda question would be the signal for their downfall within twenty-four hours of the meeting of the Chamber. . . .[87]

Monson's perceptions were confirmed, he argued, by reports in the French press. After reporting that *Le Matin*, "which on foreign questions has now become the mouthpiece of the Government," had published an article stating that the French government would not back down, the ambassador concluded with a note of alarm: "And when it is remembered that in a fortnight hence the Chambers will meet, and that the Ministers will be called upon to state their views and their determination, it cannot be denied that we are within measurable distance of very dangerous excitement."[88]

---

86. Brown, *Fashoda Reconsidered*, 96–99.
87. Quoted in Brown, *Fashoda Reconsidered*, 99–100.
88. Monson to Salisbury, 7 October 1898, no. 204, *British Documents*, 1:175.

Lord Salisbury was impressed by these arguments. Although unprepared to make territorial concessions, the prime minister was flexible on procedural matters. His hand was forced, however, by the violence of British public opinion. On 27 September, the *Daily News* reported that "[t]he chief element of danger is to be found in the widespread belief prevailing on the continent that Lord Salisbury's squeezability is unlimited."[89] These attacks were not lost on Salisbury. When Queen Victoria voiced reservations about British policy, the prime minister replied, "I deeply sympathize with your Majesty's dissatisfaction at the present deadlock. We, however, are doing nothing, but only waiting, and we cannot do anything else. No offer of territorial concession on our part would be endured by public opinion here."[90]

Despite Salisbury's flexibility, British policy remained uncompromising. In the last week of September, Salisbury agreed to let the French send a message to Marchand via the British telegraph at Cairo. However, the approval was accompanied by the threat that, if Marchand remained at Fashoda, the British would feel free to publish the diplomatic correspondence between London and Paris regarding Fashoda, a violation of diplomatic custom, and one intended to further inflame the British public.[91] Salisbury also repeated that Britain would not buy French withdrawal with territorial concessions. He pursued a deliberate policy of making Marchand's position "as untenable as possible" by denying him everything but emergency supplies.[92] French policy, in sum, reinforced Salisbury's initial views. None of Salisbury's colleagues in the cabinet supported him, however, and British strategy remained coercive.

French Compromise: 5 October to 27 October

In the second stage of the Fashoda crisis, France tried to extricate itself from a difficult situation, with very little help from Britain. While Delcassé was willing to back down and knew that he must in the end, he continued to stall in the face of further domestic turmoil. The British prime minister still sought compromise but was unable to make policy while hard-liners within the cabinet enjoyed public support. British policy remained highly coercive, but Salisbury did not engage in the kind of motivated misperception a decisional conflict approach would suggest.

89. Quoted in H. C. G. Matthews, *The Liberal Imperialists: The Ideas and Politics of a Post-Gladstonian Élite* (London: Oxford University Press, 1973), 29.

90. Buckle, *Letters of Queen Victoria*, 3:290.

91. Salisbury to Monson, 28 September 1898, no. 197, *British Documents*, 1:170–71.

92. Salisbury to Rodd, 1 October 1898, no. 201, *British Documents*, 1:173.

He was weak domestically, but he continued to appreciate the precarious nature of Delcassé's position and to advocate limited compromise.

France

Delcassé pushed the British for concessions to appease his domestic critics. On 3 October, the Brisson cabinet discussed the Fashoda issue for only the second time. At that meeting, Delcassé again explained to the other ministers that Marchand must be recalled but that territorial concessions could be secured in exchange. Courcel went to London on 4 October to negotiate with the British government and to obtain such concessions. On the next day, he met with Salisbury and, although he had been instructed to seek French claim to the entire region marked by the Bahr-el-Arab, Bahr-el-Ghazal, and Upper Nile, Courcel proposed only that France get access to the navigable portion of the Nile. The French ambassador made it clear that Marchand would withdraw if a way were made for him to do so, that is, if he were provided with food and munitions for his journey.[93] Following a 12 October meeting with Salisbury, Courcel wrote to the British prime minister outlining the full extent of French claims to the entire region in exchange for Marchand's recall.[94]

Delcassé similarly made it clear in a meeting with Monson that the French were ready to withdraw in exchange for procedural concessions. As Monson reported, ". . . he gave me to understand that if we could make things easy for him in form he would be conciliatory in substance." Delcassé needed the British to build him a "golden bridge" over which to retreat: "He was accused of being too weak, but added that, imbued as he was with the conviction that war between England and France over such a question as Fashoda would be an unparalleled calamity, he had all along been ready to discuss M. Marchand's recall, provided that it was not forced upon him as an ultimatum."[95] Several days later, Delcassé "hinted that he might have to retire on the ground of his supposed want of combativeness. . . . [H]e said more than once that any successor, whoever it might be, would be less accommodating than himself."[96]

Despite French conciliatory efforts, discouraging news from London continued. On 6 October, after meeting with the British prime minister, Courcel reported that Salisbury did not think he could wait to

---

93. Salisbury to Monson, 12 October 1898, no. 3, *Correspondence*, 898.

94. Brown, *Fashoda Reconsidered*, 101.

95. Monson to Salisbury, 11 October 1898, no. 209, *British Documents*, 1:179; Monson to Salisbury, 21 October 1898, no. 214, *British Documents*, 1:181.

96. Monson to Salisbury, 14 October 1898, FO 146/3535, 549, no. 517.

publish the blue book of diplomatic correspondence about the crisis, because the British public was already excited and public ignorance would only worsen the situation. According to Courcel, Salisbury claimed that the public was violently attacking him for his weakness on the Fashoda issue.[97] A little more than a week later, the French naval attaché in London reported that Chamberlain's return from the United States would only make Salisbury more threatening and hostile. The attaché went so far as to suggest that the British wanted war with France, that they thought that war was inevitable, and that they believed war was better now when British advantage was greatest.[98] Finally, Geoffray reported that the British press, while still aggressive, was moderating its stance. This moderation was not reflected in public opinion, however, which continued to see war as inevitable if France did not submit. The Liberal opposition, according to the French diplomat, was as intransigent as the Conservative government.[99]

Delcassé remained far more optimistic in his perceptions of British actions and his chances of securing significant concessions than the situation would seem, at first glance, to have warranted. On 5 October, he expressed his optimistic appraisal of the effect of his delaying tactics: "There has no longer been any question of unconditional withdrawal from Fashoda; the situation is still grave, but we are gaining time and time causes reflection." On the seventh, the foreign minister again wrote to his wife expressing his optimistic assumption that there was "some *detente* between England and ourselves."[100] Delcassé attributed this apparent détente to his own efforts:

Feeling between England and ourselves seems to be somewhat relaxed. My frankness and definiteness, and the resolute, though perfectly courteous and moderate, tone of my language have made some impression. I trust that the desire for an understanding with England I have freely expressed ever since taking over the Ministry, is understood to spring not from any sense of weakness, but from a general conception of policy, and that I must not be placed officially in an obligation to say "No." I hope also further reflection has brought the conviction that England's real interest lies in fostering

97. Courcel to Delcassé, 6 October 1898, no. 414, *DDF*, 632–35.

98. Ship's captain of the Fieron vessel, French naval attaché to the Vice Admiral Cavelier de Cuverville, marine chief of staff, 16 and 18 October 1898, no. 440, *DDF*, 675–77.

99. Geoffray to Delcassé, 20 October 1898, no. 443, *DDF*, 678–81.

100. Both comments are quoted in Andrew, *Théophile Delcassé*, 100.

the friendship of France, and that for this friendship a sacrifice of exclusive claims is reasonable.[101]

Delcassé still believed he could get such a pledge from Britain and was prepared to withdraw to obtain it. On 23 October, he wrote to his wife, "This week will apparently bring the *dénouement* of the Anglo-French crisis. My line is decided upon, and I have let it be known—'Recognize an outlet for us on the Nile and I shall order Marchand's withdrawal.' "[102]

It is possible, as motivational psychology suggests, that his domestic weakness motivated the foreign minister to underestimate British threats and to think his own efforts were succeeding. His optimism is more easily explained, however, as a rational interpretation of Salisbury's repeated conciliatory signals. Delcassé recognized the possibility that he might have to withdraw completely. He did not advocate total surrender and instructed Courcel to offer a "spontaneous" French withdrawal in exchange for a "spontaneous" British offer of subsequent negotiations that would preserve French access to the Nile. Nevertheless, on 24 October the foreign minister wrote, "If England does not accept my proposal, I publish Marchand's journal and recall the heroic little band. I will not murder them out there with no gain to the country."[103] These are hardly the words of a man driven by domestic vulnerability to overestimate his own ability to resist.

Delcassé's willingness to back down, while seemingly at odds with his optimistic assessment of his chances for securing concessions, was due in part to his realization of France's poor strategic position. He had always been eager to avoid war with Britain, and in October he became acutely aware of the extent of France's inferiority. Reports from a French agent in London, as well as from the chief of the naval staff, confirmed that Britain was preparing for war and that France was vastly outgunned.[104] On 22 October, Delcassé wrote, "The problem is, how to combine the demands of honour with the necessity of avoiding a naval war which we are absolutely incapable of carrying through, even with Russian help. I could not wish my worst enemies, if I have any, to have this situation facing them."[105]

The foreign minister must also have been aware of the tenor of

101. Quoted in André Maurois, *The Edwardian Era*, trans. Hamish Miles (New York: D. Appleton-Century, 1933), 91.

102. Quoted in Maurois, *Edwardian Era*, 92.

103. Quoted in Sanderson, *England, Europe, and the Upper Nile*, 349.

104. See note from an intelligence agent (extract from the archives of the minister of war), 11 October 1898, no. 430, *DDF*, 658–59; and Andrew, *Théophile Delcassé*, 102–3.

105. Quoted in Maurois, *Edwardian Era*, 91–92.

public opinion. As Monson saw it, the general feeling of the French public, "upon the broad issues of peace and war, is universally pacific. There is no general desire in this country to run the risk of war with anyone."[106] The French press remained divided, with the majority favoring compromise and moderation provided Britain gave minor substantive or, at the least, procedural compensations. *Le Matin* ran an article in mid-October that the British ambassador summarized as saying that "[t]he abandonment of Fashoda is perfectly compatible with the preservation of the national honour." On 22 October, the same paper asked, "Of what value is Fashoda to France in comparison to the price which England places upon it?" *Le Temps* argued that France should withdraw as long as "courtesy was observed toward her and . . . the question was not arbitrarily isolated from others." Similarly, the *Journal des Débats* saw no reason why Marchand should not be recalled "if we are paid for it."[107]

Yet the right-wing, anti-Dreyfusard papers remained vocally opposed to such a deal. In late September, *Le Gaulois* printed an article glorifying Colonel Henry's forgery as a patriotic act. The appearance of the article added fuel to the nationalist right. On 25 October, *Autorité* declared, "England treats us with such complete hostility and insolence that we will be obliged at one time or another to go to war with her." Three days later, *La Dépêche Coloniale* openly demanded war rather than the humiliation of withdrawing Marchand. French papers carried a manifesto on the twenty-ninth signed by many deputies protesting any settlement with the British that was not first debated in the Chamber of Deputies.[108]

Meanwhile, fears of a military coup continued in Paris. Infantry troops were ordered into Paris on 6 October to deal with the continuing strikes. On 14 October, troops occupied all the major railroad stations to counter a strike of the National Railway Workers Union, and fears of a coup increased. Colonel Douglas Dawson, Monson's military attaché in Paris, argued in mid-October that a group of dissident generals was plotting to overthrow the French government. These generals, Dawson argued, would then pursue war with England. Monson, despite his own concerns about the stability of the French government, was slow to come around to his assistant's view. On 7 October, he wrote to Salisbury that

106. Monson to Salisbury, 7 October 1898, FO 146/3535, no. 500.

107. For the quotes see, respectively, Monson to Salisbury, 10 October 1898, no. 208, *British Documents*, 1:178; and Carroll, *French Public Opinion and Foreign Affairs*, 172, 174. Also see Brown, *Fashoda Reconsidered*, 107–8.

108. See, respectively, Brown, *Fashoda Reconsidered*, 90–91; Carroll, *French Public Opinion and Foreign Affairs*, 175 for quote; and Brown, 114.

under all the outcry, the average French person desired peace.[109] By the next week, however, the ambassador was equally alarmed about the possible effects of domestic turmoil on French foreign policy. He noted on 16 October that "[t]he existing condition of unrest and suspicion is interesting to England on account of the influence it may exercise upon the foreign relations of France."[110]

Rumors surfaced that, when the Chamber of Deputies reconvened on 25 October, the troops would be used to aid the nationalists, not to prevent them from overturning the government.[111] While these rumors never materialized, the government fell on the afternoon of the twenty-fifth. Its fall was precipitated by the resignation of the minister of war, suggesting the ability of that minister to at least indirectly influence French policy.

The French position was deteriorating on all fronts. On 25 October, the British ambassador reported on the visit to Paris of Count Mouravieff, the Russian foreign minister. Monson reported that he had learned from a trustworthy source that Delcassé's advice from the Russian "was almost textually as follows: 'Do not give England any pretext for attacking you at present. At a later date an opportunity will be found by Russia for opening the whole question of Egypt.' . . . My own opinion is that Count Mouravieff neither categorically refused, nor contingently promised, the support of Russia in the present emergency."[112] France could not stand alone against England, Delcassé knew.

Throughout the remainder of the second stage of the crisis, French policy continued as it had begun—stalling and incrementally reducing demands in an attempt to trade Marchand's recall for territorial and/or procedural concessions. While Delcassé awaited a report from Marchand, French military preparations proceeded. When the report did arrive, personally delivered by Captain Baratier, who had traveled from Fashoda via Cairo, Delcassé resisted the messenger's news that Marchand was capable of holding out at Fashoda. Calling Baratier to Paris had been merely another means of stalling. Delcassé tried to impress the

---

109. Cited in Sanderson, *England, Europe, and the Upper Nile*, 359.
110. Quoted in Brown, *Fashoda Reconsidered*, 110. For other, similar views, see Maurice V. Brett, ed., *Journals and Letters of Reginald Viscount Esher*, 4 vols. (London: Ivor Nicholson & Watson, 1934), 1:220–21; and Sanderson, *England, Europe, and the Upper Nile*, 359.
111. Brown, *Fashoda Reconsidered*, 106.
112. Monson to Salisbury, 25 October 1898, no. 215, *British Documents*, 1:182. Over the next three days, however, Monson vacillated on the question of Russian intervention. See Monson to Salisbury, 27 October 1898, no. 218, *British Documents*, 1:183; Monson to Salisbury, 28 October 1898, no. 221, *British Documents*, 1:185.

captain with the lopsided nature of the Anglo-French balance of power by telling him, "You cannot desire the hostility of such a powerful State as England when we are still bleeding on our eastern frontier."[113] The foreign minister's statement suggests that it would be foolish to dismiss a systemic-level explanation, but that such an explanation is insufficient to explain Delcassé's strategy of stalling for time.

He made one final appeal to the British in the last days of October. On the twenty-seventh, Delcassé said he could not remain in office if French proposals for an outlet on the Bahr-el-Ghazal were not granted in exchange for Marchand's recall. He told Monson, "It is you who make it impossible for me to remain." Knowing France's relative weakness, Delcassé also showed the British ambassador a telegram from the *chargé d'affaires* in St. Petersburg saying that he was authorized by the Russian foreign minister to say that Russia would support France. Delcassé also claimed there were four more similar telegrams.[114] Again, on the twenty-ninth, he told Monson that whether he stayed in office depended on whether Britain agreed, in exchange for Marchand's withdrawal, to negotiate on the principle that France would be granted an outlet to the Nile.[115] Delcassé knew he could not hold Fashoda, but he still sought to extract some concessions from the British.

Britain

The British ambassador in Paris continued to receive the messages sent by Delcassé. Monson recognized the difficulty of Delcassé's position and reported that the French leader would back down if given acceptable procedural concessions. On 21 October, Monson reported, "The impression produced on me by the language employed by M. Delcassé is that the French Government foresee that they will be unable to maintain their contention as regards M. Marchand, but that, until they can announce that negotiations have begun on their claims to the west of the Nile, they will decline to withdraw him."[116]

Still, British politics propelled policy makers toward a showdown and away from any thought of compromise. Press and public opinion became more virulent. The *Daily Mail* called openly for war and exaggerated British naval preparations, running the 26 October headline "Our Ships and Men Getting Ready for the Word 'Mobilize' ". The

113. Quoted in Porter, *Career of Théophile Delcassé*, 130. Baratier took his case directly to the leaders of the colonial movement and the press, which resulted in the 29 October manifesto previously mentioned. See Brown, *Fashoda Reconsidered*, 114.

114. Monson to Salisbury, 28 October 1898, no. 221, *British Documents*, 1:184–85.

115. Monson to Salisbury, 29 October 1898, no. 222, *British Documents*, 1:186.

116. Monson to Salisbury, 21 October 1898, no. 214, *British Documents*, 1:182.

newspapers accurately displayed the unity of the British nation behind a firm policy toward France. On 10 October, the *Times* ran an article stating, "We cannot conceal from ourselves that Lord Salisbury and his colleagues have taken a position from which retreat is impossible. One side or the other will have to give way. That side cannot . . . be Great Britain." The *Morning Post* on that same day declared that "[t]he British nation is indeed united in a way that it perhaps never was." Even the Liberal newspapers joined the assault, with only the *Manchester Guardian* remaining relatively moderate.[117]

The press was not the only source of opposition to compromise. Rosebery, former prime minister and member of the Liberal opposition, gave a speech on 12 October in which he declared that any British government that showed signs of compromising with the French would fall within a week: "If the nations of the world are under the impression that the ancient spirit of Great Britain is dead or that her resources are weakened or her population less determined than ever it was to maintain the rights and honour of its flag, they make a mistake which can only end in a disastrous conflagration."[118] Later, Rosebery counseled that "a war with France would simplify differences in the future."[119]

The cabinet remained nearly as united against compromise as the public. Chamberlain returned to England in mid-October and continued his hard line toward France. The colonial secretary was afraid Salisbury would grant French concessions, raising the larger issue of French claims in the Bahr-el-Ghazal region. If the British gave in now, he claimed, the French would try again to link up with the Abyssinians to control the Upper Nile. Chamberlain argued that it was essential to stand firm both to prevent further claims by the French and to appease British public opinion. On 26 October, he wrote to Lansdowne, "My mind is uneasy about the Bahr-el-Ghazal. Heaven save us from enclaves! Either they will be worthless to the French or injurious to us. . . . I am pretty certain that this country will stand no more graceful concessions. So says all my correspondence, which has hitherto been a fair index of public opinion."[120]

Chamberlain's argument was supported by several other cabinet members. Michael Hicks Beach, chancellor of the exchequer, asserted that "this country has put its foot down and would go to war rather than yield." Beach maintained, "If, unhappily, another view should be taken elsewhere, we, the Ministers of the Queen, know what our duty de-

117. Marder, *Anatomy of British Sea Power*, 321; Lebow, *Between Peace and War*, 322; Sanderson, *England, Europe, and the Upper Nile*, 348.

118. Quoted in Garvin, *Life of Joseph Chamberlain*, 3:227.

119. Quoted in Matthew, *Liberal Imperialists*, 204.

120. Garvin, *Life of Joseph Chamberlain*, 3:227–30, quote at 229 n. 1.

mands. It would be a great calamity. . . . But there are greater evils than war."[121] Similar views were also voiced by Goschen, the first lord of the admiralty.[122]

Salisbury continued to espouse more moderate views, but the difference between the two groups was slight. The prime minister ordered Kitchener to make suggestions for possible territorial concessions to the French. On 8 October, the sirdar proposed a delineation "granting large concessions to France, that might from a military point of view . . . be given them without injuring our position in this part of Africa."[123] Again on the twelfth, Salisbury showed signs of compromise in his meeting with the French ambassador to London and agreed to consider Courcel's proposal for exchanging Marchand's withdrawal for territorial concessions. Salisbury suggested that Courcel submit his proposals in writing.[124] In short, neither the depth of public opinion nor his own domestic weakness ever convinced Salisbury to advocate unbridled coercion.

Despite Salisbury's predilection for compromise, British strategy during the second stage of the Fashoda crisis continued to be almost exclusively coercive. On 6 October, Salisbury told Monson that he had warned Courcel, "M. Marchand's was a secret expedition into a territory already owned and occupied, and concerning which France had received repeated warnings that a seizure of land in that locality could not be accepted by Great Britain."[125] Salisbury briefly showed a willingness to compromise when he asked Courcel to submit French proposals, but this was quickly shelved when the extent of the French demands became clear on 13 October.[126] The most dramatic British move in this phase of the conflict was the publication of the government's blue book on 10 October. Issued largely in response to Trouillot's 26 September disclosure, this collection included the diplomatic correspondence between France and Britain concerning Fashoda, and its publication was a clear violation of diplomatic custom and a rejection of French requests for concessions.[127]

---

121. Quoted respectively in Sanderson, *England, Europe, and the Upper Nile*, 347; and Langer, *Diplomacy of Imperialism*, 553.

122. Jay, *Joseph Chamberlain*, 211–12; Robinson, Gallagher, and Denny, *Africa and the Victorians*, 373.

123. Kitchener to Cromer, 8 October 1898, enclosure 1 in Cromer to Salisbury, 9 October 1898, no. 207, *British Documents*, 1:177–78.

124. Sanderson, *England, Europe, and the Upper Nile*, 346.

125. Salisbury to Monson, 6 October 1898, no. 1, *Correspondence*, 891.

126. Sanderson, *England, Europe, and the Upper Nile*, 346–47; Brown, *Fashoda Reconsidered*, 101.

127. *Egypt No. 2*, *Correspondence*, was published on 10 October, and *Egypt No. 3* was published on 23 October.

The cabinet met on 27 October to consider the French offer of a "spontaneous" recall of Marchand if Britain would "spontaneously" offer negotiations granting France access to the Nile. Although there was considerable difference of opinion throughout the meeting, the outcome was as inflexible as previous British policy—a demand for unconditional French withdrawal. Most of the cabinet, with the exception of the prime minister, expressed the view that war was likely and that it was better now than later. Chamberlain, and perhaps Goschen, even spoke in favor of preventive war and argued for an immediate ultimatum, while Salisbury supported a peaceful solution. The outcome was a compromise between the two positions, although one that leaned heavily toward the coercive side. There would be no promises about access to the Nile; Marchand must withdraw unconditionally. Only after he had been withdrawn would the relevant issues, including access, be considered. If the French refused to recall Marchand, however, the British would not interfere or fix any date by which he must withdraw. It was thereby "left to France to adopt any active measures that would precipitate a conflict." The British navy also was put on a war footing.[128] Salisbury clearly lacked the support of his colleagues for a conciliatory approach.

French Capitulation: 27 October to 4 November

France backed down completely in the final stage of the crisis. Delcassé was a relatively unitary executive, but he enjoyed little autonomy from Parliament and was vulnerable to societal pressures. For this reason, public opinion undermined his initial policy, and British intransigence made his goals impossible. Procolonial sentiment in France nevertheless compelled the foreign minister to hold out dangerously long for concessions. Once Delcassé capitulated, British strategy shifted very slightly to more accurately reflect Salisbury's concerns. Britain provided minimal concessions once Marchand withdrew. Such limited concessions were not enough, however, to prevent lingering hostility in Anglo-French relations after the immediate crisis ended.

France
By 27 October, Delcassé knew he would have to back down completely in the face of British firmness. His ambassador in London heeded the

---

128. The quote is from Darrell Bates, *The Fashoda Incident of 1898: Encounter on the Nile* (Oxford: Oxford University Press, 1984), 158. See also Brett, *Journals and Letters of Reginald Viscount Esher*, 1:221–22; Brown, *Fashoda Reconsidered*, 113; Buckle, *Letters of Queen Victoria*, 299; and Sanderson, *England, Europe, and the Upper Nile*, 350.

warning of British public opinion. On 29 October, Courcel recommended the immediate recall of Marchand while it was still possible to preserve French honor and to explain the retreat by reference to local difficulties. "We must deceive ourselves no more," he argued; "we won't obtain any compromise on this point."[129] Although he believed Salisbury wanted to give France some face-saving concessions, Courcel recognized that British public opinion would not allow it.

French policy continued to be one of incremental retreat and an attempt to inch away from conflict while securing even minor, procedural concessions. In their 27 October meeting, Courcel told Salisbury that "Fashoda could never furnish the outlet on the Nile which France might obtain; and that therefore it was of no use to her. He [Courcel] thought it therefore not improbable that M. Marchand would receive orders to retire."[130] Meanwhile, Delcassé had agreed to stay on as foreign minister in a new French cabinet. On 3 November, the new government voted to withdraw Marchand from Fashoda.

The complete surrender of Delcassé and his government was tolerable to the French public. On 4 November, *Le Matin* proclaimed that "the national honor is never at stake in colonial enterprises. These only represent a business policy." However, even *Le Matin* and the other moderate journals were offended by England's refusal to grant concessions.[131] The rightist and nationalist press were more violent, going as far as to discuss the possibility of an alliance with France's rival, Germany.[132] Despite the virulence of colonialist sentiment and the weakness of Delcassé's position, he recognized that the majority of the French were anticolonialist, and he backed down.

Britain

The British ambassador in Paris remained sensitive to the precarious position of the French government. To the end, Monson argued that Delcassé's resignation would not lead to French compromise: "I doubt whether any new Government would venture to start on its career under the accusation of having commenced by truckling to English demands." He noted that although the *Groupe Colonial* in the Chamber of Deputies was weaker, it still included "a few Deputies with influence enough to excite an angry debate on any Colonial question in which there is

---

129. Courcel to Delcassé, 29 October 1898, no. 465, *DDF*, 727.
130. Courcel's statement to Salisbury is recounted in Salisbury to Monson, 30 October 1898, no. 223, *British Documents*, 1:187.
131. Carroll, *French Public Opinion and Foreign Affairs*, 175–76.
132. Carroll, *French Public Opinion and Foreign Affairs*, 176–81.

friction with England."[133] Monson was concerned about the effect of British military preparations—especially newspaper accounts of those preparations—on French public opinion. The British ambassador still did not recognize the exact nature of Delcassé's position or the inevitability of his capitulation.[134]

Salisbury remained conciliatory, but public opinion was taking its toll. On 26 October, the French ambassador cabled Paris that British public opinion was increasingly aroused and that "[i]n all the classes of the population, the idea is spreading that war is the only possible outcome. . . ." Salisbury refused to meet with the French ambassador before meeting the cabinet, Courcel reported, "so as not to be suspected of having given in personally to the solicitations of the French ambassador."[135] Again, two days later, Courcel reported Salisbury's statement that British public opinion would not allow negotiations until France left Fashoda.[136] Although Courcel was convinced, based on the prime minister's earlier statements, of Salisbury's goodwill, he noted that no British minister would be able to withstand the public outcry caused by a French presence in the Bahr-el-Ghazal region. Salisbury was stalling for time in order to let British passions subside. For the present, he could not let the public see that he was any more conciliatory than his colleagues.[137]

Chamberlain remained as hard-line as ever. On 4 November, after the French decision to withdraw was known, he stated that this would not end the conflict: "The time has come where England and France have to settle all their differences once and forever." In contrast, Salisbury continued to advocate concessions, and Chamberlain questioned the prime minister's resolve:

> I am afraid Lord Salisbury himself has not got the strength of mind to bring about the necessary crisis and choose the right moment to strike like Bismarck did at Ems. You may be certain, however, that all my colleagues, even Mr. Arthur Balfour, are of the same opinion as I am namely that Lord Salisbury's policy "peace at any price" cannot go on any longer and that England has to show to the whole world that she *can act*. I consider that the present moment is very favourable for us and you will see what is going to

---

133. For the quotes see, respectively, Monson to Salisbury, 30 October 1898, no. 225, *British Documents*, 1:188; and Sanderson, *England, Europe, and the Upper Nile*, 353.

134. See Monson's private correspondence to Salisbury, 4 November, quoted in Andrew, *Théophile Delcassé*, 111.

135. Courcel to Delcassé, 26 October 1898, no. 455, *DDF*, 708–9.

136. Courcel to Delcassé, 28 October 1898, no. 459, *DDF*, 720.

137. Courcel to Delcassé, 29 October 1898, no. 465, *DDF*, 727–32.

happen as soon as our war preparations are finished. . . . [A]s soon as we are ready we shall present our bill to France *not only in Egypt* but all over the globe, and should she refuse to pay, *then war.* Christmas may pass over quietly but what will happen in January or February nobody can foretell.[138]

British strategy changed only slightly during the last stage of the crisis, reflecting Salisbury's concern that France be given some concessions as a way of gracefully backing down. On 28 October, at the French ambassador's request, Salisbury provided an "unofficial" *aide-memoire* stating that "whatever was at present abnormal in the diplomatic relations between the two countries would cease" following the issuance of Marchand's orders to withdraw from Fashoda. Also at France's request, Britain provided written confirmation that it had never formally demanded Marchand's recall.[139] Orders were issued to the British commanders-in-chief on 31 October and 4 November to avoid provoking the French by mobilizing the navy.[140]

The British had won the crisis—France was abandoning Fashoda— but at least Salisbury and Monson were skeptical about the extent of the British victory. The ambassador predicted that a humiliated France would use the next few years to dramatically increase its naval strength: "France appears to me to be staggered; and in consequence calls herself humiliated. I should like to think that the feeling of resentment will be transitory; but the contrary is, I fear, the more likely."[141] Salisbury wondered aloud about the value of British spoils: "[W]e have been so anxious to establish our position against the French, that we have half pledged ourselves to liabilities which will furnish subjects of penitent reflection to the Treasuries both of England and of Egypt."[142] The minor British concession allowed France to save some dignity in an otherwise humiliating retreat. Such concessions as were given, however, were very little and very late.

Outcome and Aftermath

The immediate outcome of the Fashoda crisis was a British diplomatic victory followed by several years of hostile relations between the two

---

138. Quoted in Garvin, *Life of Joseph Chamberlain*, 3:232.
139. Sanderson to Courcel, 28 October 1898, no. 220, *British Documents*, 1:184. On Salisbury's *aide-memoire*, see Sanderson, *England, Europe, and the Upper Nile*, 350–51.
140. Marder, *Anatomy of British Sea Power*, 321–22.
141. Monson to Salisbury, 11 November 1898, no. 233, *British Documents*, 1:192.
142. Quoted in Grenville, *Lord Salisbury and Foreign Policy*, 232.

countries. The three months immediately following the French defeat were particularly tense, with relations spiraling close to war on several occasions. The humiliating nature of the French defeat inspired intense anti-British sentiment. Concerns were frequently voiced that England might be preparing to attack France. Both the French minister of the navy and the naval chief of staff expressed concerns about the possibility of a preventive war launched by Britain, and France responded with its own military preparations. In late December, Delcassé noted "the persistent armaments of Great Britain" and concluded that British military preparations, "by their very activity, seem to imply the possibility of a conflict." Delcassé even discussed the possibility of a rapprochement with Germany.[143] Tensions reached their height in early January 1899. At that time, the French foreign minister warned Monson that, if war came, France would continue to fight even if its fleet were destroyed, to secure a favorable change in the European situation.[144]

British suspicions and hostile behavior also continued after the resolution of the immediate crisis. The British admiralty was wary of French military preparations throughout November 1898. Until late January 1899, British naval preparations continued; the Navy remained at maximum preparedness and continued to commission the reserve fleet. It was not until early 1899 that British military leaders and policy makers recognized the largely defensive nature of French actions.[145]

Because of these tensions, Anglo-French talks did not begin formally until January 1899. The agreement reached on 21 March delimited a boundary separating French Africa from the British Sudan, and both parties agreed not to acquire territory or political influence in the other's sphere. This line, which followed the Nile-Congo watershed, excluded France from the entire Bahr-el-Ghazal region.[146] Relations between France and Britain remained tense for several years, although the removal of the African conflict opened the way for future improvement. The Fashoda crisis was, however, the last episode of intense Anglo-French hostility, and the 1904 *Entente Cordiale* definitively settled the Egyptian question.

---

143. Delcassé's comments are quoted in Marder, *The Anatomy of British Sea Power*, 334–35; also see Andrew, *Théophile Delcassé*, 111–12. This was not French paranoia; the Germans also thought England would launch a preventive war. See Marder, 332; and Sanderson, *England, Europe, and the Upper Nile*, 363.

144. Sanderson, *England, Europe, and the Upper Nile*, 364–65.

145. Marder, *Anatomy of British Sea Power*, 330; Sanderson, *England, Europe, and the Upper Nile*, 364–65.

146. The text of the 21 March agreement appears in *Correspondence*, 958–59.

Conclusions

In many respects, the French decision to back down in Fashoda was overdetermined. A complete explanation includes consideration of the international setting, domestic political context, and Delcassé's beliefs. But international structure alone is insufficient to explain the outcome, and Delcassé's beliefs would not have mattered (since he would not have been in a position to set policy) were it not for the structure of the French state.

Britain's coercive policy successfully resolved the Fashoda conflict, despite the volatile nature of French domestic politics, because it demonstrated to the French public the futility of Delcassé's hard-line, colonial policies. The existence of private actors who vocally advocated colonial expansion made it difficult for Delcassé to back down and led him to engage in delaying tactics as he attempted to gain even modest concessions from the British. However, the majority of the French press and public was opposed to war and indifferent to the future of Fashoda. This fact ultimately forced Delcassé to back down. In short, the structure of the French state gave him a wide degree of latitude within the cabinet, but the significant role of the Assembly meant that he was susceptible to societal pressures.

French policy failed to influence Britain to any noticeable extent, largely because of domestic factors. While Britain enjoyed strategic superiority, the British prime minister was willing to grant concessions in exchange for French withdrawal from Fashoda. State structure determined the policy-making process. The diffuse, nonautonomous nature of British authority meant that coalition politics prevailed. French intransigence eroded the credibility of the moderate prime minister's arguments and supported the more hawkish views of his colleagues, preventing compromise. This argument does not refute the conventional wisdom about the Fashoda crisis: an initially coercive British strategy succeeded because the balance of interests favored London. Yet this systemic argument only provides a persuasive explanation of the evolution and outcome of the Fashoda crisis once it is supplemented by an analysis of the domestic sources of national interest.

While international structural and domestic institutional approaches complement one another, motivational psychology fails to explain the decision-making process or the outcome of the crisis. The French government found itself in a decidedly vulnerable position at home as well as abroad. Delcassé stalled for time in order to have some concessions to present to the colonialists, but domestic vulnerability did not prevent him from compromising. Britain's coercive policy increased the domestic opposition to Delcassé's original policy and forced the foreign minister to concede. If anything, the weakness of the French government actually compelled him to compromise. While Delcassé may have wishfully thought he could obtain concessions from the British, there is a simpler explanation for his behavior: Salisbury's conciliatory stance led the French foreign minister to believe Britain would compromise.

A motivated bias explanation fails in the British case, as well. Lebow argues that "[t]he psychological impact of Salisbury's success in mobilizing British public opinion and readying the navy for war cannot be underestimated. Salisbury appeared to be deliberately courting war. . . ."[147] It seems far more likely, however, that public opinion was driving the prime minister than that the prime minister was leading public opinion. Domestic weakness never motivated him to overestimate French hostility or to advocate coercive policies. Instead, Salisbury consciously noted the imperatives of British public opinion and conceded the need for continued belligerence. French strategy influenced British policy by influencing the distribution of power within the British cabinet. A thorough explanation of the evolution of the Fashoda crisis recognizes differences in decision making among states and considers the interaction of strategy and state structure.

---

147. Lebow, *Between Peace and War*, 323.

5

The Berlin Crisis, 1958–61

Conventional wisdom on the 1958–61 Berlin crisis attacks the Eisenhower administration's hesitant response in the face of a direct Soviet challenge.[1] According to this school, Khrushchev saw initial U.S. willingness to negotiate as evidence of fear and weakness. By the time the United States shifted to more coercive rhetoric later in the crisis, it was too late; Soviet leaders already had formed their perceptions of an irresolute adversary that could be exploited.

Students of Soviet domestic politics describe a different scenario. Their work points to the conclusion that U.S. strategy was effective given the situation and that the more initially coercive strategy suggested by deterrence theorists only would have escalated the conflict. Their findings parallel the policy prescriptions of cooperation theory. Khrushchev was in a vulnerable position domestically and needed a foreign policy victory to promote his domestic agenda and reduce defense spending. Initial U.S. conciliation allowed him to claim such a victory. He perceived the U.S. president as a reasonable, not irresolute, adversary and responded with concessions, not further threats.[2]

This second school paints a more accurate, if incomplete, picture of the evolution of the Berlin crisis, in which initially conciliatory bargaining strategies contributed to a peaceful outcome by interacting with the domestic political environment in both the United States and the Soviet Union. Domestic structure influenced decision making in a paradoxical

---

1. The classic work is Jack M. Schick, *The Berlin Crisis, 1958–1962* (Philadelphia: University of Pennsylvania Press, 1971). Also see Alexander L. George and Richard Smoke, *Deterrence in American Foreign Policy: Theory and Practice* (New York: Columbia University Press, 1974); James L. Richardson, *Germany and the Atlantic Alliance: The Interaction of Strategy and Politics* (Cambridge: Harvard University Press, 1966); Snyder and Diesing, *Conflict among Nations*; and Hans Speier, *Divided Berlin: The Anatomy of Soviet Political Blackmail* (New York: Praeger, 1961).

2. The most explicit exposition of this argument is Richter, *Khrushchev's Double Bind*. Also see Linden, *Khrushchev and the Soviet Leadership*; Robert M. Slusser, *The Berlin Crisis of 1961: Soviet-American Relations and the Struggle for Power in the Kremlin, June-November 1961* (Baltimore: Johns Hopkins University Press, 1973); and Tatu, *Power in the Kremlin*.

manner, however. Soviet foreign policy was the product of compromise among a coalition of elites, and the secretary general was constrained by his domestic opposition. Presidents Eisenhower and Kennedy, in contrast, both enjoyed significant freedom of action in the foreign policy arena.

Unlike the Crimea and Fashoda cases, the U.S. and Soviet bargaining strategies in the Berlin crisis were highly mixed. Nevertheless, a general pattern emerges: both states employed initial accommodation followed by coercion. In the Soviet Union, where foreign policy authority was dispersed among many executive offices but where no effective national legislature existed, initial U.S. restraint garnered credibility for Khrushchev's moderate foreign policy. The subsequent U.S. shift to coercion undermined the Soviet leader's domestic support and led to a more coercive Soviet response. In the United States, the decision-making process was very different; initial Soviet restraint reinforced Eisenhower's preexisting beliefs—his desire for cooperation with the Soviets and his doubts about the legitimacy of the status quo in Berlin. The major policy shift occurred only in 1961, when John F. Kennedy became president.

A brief discussion of the origins of the conflict follows, after which I present alternative explanations for the outcome. I next examine the structure of foreign policy authority in Washington and Moscow and then provide a detailed analysis of bargaining in the six phases of the crisis. Like the two previous chapters, this one chronologically examines the sequence of bargaining tactics, decision-makers' perceptions, and policy responses.

Origins of the Conflict

The 1958–61 Berlin crisis had its roots in the division of Germany by the victorious allies at the Yalta and Potsdam Conferences in 1945. Soon after the war, U.S. emphasis on German economic recovery clashed with Soviet attempts to squeeze war reparations from the defeated Germany. Following currency reform in the Western sectors and Western planning for a separate West German state, these disputes culminated in the 1948–49 Berlin crisis. In that confrontation, Stalin blockaded the city of Berlin for nearly a year, while the United States airlifted supplies to the residents.

The second Berlin crisis had its immediate origins in four areas.[3]

---

3. See Linden, *Khrushchev and the Soviet Leadership*, esp. 82–87; Richter, *Khrushchev's Double Bind*, chap. 5; George and Smoke, *Deterrence in American Foreign Policy*, 394–95; and J. M. Mackintosh, *Strategy and Tactics of Soviet Foreign Policy* (New York: Oxford University Press, 1963), chap. 17.

First, Khrushchev sought recognition of East Germany by the West. Second, the Soviet leader was under pressure at home and may have required a foreign policy victory to win support for his proposed reductions in troop levels and defense spending. Third, by 1958 the number of young skilled East Germans fleeing to West Berlin had reached ten thousand a month. Finally, the Soviets wanted to prevent German acquisition of nuclear weapons; the December 1957 NATO foreign ministers' meeting in Paris had outlined a plan for stationing intermediate range missiles in Europe. Each of these factors influenced Khrushchev in the fall of 1958 as he prepared to issue an ultimatum to the West: settle the status of West Berlin within six months or the Soviets would give the East Germans control of access to the city.

Alternative Explanations

International Structure

The international structure provides a parsimonious explanation of the Berlin crisis: Soviet and American interests were fundamentally compatible, and both states employed the initially cooperative strategy that allowed compromise, given their interests. U.S. and Soviet interests on the eve of the crisis resembled a game of Prisoners' Dilemma.[4] Each state preferred compromise to conflict over Berlin, but each preferred the institutionalization of its own view of the status quo to compromise. For the Soviets, this included the removal of the Western powers from Berlin. U.S. and Soviet strategies appeared at times to be crazy hybrids of coercive and conciliatory tactics, but following Khrushchev's ultimatum, both states adopted the initially conciliatory strategy prescribed by cooperation theory. The interaction of strategy and international structure produced the cooperative outcome.

Yet a systemic account of the Berlin crisis only provides determinate and accurate predictions once we assume these preferences are correct; it fails to explain the sources of actors' preferences. Within the broad parameters set by American political culture, the president formulated U.S. interests, so those interests cannot be determined independent of the beliefs of the individual holding office at any given moment. For instance, U.S. strategy shifted considerably when the more hawkish Kennedy assumed office. In contrast, Soviet interests reflected the composite, if autonomous, nature of decision making within the Politburo.

---

4. See Snyder and Diesing, *Conflict among Nations*, 92.

Motivated Bias

Although he cannot be described as "vulnerable" in the same sense as can Lord Aberdeen, the British prime minister during the Crimean crisis, Nikita Khrushchev faced significant domestic opposition during his abbreviated tenure as general secretary. Nevertheless, motivational psychology fails to adequately explain the evolution and outcome of the Berlin crisis. There is little evidence that Khrushchev actually engaged in motivated misperception. While he did respond to U.S. threats in the later stage of the crisis with renewed threats of his own, Khrushchev continued to describe Eisenhower as a "realist" who wanted compromise. Despite domestic weakness, Khrushchev seems to have neither overestimated his opponent's hostility nor ignored U.S. threats.

It is possible that his precarious domestic situation motivated the general secretary to believe that the United States sought compromise and that his own ultimatum and subsequent concessions were working. The kind of detailed evidence necessary to support this argument over one that focuses on the direct influence of domestic politics is not yet available on the Khrushchev period. Even if it were, such an argument would raise another problem; it would prevent the generation of determinate predictions about the influence of domestic vulnerability on foreign policy. In short, his domestic weakness could have motivated Khrushchev to see the United States as either overly hostile or overly cooperative and to engage in either coercive or conciliatory behavior.

Cognitive and Bureaucratic Explanations

As in the two previous cases, cognitive and bureaucratic explanations each explain part of the process of bargaining during the Berlin crisis. Again, the organization of foreign policy authority within the adversary states determines the usefulness of these two approaches. Cognitive psychology best describes the bargaining process in Washington from 1958 to 1961. Both U.S. presidents interpreted Soviet policy according to their own tactical beliefs. Initial Soviet restraint reinforced Eisenhower's belief in the efficacy of conciliation and the possibility of cooperating with Moscow. U.S. policy on Berlin only shifted noticeably when Kennedy assumed office in 1961. Ironically, given the political systems of the two states, coalition politics prevailed in Moscow, not in Washington. The initially conciliatory U.S. strategy improved Khrushchev's domestic incentives and resources, while subsequent U.S. threats eroded the credibility of the general secretary's moderate policy prescriptions.

The decision-making processes within the two states were the reverse of what might be expected, given the states' overall political structures. Alexis de Tocqueville once lamented, "Foreign politics demand scarcely any of those qualities which are peculiar to a democracy; they require, on the contrary, the perfect use of almost all those in which it is deficient."[5] Nevertheless, in the late 1950s and early 1960s the United States was a "strong state" in an international crisis. The president was a highly unitary actor who enjoyed extensive autonomy from Congress on such matters. The Soviet premier, by contrast, was more constrained. While no true national legislature existed, Khrushchev shared foreign policy authority with other high-ranking members of the Politburo. Two components of state structure—the organization of the executive and the degree of executive autonomy from a national legislature—together determined the process by which crisis bargaining occurred and the usefulness of existing cognitive and bureaucratic explanations. I now turn to an examination of those institutional constraints.

State Structure and the Decision-Making Process in Moscow and Washington

The Soviet Union

Like every general secretary before and after him, Khrushchev sat atop a large, highly centralized bureaucracy. Although the Soviet Union is most commonly viewed as an autocratic state with a unitary leader, the state's political institutions required the Soviet leader to seek the support of his colleagues within the Party leadership if his policies were to be adopted and successfully implemented. There existed no effective national legislature to constrain a Soviet leader's ability to formulate effective foreign policy, but decision making within the executive element of the government was a collective enterprise. In the words of one student of Soviet politics, the Presidium (Politburo) was a "battleground" among the competing interests of the "oligarchy."[6]

While it was authoritarian, the Soviet state could not be considered a unitary actor. Factional struggles influenced foreign policy making in Moscow, just as they had in the parliamentary democracy of nineteenth-century Britain, because of the collective nature of executive decision making. Indeed, the Presidium, "the real cabinet of the Soviet system,"[7] had approximately fifteen members at any given time. Although the

---

5. *Democracy in America* (New York: Random House, Modern Library, 1950), 126.

6. Gelman, *Brezhnev Politburo*, esp. 230–31 n. 1.

7. Jerry F. Hough and Merle Fainsod, *How the Soviet Union is Governed* (Cambridge: Harvard University Press, 1979), 466.

general secretary was a first among equals, other high-ranking members of the Presidium regularly participated in domestic and foreign policy decisions. Many students of Soviet politics have long recognized the existence of different Soviet groups or factions struggling for power and of the tactical need of Soviet leaders to build coalitions in support of a preferred strategy. In May 1957, for example, Khrushchev alluded to a "heated" policy debate within the Presidium that was only settled by a vote of the members.[8] Some scholars go so far as to assert that the principle of collective leadership even dominated decision making during the height of Stalin's autocratic rule.[9]

Although executive authority for foreign policy in the Soviet Union was diffuse, one dramatic difference remained between the Soviet Union under Khrushchev and a state like Britain under Aberdeen or Salisbury: the foreign policy executive enjoyed significant autonomy from a national legislature. Such a legislature existed, but because of the autocratic nature of the political system, it did not function as a constraint on the Soviet elite. According to the Soviet constitution, the two houses of the Supreme Soviet—the Council of the Union and the Council of Nationalities—were the highest legislative bodies of the state. In reality, both bodies performed largely symbolic roles and "the real parliament [was] the party Central Committee."[10] The Party Congress selected the Central Committee to govern between meetings of the Congress, but the Central Committee met rarely and briefly and did not provide a forum for active debate.

It reached the height of its influence in the 1957 attempt to oust Khrushchev. After his opponents called for his resignation, Khrushchev resisted and convened the Central Committee, which overwhelmingly supported him. While this event is significant, there are two reasons why

---

8. *New York Times*, 11 May 1957, cited in Linden, *Khrushchev and the Soviet Leadership*, 41. Also see Breslauer, *Khrushchev and Brezhnev as Leaders*; Herbert Alexander Dallin, "Soviet Foreign Policy and Domestic Politics: A Framework for Analysis," *Journal of International Affairs* 23 (1969): 250–65; Herbert S. Dinerstein, *The Making of a Missile Crisis, October 1962* (Baltimore: Johns Hopkins University Press, 1976); Franklyn Griffiths, "A Tendency Analysis of Soviet Policy-Making," in H. G. Skilling and Franklyn Griffiths, eds., *Interest Groups in Soviet Politics* (Princeton: Princeton University Press, 1971); Jiri Valenta, *Soviet Intervention in Czechoslovakia, 1968: The Anatomy of a Decision* (Baltimore: Johns Hopkins University Press, 1979), 17–20; and the works cited in n. 2 of this chapter.

9. Hough and Fainsod, *How the Soviet Union is Governed*, 473; Linden, *Khrushchev and the Soviet Leadership*, 11, 13. Nevertheless, Stalin's death marked a significant change in the institutional structure of the Soviet state.

10. Hough and Fainsod, *How the Soviet Union is Governed*, 362. The following discussion of the Central Committee draws on Hough and Fainsod, 455–66.

the influence of the Central Committee should not be exaggerated based on this incident. First, it remains unclear whether real power resided in the Central Committee, where Khrushchev controlled a majority of the votes, or in the Presidium, where the anti-Party group was defeated even before the Central Committee assembled. While Carl A. Linden argues that Khrushchev convinced several weaker members of the opposing coalition within the Presidium to support him in exchange for a promise not to retaliate,[11] the general secretary's task was made easier by the knowledge that his control of the Central Committee meant the outcome was a foregone conclusion. Second, even if the Central Committee did play a decisive role in the 1957 struggle, it does not follow that the body was influential in the foreign policy-making process or that it was capable of threatening the continued existence of the Soviet government. In 1957, the Central Committee was convened to support the sitting general secretary against a group easily labeled "anti-Party," not to threaten the government's authority.

In sum, the Soviet Union of the late 1950s and early 1960s was a type III (diffuse, autonomous) state. Decision making within the Presidium was far from collective in the true sense of that word, but it was impossible for a general secretary to implement a policy proposal against the sustained opposition of his colleagues. Any policy had to have the support of, or at least could not solicit the active opposition of, a majority of the members of the decision-making elite. Lest the potential influence of domestic factors be overstated, we also must remember that the national legislature exercised no real control over the foreign policy-making process. Juridical authority for foreign policy resided in the Presidium, and the Central Committee had insufficient power or authority to demand accountability.

The Khrushchev Presidium

The collective, if autonomous, structure of the Soviet state distinguishes the full members of the Presidium as the key decision makers and identifies the nature of the domestic incentives the Soviet leaders faced. Yet state structure alone cannot explain the outcome of the crisis; we must also examine the foreign policy orientation of the Khrushchev regime.

While Nikita Khrushchev was no dove, his strategic beliefs were considerably more moderate than many of his colleagues within the Presidium. Jack Snyder's description of the general secretary's belief in "offensive détente" suggests that Khrushchev's beliefs were more mixed

---

11. *Khrushchev and the Soviet Leadership*, 43–44.

than those of most decision makers examined in this study.[12] The Soviet leader believed in the possibility and desirability of "peaceful coexistence" with the West, a belief that led him to call for arms control and a nuclear test ban. It also led, according to Linden, to Soviet restraint in crises over Taiwan and Lebanon.[13]

Khrushchev's belief in détente stemmed from a conviction that war, while unlikely, would be disastrous. At an April 1957 press conference, he stated, "All now consider that an atomic war would be terrible for humanity. That means the US and the USSR, England, France and all other governments . . . must, if they don't want to go on the dangerous path of adventurism, agree that the single way out is coexistence."[14] War was no longer inevitable; it was now possible to exclude "world war from the life of society even before the complete triumph of socialism, even with capitalism existing in part of the world."[15] While Khrushchev held a fairly optimistic image of the international system, he argued that peaceful coexistence could only come about through Soviet military strength. The correlation of forces was shifting in Moscow's favor, and the West was less likely to attack, "not because the imperialists have become wiser or kinder, but because they have become weaker." Soviet strategic nuclear forces, in particular, would have a "strong sobering" influence on the "imperialist aggressors."[16]

Finally, the general secretary had a relatively benign, or at least highly differentiated, view of the adversary. He believed the United States would not attack the Soviets or risk provoking them to war. Khrushchev claimed in 1956 that "signs of a noted sobering are beginning to appear among Western ruling circles," and that President Eisenhower "showed some inklings of a desire to enter a path to establish mutual understanding."[17] The general secretary maintained that while some imperialist leaders sought conflict, the U.S. president was a realist who recognized Soviet strength and the need for compromise.

Khrushchev can be labeled a moderate only because many of his

12. "The Gorbachev Revolution: A Waning of Soviet Expansionism?" *International Security* 12, no. 3 (winter 1987/88), 103–6; Snyder, *Myths of Empire*, chap. 6.

13. *Khrushchev and the Soviet Leadership*, 82 (also see 51).

14. Quoted in James Gerard Richter, "Action and Reaction in Khrushchev's Foreign Policy: How Leadership Politics Affect Soviet Responses to the International Environment," (Ph.D. diss., Berkeley, 1989), 312–13.

15. *Pravda*, 11 November 1958, quoted in Linden, *Khrushchev and the Soviet Leadership*, 85.

16. See respectively *Pravda*, 27 March 1959, quoted in Arnold Horelick and Myron Rush, *Strategic Power and Soviet Foreign Policy* (Chicago: University of Chicago Press, 1961), 55; and *Pravda*, 7 March 1954, quoted in Richter, "Action and Reaction," 173.

17. *Pravda*, 1 May 1956, quoted in Richter, "Action and Reaction," 274.

colleagues possessed dramatically different foreign policy beliefs.[18] The general secretary was criticized from the "right" by more dovish members of the Soviet elite, such as Deputy Premier Anastas Mikoyan. While Mikoyan supported the notion of peaceful coexistence, he was critical of Khrushchev's "waste of human and material resources on military goals" as a means of securing peace.[19] Reportedly, Mikoyan was the first member of the Soviet elite to publicly advance the argument that there were "realists" within the ruling circles in the West.[20]

The military opposed Khrushchev on different grounds. As Snyder observes, "During this period, the strategic ideology of the Soviet military stressed straightforward threat inflation, denying that there were any 'realists' in the West who could be partners in arms control, or for that matter, who could be intimidated by Khrushchev's brinksmanship into accepting détente on Soviet terms."[21] Although R. D. Malinovsky recognized the existence of some "sober" elements of the Western elite, the minister of defense also argued that "the existence of inner contradictions in the aggressive blocs, especially NATO, in no wise reduces the great threat to the peace and security of the peoples. Moreover, the more obvious the failure of the aggressive policy becomes, the greater will become the danger of a military adventure."[22]

Snyder includes Frol Kozlov in this group because of his ties to the military-industrial complex. Kozlov held a hostile image of the West and believed that the antidote was Soviet military strength. He noted, "Lacking confidence in the stability of their economic system, the imperialists are seeking a way out of their economic difficulties not through peaceful competition but through intensifying the arms race, militarizing the economy, and preparing for a new war."[23]

Finally, the general secretary was attacked from the "left" by the ideological hard-liner Mikhail Suslov. In fact, it was the orthodox party theoretician who later initiated Khrushchev's removal from office. Unlike the general secretary, Suslov saw an aggressive opponent and believed war was likely. A 1949 conference resolution based on a speech by

18. The following discussion draws heavily on Richter, *Khrushchev's Double Bind*; and Snyder, "The Gorbachev Revolution."

19. Quoted in Richter, *Khrushchev's Double Bind*, 85. Also see Tatu, *Power in the Kremlin*, 29.

20. Christer Jönsson, *Soviet Bargaining Behavior: The Nuclear Test Ban Case* (New York: Columbia University Press, 1979), 154.

21. *Myths of Empire*, 242. Also see Jönsson, *Soviet Bargaining Behavior*, chaps. 11–13.

22. Quoted in Jönsson, *Soviet Bargaining Behavior*, 155.

23. Quoted in Jönsson, *Soviet Bargaining Behavior*, 155. Also see Linden, *Khrushchev and the Soviet Leadership*, 50–51; and Snyder, "The Gorbachev Revolution," 100.

Suslov concluded that the "Anglo-American imperialists" hoped "to gain world domination": "Historical experience teaches that, the more hopeless things are for imperialist reaction, the more it rages and the greater the danger of military adventures."[24]

The collective, if autonomous, structure of foreign policy authority determined the process of crisis bargaining within Moscow, but U.S. policy only succeeded because of Khrushchev's moderate foreign policy outlook. Initial U.S. restraint reinforced the credibility of Khrushchev's strategic arguments in the early phase of the crisis and bolstered his domestic support. When U.S. policy shifted later in the conflict, U.S. coercive tactics and rhetoric inadvertently reinforced Khrushchev's opposition, resulting in a hardening of Soviet policy.

The United States

In 1957, Edward S. Corwin noted that "the history of the presidency is a history of aggrandizement."[25] Although frequently depicted as weak, particularly in relation to Congress, the American president possessed enormous freedom of action on foreign policy. Indeed, decision making within the United States in the 1950s and 1960s was unitary and autonomous. Woodrow Wilson put it succinctly: "The initiative in foreign affairs, which the President possesses without any restriction whatever, is virtually the power to control them absolutely."[26]

Within the executive element of the government, the U.S. president was and is the undisputed, sole voice in foreign policy. His cabinet and trusted advisors often function as an advisory group during crises, but they have no constitutionally granted or traditionally assumed powers as a decision-making unit; the power and authority of individual cabinet members derive from their personal relationship to the president.

Although certainly not as free as a nineteenth-century Russian czar, in a foreign policy crisis the American president of the 1950s and 1960s was relatively autonomous from the national legislature. This autonomy derived in part from the president's constitutionally granted authority to make treaties, appoint and receive ambassadors, and, most important, command the armed forces. The Constitution is not silent on congres-

---

24. Quoted in Marshall D. Shulman, *Stalin's Foreign Policy Reappraised* (Cambridge: Harvard University Press, 1963), 119. On Suslov's conservative opposition, see Linden, *Khrushchev and the Soviet Leadership*, 44–45, 56–57; Roy Medvedev, *All Stalin's Men* (Garden City, NY: Anchor Press, 1984), chap. 3; and Tatu, *Power in the Kremlin*, 30–33.

25. *President*, 29–30.

26. *Constitutional Government in the United States* (New York: Columbia University Press, 1911), 77.

sional authority, however, granting the legislative body the power to advise and consent, confirm executive appointments, control the purse strings, and, most important, declare war. The U.S. Constitution has, in fact, been frequently referred to as "an invitation to struggle for the privilege of directing American foreign policy."[27]

Rather than deriving exclusively from the Constitution, the president's foreign policy powers evolved slowly and sporadically. Although the executive and the legislature have each dominated decision making in different periods of American history, the president has consistently gained and consolidated his authority.[28] Even John Rourke, an ardent critic of the widely accepted notion that an "imperial presidency" existed from World War II through the early 1970s, concedes that in an international crisis Congress deferred to the president: "When an issue remained purely foreign in its perceptual focus, the president normally prevailed."[29]

Legislative passivity in the face of intermittent presidential willingness to consult indicates the extent to which presidential predominance was firmly entrenched in the American political system. Eisenhower was unique in the extent to which he sought congressional input, but leaders of Congress always demurred. In the Dien Bien Phu crisis of 1954, for example, Representative Sam Rayburn told the president that congressional Democrats were "ready to cooperate in a sound foreign policy" if they only knew "what that policy is."[30] When Eisenhower consulted Capitol Hill on the brewing Middle East crisis three years later, Representative John McCormack suggested that the president possessed the authority to act as commander in chief and did not need to seek congressional authorization to provide aid to the region.[31] The Taiwan Straits crisis similarly led Senator Mike Mansfield to bemoan Eisenhower's attempt to consult Congress on the Formosa Resolution: "I don't like to see the President reducing the power he has under the Constitution.

27. Corwin, *President*, 171.

28. Daniel S. Cheever and H. Field Haviland, Jr., *American Foreign Policy and the Separation of Powers* (Cambridge: Harvard University Press, 1952); Corwin, *President*, chaps. 5–6; Crabb and Holt, *Invitation to Struggle*; Clinton Rossiter, *The American Presidency*, rev. ed. (New York: Harcourt Brace, 1960); Schlesinger, *Imperial Presidency*, esp. chaps. 3–5; Wilson, *Constitutional Government*.

29. *Congress and the Presidency in U.S. Foreign Policymaking: A Study of Interaction and Influence, 1945–1982* (Boulder: Westview Press, 1983), 79. On the power of the president in a crisis, see Waltz, *Foreign Policy and Democratic Politics*, chap. 10.

30. *New York Times*, 14 May 1954, 1, quoted in Waltz, *Foreign Policy and Democratic Politics*, 113–14.

31. Dwight D. Eisenhower, *The White House Years*, 2 vols. (New York: Doubleday, 1965), 2:179.

And I don't like to see Congress taking power which normally should be in the hands of the Executive."[32]

As my analysis of the Berlin crisis indicates, neither the Eisenhower nor the Kennedy administration shared a single set of foreign policy beliefs. While domestic factions flourished, the president's authority to make foreign policy was unchallenged. In this sense only, the United States during the mid-twentieth century was as strong a state as czarist Russia. Because the United States was a unitary, autonomous state, Soviet strategy influenced U.S. policy through its impact on the presidents' beliefs.

Eisenhower and Kennedy
American political culture, particularly the social consensus for containment that dominated political discourse in the 1950s, strongly influenced the core beliefs of the foreign policy elite. Presidents Eisenhower and Kennedy shared the consensus view of the threat posed by the Soviet Union and of the need to resist Soviet aggression. The two presidents differed, however, in their intermediate beliefs about domestic dynamics within the Soviet Union and, more noticeably, in their tactical beliefs about the efficacy of force as an influence tactic.

While Eisenhower has been described accurately as an "unremitting anticommunis[t]" and "a thoroughgoing Cold Warrior,"[33] his tactical foreign policy beliefs prior to the Berlin crisis identify him as a relative moderate and perhaps, as Khrushchev claimed, a realist. Following World War II, Eisenhower repeatedly expressed a concern to avoid war with the Soviets. He opposed the division of Germany, because such a division would make cooperation with the Soviets difficult. In May 1945, Eisenhower went so far as to compare the U.S.-Soviet relationship to the Anglo-American alliance. He concluded that "[t]he more contact we have with the Russians, the more they will understand us and the greater will be the cooperation. . . . [N]ow, in peace, the motive for cooperation is the betterment of the lot in life of the common man. If we can create singleness of purpose on this theme, as we did to win the war, then peace should be assured."[34] Russian intentions were relatively be-

32. Minority Leader Joseph Martin similarly told Eisenhower that he did not need congressional authorization to act. For this and the Mansfield quote, see Rourke, *Congress and the Presidency*, 207.

33. See respectively H. W. Brands, Jr., *Cold Warrior: Eisenhower's Generation and American Foreign Policy* (New York: Columbia University Press, 1988), 199; and Michael R. Beschloss, *Mayday: Eisenhower, Khrushchev, and the U-2 Affair* (New York: Harper & Row, 1986), 70.

34. Stephen E. Ambrose, *Eisenhower*, 2 vols. (New York: Simon and Schuster, 1983–84), 1:399–402, quote at 402.

nign: "There is no one thing, I believe, that guides the policy of Russia more today than to keep friendship with the United States."[35]

While Eisenhower was often suspicious of Soviet intentions, his faith in peaceful diplomacy never wavered. His lecture to Syngman Rhee in 1954 on the need for peace was representative of many Eisenhower remarks: "[L]et me tell you that if war comes, it will be horrible. Atomic war will destroy civilization. It will destroy our cities. There will be millions of people dead. War today is unthinkable with the weapons which we have at our command. If the Kremlin and Washington ever lock up in a war, the results are too horrible to contemplate. I can't even imagine them."[36] Eisenhower advocated a relatively conciliatory approach to the Soviets that relied on negotiations, not coercion. He objected, for instance, to the use of the atomic bomb in 1945, because it would provoke the Soviets.[37] In 1954, Eisenhower told a group of foreign service officers that there was no longer "any alternative to peace": "The soldier can no longer regain a peace that is useable to the world."[38] In his relations with the Soviets, at least, Eisenhower was committed to peace and to cautious diplomacy as a means of achieving it.

John Kennedy was a bird of a different feather: he was more skeptical of Soviet intentions and placed more faith in the efficacy of force. He was not a true hard-liner; Kennedy attributed both expansionist and security goals to the Soviets. He commented in 1959, "I don't think that there is any button that you press that reaches an accommodation with the Soviet Union which is hard and fast. . . . What it is is a constant day-to-day struggle with an enemy who is constantly attempting to expand his power."[39] Even Soviet restraint was evidence of hostility; Kennedy noted that at the 1955 Geneva summit "[t]he barbarian may have taken the knife out of his teeth to smile, but the knife itself is still in his fist."[40]

Kennedy was critical of negotiations as a means of securing Soviet cooperation. His campaign rhetoric focused on the "missile gap" and the need for a stronger defense. If there were any hope of long-term cooperation, it would be based on respect for American strength, not on Soviet restraint. On the occasion of the introduction of his June 1960

---

35. November 1945, quoted in Ambrose, *Eisenhower*, 1:447.

36. Quoted in Brands, *Cold Warriors*, 198.

37. Blanche Wiesen Cook, *The Declassified Eisenhower: A Divided Legacy* (Garden City, NY: Doubleday & Company, 1981), 40, 42, 59.

38. Quoted in Robert A. Divine, *Eisenhower and the Cold War* (New York: Oxford University Press, 1981), 116.

39. Quoted in Michael R. Beschloss, *The Crisis Years: Kennedy and Khrushchev 1960–1963* (New York: Edward Burlingame, 1991), 20.

40. Quoted in Beschloss, *Crisis Years*, 19.

plan to increase defense spending, Senator Kennedy attacked Eisenhower: "As a substitute for policy, President Eisenhower has tried smiling at the Russians, our State Department has tried frowning at them, and Mr. Nixon has tried both. . . . So long as Mr. Khrushchev is convinced that the balance of power is shifting his way, no argument of either smiles or toughness—neither Camp David talks nor Kitchen Debates—can compel him to enter fruitful negotiations."[41]

Both Eisenhower's and Kennedy's foreign policy beliefs were crucial to the effectiveness of Soviet policy during the Berlin crisis, because of the unitary, autonomous organization of authority in the United States. Soviet restraint reinforced Eisenhower's relatively moderate beliefs, and the subsequent hardening of Soviet policy indicated to the American president that the Soviet leader faced domestic opposition. The more hawkish Kennedy was less willing to cut Khrushchev any slack and came to office prepared to implement a tougher line toward Moscow. The following section details the interaction of U.S. and Soviet policies and their impact on the opponent's domestic political situation.

The Berlin Crisis

The crisis can be divided into six phases: (1) the Soviet presentation of and subsequent attempts to back away from the November 1958 ultimatum; (2) the Geneva Conference from May to August 1959; (3) Khrushchev's visit to Camp David and its aftermath, September 1959 to May 1960; (4) the confrontation from May 1960 to February 1961; (5) the early months of the Kennedy administration, February to June 1961; and (6) the resolution of the conflict from June to October 1961.

The Soviet Challenge and Withdrawal: November 1958 to May 1959

In the first stage of the crisis, Khrushchev followed his coercive challenge with more conciliatory, but mixed, tactics. Despite the ultimatum, Eisenhower perceived Soviet moves according to his beliefs: Khrushchev's aims in Berlin were limited and were motivated largely by security considerations. Contrary to the predictions of deterrence theory, which suggests he should have sought to exploit Western concessions, Khrushchev initially responded with concessions of his own. U.S. restraint quieted domestic opposition and allowed him to follow his own policy preferences.

---

41. *Congressional Record*, 14 June 1960, quoted in Beschloss, *Crisis Years*, 22–23.

Soviet Union
The Berlin crisis began with Khrushchev's 10 November challenge. In a speech to the Soviet-Polish Friendship Meeting in Moscow, he claimed "[t]he time has obviously arrived for the signatories of the Potsdam Agreement to renounce the remnants of the occupation regime in Berlin and thereby make it possible to create a normal situation in the capital of the German Democratic Republic."[42] His threat to turn control of Berlin over to the East Germans was accompanied by menacing actions, such as the 14 November detention for eight and a half hours of a U.S. military convoy on the autobahn outside Berlin.

The Soviets issued the Berlin ultimatum on 27 November in identical notes to the three Western powers occupying Berlin. It proposed negotiations to make West Berlin a demilitarized, free city but threatened that, if no agreement were reached within six months, the Soviets would turn over control of access to the city to the East Germans: "The U.S.S.R. does not seek any conquests. All it wants is to put an end to the abnormal and dangerous situation which has developed in Berlin because of the continued occupation of its western sectors by the United States, the United Kingdom and France."[43]

Almost immediately after the Soviets issued this ultimatum, they began to water it down. On 28 November, a Soviet diplomat in East Berlin stated that Moscow would be flexible about the deadline.[44] The next day, in a press conference at the Albanian Embassy reception in Moscow, Khrushchev qualified his threat saying, "We put this question, not in the nature of an ultimatum, but suggesting a six-month time-limit for a comprehensive discussion on it, for meetings with representatives of western powers, to discuss the Soviet government's proposals if the western powers show readiness to discuss this question."[45] The issue did not have to be settled; negotiations merely had to begin.

In January 1959, Mikoyan visited the United States and continued relaxing the Soviet challenge. Throughout his trip, the deputy premier advocated negotiations, and on his return to Moscow he stated at a news conference, "We have not issued any ultimatums to anyone and have not

42. U.S. Senate Committee on Foreign Relations, *Documents on Germany, 1944–1970*, 92d Cong., 1st sess., 1971, 350–54, quote at 353 (hereinafter *Documents on Germany*). Several students of the crisis argue that Khrushchev simply got carried away during the course of his comments and did not intend to issue such a strong challenge to the West. See the works cited in George and Smoke, *Deterrence in American Foreign Policy*, 397.
43. George D. Embree, ed., *The Soviet Union and the German Question September 1958–June 1961* (The Hague: Martinus Nijhoff, 1963), 23–40, quote at 35.
44. *New York Times*, 29 November 1958, 1, cited in Schick, *Berlin Crisis*, 16–17.
45. Embree, *German Question*, 48.

threatened anyone. . . . The main thing in our proposal is not the date for ending the talks, but the talks themselves, the necessity of their being held."[46] While Soviet threats continued, Moscow couched its warnings in claims to be restoring the status quo. According to a 12 December TASS statement, "There is only one basis for the solution of the German problem—recognition of the existence of the two German states, that is to say, recognition of the actual situation prevailing in Germany."[47]

On 10 January 1959, the Soviets presented the United States with a draft peace treaty concerning Germany. The treaty would have banned the production or stationing of nuclear weapons on German territory and would have prevented Germany from joining a military alliance against any of the victors from World War II, unless all four of the Allies were also members. The accompanying note cited "the completely abnormal situation which has developed as a result of the delay in solving one of the most important international postwar problems—the conclusion of a peace treaty with Germany."[48]

Menacing rhetoric and actions continued throughout early 1959, resulting in a mixed bargaining strategy. Nevertheless, the Soviet Union had toned down its harsh rhetoric almost immediately after issuing the ultimatum on Berlin. The shift to a more conciliatory policy was noticeable in Khrushchev's qualifications, as well as in Mikoyan's visit to the United States. Throughout this early phase of the conflict, in sum, Khrushchev premised Soviet actions on a definition of the status quo as a divided Germany within which the city of Berlin was an anomaly.

United States

Eisenhower was not alarmed by initial Soviet actions. Consistent with his prior beliefs, he advocated restraint. Although the British prime minister sent a letter to Khrushchev reaffirming Britain's commitment to Berlin, the United States did not act.[49] Eisenhower's initial response was to state that there was little reason to worry and that the United States should avoid any provocative actions. In his memoirs, Eisenhower notes that "[w]hen the news of Khrushchev's statement first broke, there was no reason for an immediate public reply by the United States government; too much eagerness to counter Khrushchev's statement would give the impression that our government was edgy."[50]

---

46. Embree, *German Question*, 102–3.
47. Embree, *German Question*, 55.
48. Embree, *German Question*, 81. For the complete text of the treaty, see Embree, 89–100.
49. George and Smoke, *Deterrence in American Foreign Policy*, 407.
50. Eisenhower, *White House Years*, 2:331.

The president's optimism extended to the 27 November note. He was vacationing in Augusta when he received the news in a telegram from his secretary of state. Eisenhower's memoirs record his cavalier response: "Foster had more to report. The State Department had just received a note from Moscow that seemed to defer any move on Khrushchev's part for six months, during which time negotiations over Berlin should take place." Although the president admitted that the note "had the tone of an ultimatum," he also admitted that he "would be willing to study the possibility of creating a free city . . . if it included *all of Berlin*, East and West. . . ."[51]

U.S. policy reflected Eisenhower's conciliatory preferences. In fact, Secretary of State Dulles displayed an uncharacteristic flexibility and willingness to negotiate in the first public U.S. response to the Soviet challenge. In his 26 November news conference, Dulles noted the limited aims of the Soviets:

> . . . [N]othing that has been said recently indicates that there is any intention or desire on the part of either of [sic] the Soviet Union itself or the puppet regime, the GDR, to stop access to and from Berlin. The only issue that seems to have been raised is whether or not the Soviet Union can itself dispose of its responsibilities in the matter and turn them over to the GDR. But there has not been any intimation of any kind that the result of that would be a stoppage. It would be a shift of responsibility and authority. . . . The motivation at the present time would be not a purpose to drive us out of Berlin or to obstruct access to Berlin but to try to compel an increased recognition and the according of increased stature to the GDR.[52]

Dulles's most famous statement of the day came in response to a reporter's question on whether the United States might deal with the East Germans as "agents of the Soviet Union." The secretary responded, "We might, yes. There are certain respects now in which minor functionaries of the so-called GDR are being dealt with by both the Western Powers, the three allied powers, and also by the Federal Republic of Germany."[53] This represented a substantial shift in U.S. policy, which had held the Soviets responsible for the actions of the East Germans in Berlin. At the same time, however, Dulles's public comment on leaving a 30 November meeting with Eisenhower demonstrated the limits of

---

51. Eisenhower, *White House Years*, 2:333–34.
52. *Documents on Germany*, 358–59.
53. *Documents on Germany*, 355–56.

U.S. accommodation: "The President reiterated our government's firm purpose that the United States will not enter into any arrangement or embark on any course of conduct which will have the effect of abandoning the responsibilities which the United States, with Great Britain and France, has formally assumed for the freedom and security of the people of West Berlin."[54]

U.S. policy continued to reflect Eisenhower's flexibility and optimism in the aftermath of the Soviet ultimatum. On 15 December, Dulles recommended to the NATO Ministerial Council meeting that the organization enter into broad negotiations with the Soviets. This recommendation was embodied in the NATO Council declaration of the next day.[55] The United States issued an official response on 31 December in a note to the Soviets informing them that the United States would not accept the unilateral denunciation of the Potsdam Agreements and would continue to hold the Soviet Union responsible for actions in East Berlin. Although the note rejected the Soviet free-city proposal, it concluded with a call for negotiations. The United States was willing, it said, "to discuss the question of Berlin in the wider framework of negotiations for a solution of the German problem as well as that of European security."[56]

Even following the Soviet presentation of a draft peace treaty on 10 January 1959 and Mikoyan's visit to the United States, U.S. policy remained accommodative. Dulles referred to the presence of the deputy premier in the United States as evidence of Soviet willingness to negotiate. In a press conference on 13 January the secretary of state observed that Mikoyan had "made clear that there was no intention on the part of the Soviet Union to have their note treated as . . . an ultimatum with a fixed time limit." He added, "There seems to be a sharp difference of opinion as to what we talk about, but there is at least a common denominator, I think, in terms of a feeling that there should be discussions."[57] In the same press conference, Dulles eased the requirements for the reunification of Germany. To a reporter's question, he responded that free elections were "a natural method" of reunification, but that he "wouldn't say that it is the only method by which reunification could be accomplished." On January 27, he elaborated that he could conceive of a German confederation as a means of reunification.[58]

Dulles himself did not entirely agree with these early statements of

---

54. Quoted in Jean Edward Smith, *The Defense of Berlin* (Baltimore: Johns Hopkins Press, 1963), 185.

55. Schick, *Berlin Crisis*, 20, 34.

56. *Documents on Germany*, 382.

57. Quoted in Schick, *Berlin Crisis*, 37–38.

58. Schick, *Berlin Crisis*, 37–39, quote at 37.

U.S. policy, which suggests the importance of Eisenhower's moderate beliefs in shaping U.S. policy. In a 25 January essay entitled "Thinking Out Loud by John Foster Dulles," the secretary of state privately questioned his own public stand and noted that dealing with the GDR government as an agent of the Soviet Union represented a major Soviet gain.[59] A 29 January telegram to the U.S. ambassador in Bonn revealed Dulles's impression of Mikoyan's visit. While he agreed that "Mikoyan took some pains to convey by his manner an apparent willingness to be conciliatory," the secretary of state noted,

> Nevertheless, at no point did he hint that, failing agreement with the Western powers by May 27, the Soviets would be deterred from turning over their responsibilities to the Pankow regime. . . . [I]t would have been contrary to the normal techniques employed by the Soviets to compromise or retreat at this early stage. They may be expected to press their demands until they have satisfied themselves that we are prepared to fight over Berlin. . . . It is probable that, among his purposes, Mikoyan came to the United States to assess the strength of our determination on [Berlin] as well as the general fiber of the country.[60]

Dulles's skepticism and hard-line preferences were shared by the French (who feared a repeat of the 1936 German occupation of the Rhineland) but were strongly opposed by the British. The French press noted the conciliatory nature of Moscow's 10 January note and general Soviet willingness to talk, but President DeGaulle was unwilling to negotiate under duress. He argued instead that a conference should be held only after the 27 May deadline passed.[61] The British favored a more conciliatory approach, including an early conference with the Soviets.

59. *Declassified Document Reference Service* (hereinafter *DDRS*), 1987, Department of State (hereinafter DOS), no. 1378; *DDRS*, 1988, DOS, no. 2067. On the difference between Dulles's public statements and his "behind the scenes activity," see Roscoe Drummond and Gaston Coblentz, *Duel at the Brink: John Foster Dulles' Command of American Power* (Garden City, NY: Doubleday, 1960), 201–10; and Townsend Hoopes, *The Devil and John Foster Dulles* (Boston: Little, Brown, 1973), 464.

60. At the same time, however, Dulles recognized the need for some "face-saving camouflage" if the Soviets were to alter their demands on Berlin. See Dulles, telegram to the American embassy in Bonn, Paris, and London, 29 January 1959, *DDRS*, 1981, DOS, no. 518A, 1–3.

61. See *Current Intelligence Weekly*, 15 January 1959, *DDRS*, 1988, Central Intelligence Agency (hereinafter CIA), no. 1181; Schick, *Berlin Crisis*, 54–55, 64; and Dulles, memorandum of conversation with Couve de Murville, 7 February 1959, *DDRS*, 1983, DOS, no. 904.

Earlier British plans had gone as far as to suggest Western withdrawal from Central Europe. Against U.S. opposition, Prime Minister Macmillan visited Moscow from 21 February to 3 March for bilateral talks with Khrushchev.[62] Not surprisingly, the West Germans leaned more toward the French than the British position.

Although the bulk of my argument focuses on the two chief antagonists in the Berlin crisis, the United States and the Soviet Union, Eisenhower also spoke and acted on behalf of the Western alliance. From the beginning, the President was constrained by U.S. relations with its allies and, particularly, by relations with its German client, which for obvious reasons opposed any serious, substantive concessions.[63] To some extent, Eisenhower had to satisfy U.S. alliance partners, but he did not face any significant domestic opposition and his actions reflected his prior beliefs.

On 16 February, the United States sent a note to the Soviet Union proposing a foreign ministers' conference. Even though the French, the West Germans, and some elements of the U.S. administration advocated a more hawkish response, Western policy was restrained. It was not, however, as conciliatory as the British suggested.

Soviet Union

The Soviet response to initial U.S. conciliation was more favorable than predicted by deterrence theory, because Western policy allowed Khrushchev to claim a much needed foreign policy success. Soviet statements in early 1959 appear to support the conclusion that early conciliation led the Soviets to view the West as weak. On 29 January, "a speaker from the main political administration of the Soviet armed forces" noted as evidence of Western weakness Dulles's "retreat" from his previous position on free elections as the requirement for reunification and his discussion of the idea of a German confederation.[64] Yet Soviet perceptions of the initial U.S. bargaining moves were both more favorable and more complex than this account suggests.

Khrushchev and Mikoyan perceived the early U.S. readiness to negotiate and showed no indication of exploiting it. On 24 January, in response to a reporter's question on whether a German confederation was now acceptable to the United States, Mikoyan responded, "I cannot

62. Schick, *Berlin Crisis*, 54, 58–60.

63. On the dynamics of coalition maintenance, see Jack Snyder, "East-West Bargaining Over Germany: The Search for Synergy in a Two-Level Game," in Evans, Jacobson, and Putnam, *Double-Edged Diplomacy*; and Marc Trachtenberg, *History and Strategy* (Princeton: Princeton University Press, 1991), chap. 5.

64. *CIA Current Intelligence Weekly Summary*, 29 January 1959, *DDRS*, 1988, CIA, no. 1812, 2–3.

assert that, but one cannot disregard a statement made by Mr. Dulles at a press conference. Unlike previous statements, he said that free elections were not the only way to German unification. This is a very interesting statement." One week later, the deputy premier noted the lack of references in U.S. statements to the cold war concepts of "containment," "rollback," and "liberation": "One might conclude from these statements by the President and the Secretary of State that they are now inclined to recognize the principle of peaceful coexistence of countries with different social and political systems. If this is the case, it is of great positive significance for peace."[65]

Khrushchev, too, correctly perceived Western flexibility and attributed it to an ongoing struggle between realist and imperialist forces in the West. He praised those "persons in the West who look at the international situation soberly," but he noted that there were also forces in the United States "who favor continuing the 'cold war.' "[66] Khrushchev labeled both Eisenhower and Dulles as realists. In his concluding speech to the Twenty-first Congress in early February, the Soviet leader noted that Eisenhower, despite his background, did not "belong to those military people who in deciding conflicting questions rely only on guns and want to decide all problems by the force of arms." Similarly, in May 1959, Khrushchev noted that the secretary of state had "in the last months of his life showed a more sober understanding of the evolved international situation."[67]

References to realist forces in the West increased with the lifting of the ultimatum on 2 March 1959. In a 19 March news conference, Khrushchev again praised Eisenhower's realism and willingness to negotiate. While noting "threatening" and "contradictory" language in Eisenhower's statements, Khrushchev focused on the accommodative: "[T]here is still a sound grain of reason in this statement of President Eisenhower's. And we welcome it. This grain can sprout and force its way into the open once the hedging has been removed."[68]

Throughout March, Khrushchev continued to tone down the ultimatum, stating to Western leaders in a speech at Leipzig, "If you, gentlemen, are willing to speak with us reasonably we can postpone this date from May 27 to, say June 27. Let us postpone it to July, if you like." At a 19 March press conference, he stated, "It must be said that there has been no

65. For the first quote see Embree, *German Question*, 104; for the second see *Pravda*, 1 February 1959, 8–9, translated in *Current Digest of the Soviet Press* (hereinafter *CDSP*), 11, no. 9 (1 April 1959): 58.

66. Speech at Tula, 17 February 1959, in Embree, *German Question*, 106.

67. Quoted in Richter, *Khrushchev's Double Bind*, 60.

68. Embree, *German Question*, 143.

'extension of the time limit,' because, as I have already explained, no time limits in the nature of an ultimatum have been set for the implementation of our proposals on the Berlin question in general." More surprisingly, Khrushchev noted that the West had legal rights for its occupation of Berlin ensuing from the defeat of Germany in World War II.[69]

Even Mikhail Suslov, Party theoretician and generally a hard-line opponent of Khrushchev, toned down his confrontational stance. His statements portrayed the United States less starkly and stereotypically, he advocated negotiations to reduce international tensions, and he made arms control a high priority. In March, Suslov stated publicly that the Soviet Union and the United States "must seek and find a common language."[70]

As relations with the West eased, Khrushchev turned his attention and his ire on the West German leader Adenauer. On 19 March, the chairman warned that Adenauer should "know that the first country to perish in modern war would be West Germany, because it is being converted into a springboard for nuclear weapons to be used against other countries."[71] James G. Richter argues that as the United States demonstrated its willingness to negotiate, Khrushchev began to view Adenauer as the major obstacle to a summit meeting.[72]

In contrast to the predictions of deterrence theory, Khrushchev did not perceive initial U.S. accommodation as indicating weakness. He did not raise his demands or increase his threats in an attempt to exploit U.S. weakness. Instead, early U.S. conciliation was taken as evidence of a reasonable opponent, and Khrushchev offered further concessions. This was true largely because Khrushchev needed a foreign policy success, and early U.S. restraint allowed him to claim one.

United States

The mixed Soviet strategy gave both hard- and soft-liners ample ammunition to support their view. The allies continued to be split in their preferences. In late March, the French foreign minister summed up the differences: "[Britain is willing] to exhibit flexibility at [the] outset [of] negotiations with [the] Soviets while [the] French feel [the] West must be tough."[73]

---

69. For the quotes see Embree, *German Question*, 131 and 152, respectively. See also 146.

70. *Pravda*, 20 March 1959, quoted in Richter, *Khrushchev's Double Bind*, 121.

71. Embree, *German Question*, 147.

72. "Action and Reaction," 426–28.

73. Herter, telegram to the American embassy in Paris, 31 March 1959, *DDRS*, 1987, DOS, no. 709, 1.

A terminal illness forced Dulles to take a leave beginning in 1959. Nevertheless, Eisenhower's relatively benign view of Soviet intentions and his advocacy of restraint continued to be disputed by members of his administration, especially by Dean Acheson, former secretary of state and an advisor to President Eisenhower. Acheson believed the Soviets had initiated the crisis to test U.S. resolve and he advocated a determined response. In a March 1959 article, he proposed a significant increase in U.S. military power, a buildup of NATO strength on the continent, and a crash intercontinental ballistic missile program. Throughout the spring, Acheson repeatedly called for a general national mobilization in response to the Soviet challenge.[74]

These views were at odds with those of the president. The president opposed what he termed appeasement, but he concluded that, "[o]n the other hand, this does not mean that we will not negotiate. We will negotiate whenever we can and are making many efforts in that direction."[75] Eisenhower claims to have recognized Khrushchev's concessions in lifting the ultimatum in early 1959. According to the president's memoirs, during February and March "Premier Khrushchev executed a remarkable diplomatic retreat. So skillful and subtle was each step backward that its significance was hardly noticed and for this reason the retreat, although absolute, caused scarcely any loss in Khrushchev's public standing. The Western governments deliberately encouraged this evolution."[76] The president also publicly disagreed with Acheson's advocacy of a tougher stance, asking at a press conference on 4 March, "Now, did you ever stop to think what a general mobilization would mean in a time of tension?" Even if Congress allocated additional funds for conventional forces, Eisenhower said he would refuse to spend them.[77] Finally, and most significantly, in his television address to the nation on 16 March, he concluded that "our final choice is negotiation. . . . We will do everything within our power to bring about serious negotiations and to make these negotiations meaningful."[78] Although Eisenhower later claimed he did not intend to be conciliatory, at the time he favored a moderate stance toward the Soviets and he did not perceive the situation

74. Schick, *Berlin Crisis*, 49–50, 147–48.

75. Memo of conference with the president, 6 March 1959, *DDRS*, 1981, White House (hereinafter WH), no. 597B, 6. On Eisenhower's opposition to appeasement, also see *Department of State Bulletin*, 27 April 1959, 582, quoted in Smith, *Defense of Berlin*, 201–2.

76. Eisenhower, *White House Years*, 2:342.

77. See Ambrose, *Eisenhower*, 2:518 for the quote; and *New York Times*, 12 March 1959, 12, cited in Schick, *Berlin Crisis*, 51.

78. *Documents on Germany*, 418.

in Berlin to be a crisis. Instead, Eisenhower believed that the United States could expect several decades of ongoing conflict.[79]

Over the opposition of Acheson and the French, Eisenhower continued to implement a largely accommodative bargaining strategy. Following the invitation to the Soviets to participate in a foreign ministers' meeting preparatory to a U.S.-Soviet summit, the president made further concessions on disarmament. On 13 April, he wrote to Khrushchev saying that the United States no longer would insist on a comprehensive test ban but would be willing to proceed in stages. A week later, Eisenhower proposed a ban on atmospheric testing of nuclear weapons.[80]

While executive decision making was unitary, it was not immune to social pressures. As was his habit, Eisenhower consulted with congressional leaders over Berlin and the related issue of his plan to cut thirty thousand army troops, which was consistent with his policy of "massive retaliation."[81] Congressional leaders strongly criticized the president's policy, but in the end, Eisenhower refused to increase military forces. According to John Eisenhower's memorandum of his 6 March conference with the president, the chair of the Senate Armed Services Committee, Richard Russell, "assured the President that consultation with Congress would not be necessary, but that the initiative is his and Congress will support it."[82] To Russell's remark, "If you have to act, Mr. President, you go ahead and act, don't come to us," Eisenhower reportedly responded, "Oh, I certainly intend to."[83]

While Eisenhower dismissed congressional opposition to his policy, the president and his advisors still worried about public opinion. For example, the report of an interdepartmental group charged with the task of planning U.S. policy on Berlin noted that "the Western Powers" needed to "give sufficient evidence of their flexibility and desire for a peaceful solution so as to hold the support of public opinion. . . ."[84] While such statements refute the assertion that societal pressures were absent because of congressional acquiescence, they are easily explained by the existence of an effective national legislature that limited executive

79. Bryce Harlow, staff notes, 26 March 1959, *DDRS*, 1978, WH, no. 118C, 1. For Eisenhower's claim that he misspoke himself in his address, see Eisenhower, *White House Years*, 2:350.

80. Ambrose, *Eisenhower*, 2:521–23; Eisenhower, *White House Years*, 2:479.

81. The following discussion draws on Richard K. Betts, *Nuclear Blackmail and Nuclear Balance* (Washington, DC: Brookings Institution, 1987), 85–88.

82. Quoted in Betts, *Nuclear Blackmail*, 87.

83. Steve Neal, *The Eisenhowers* (Lawrence: University of Kansas Press, 1978), 402. Also see Eisenhower, *White House Years*, 2:349.

84. CIA memorandum, "U.S. Negotiating Position on Berlin—1959–62," 13 July 1959, *DDRS*, 1989, CIA, no. 3024, 3.

autonomy on domestic issues. Still, while concerns over public opinion existed, they did not drive U.S. strategy; no private groups mobilized to influence policy; and Congress remained largely on the sideline while Eisenhower charted the U.S. response.

The Geneva Conference: May to August 1959

The first of two phases of the foreign ministers' conference opened in Geneva on 11 May. Christian Herter, who had succeeded Dulles as secretary of state, presented the Western proposals three days later. They included four stages: (1) the reunification of Berlin through free elections held under UN supervision; (2) the creation, by the four powers, of a "Mixed German Committee" to draft an electoral law; (3) elections within two and a half years for an all-German Assembly that would draft a constitution and form an all-German government; and (4) the conclusion by that government of a final peace settlement.[85] Gromyko introduced a draft treaty on 15 May, and Khrushchev rejected the Western plan on the following day. Much of the negotiations then moved into more informal channels, and on 26 May the United States agreed to enter into discussions on the fate of Berlin only, rather than on the broader German issue, thereby "untying the Western package." The Soviets rejected this concession and suggested the establishment of an international commission to oversee the free-city status of West Berlin.[86]

On 10 June, Foreign Minister Gromyko introduced slightly different Soviet proposals regarding Berlin and a peace treaty with Germany. The offer extended the Western occupation of Berlin for one year dependent on (1) the reduction of Western forces in Berlin to "token contingents," (2) the termination of "hostile propaganda" in West Berlin aimed at East Germany, (3) the liquidation of organizations in West Berlin "engaged in espionage and subversive activities," and (4) an agreement not to place nuclear weapons or bases in the city of Berlin. The Soviets proposed that during the year, the two Germanies should establish an all-German committee to discuss reunification and a peace treaty. The new Soviet proposal effectively restored the previous deadline threat. Herter immediately rejected it as unacceptable because of its substance and the time limit, stating, "The latest Soviet proposal appears to have set us back not just to May 11, when this Conference opened, but to November, 1958, when the Soviet Union fabricated the Berlin crisis and insisted that its terms be accepted by May 27, 1959. We

---

85. *Documents on Germany*, 427–31.
86. Schick, *Berlin Crisis*, 80, 84.

are unwilling to negotiate under this threat."[87] Additionally, Eisenhower sent a letter to Khrushchev on 15 June saying that the new Soviet position made a summit impossible without some prior progress at the foreign ministers' meeting.[88]

The Western foreign ministers submitted their second and final set of proposals to the conference on 16 June. They made no mention of Allied occupation rights, asking only that there should continue to be free, unrestricted access to Berlin. The United States, Britain, and France also agreed to limit total Western forces in Berlin to their present levels and not to arm them with nuclear weapons. Despite these concessions, the Soviets rejected the plan and the conference recessed on 20 June. Before adjourning, the Soviets restated their demands to include (1) reducing the number of Western troops in West Berlin, (2) stopping subversive activity in West Berlin, and (3) no storage of nuclear weapons in West Berlin.[89]

As the following discussion illustrates, Eisenhower invited Khrushchev to the United States for summit talks, despite Soviet intransigence at Geneva. Throughout this stage of the conflict, Khrushchev maintained his positive image of Eisenhower and did not seek to exploit Western concessions. Soviet strategy nevertheless continued to include coercive elements, probably in response to domestic criticism.

United States

In the early stages of the Geneva conference, U.S. officials began to detect a hardening of the Soviet position and to recognize an incompatibility between the two sides' demands. On 3 June, Eisenhower reiterated his "position that a summit meeting based on nothing more than wishful thinking would be a disaster."[90] Nevertheless, he made concessions. Undersecretary of state Robert Murphy met the Soviet deputy premier, Frol Kozlov, on 12 June as the Soviet was departing the United States. Murphy passed along a letter from Eisenhower to Khrushchev and, on behalf of the president, invited the Soviet leader to the United States for a summit meeting at Camp David. Eisenhower later claimed Murphy misunderstood his instructions and was only supposed to invite Khrushchev contingent on progress in the second round of talks at Ge-

---

87. *Documents on Germany*, 464. For the Soviet proposal, see *Documents on Germany*, 459–61.
88. Eisenhower, *White House Years*, 2:400.
89. Embree, *German Question*, 175.
90. Eisenhower, *White House Years*, 2:399.

neva. However, on 17 June the president publicly stated that lack of progress on the Berlin issue did not preclude a summit meeting.[91]

The latter sentiment is much closer to the president's statements at the time than to his subsequent recollections. Eisenhower warned Herter not to employ provocative language in his 22 June speech, and on 1 July the president indicated a readiness to back down further: "The President said what we have to do is to 'thaw out' the Russian defenses. About Berlin we say we will never have our rights there diminished. The Russians say this is an illogical position. We admit it is illogical, but we will not abandon our rights and responsibilities—*unless there is a way made for us to do so.*"[92]

The Geneva conference reconvened on 13 July 1959, but there was little progress before it closed again on 5 August. The West's final proposals, submitted on 28 July, contained significant concessions. Whereas the 16 June plan had stated that the proposed arrangements would remain in force until reunification (unless altered by four-power agreement), the final proposal called for an interim agreement of five years, thereby severing the connection between the settlement of the Berlin issue and the question of German reunification.[93] Eisenhower continued to implement a primarily accommodative policy, despite his fear of the consequences of appearing to give in to aggression.

Soviet Union

The Soviets continued to engage in a mixed bargaining strategy, but Khrushchev's perceptions of Eisenhower were of a reasonable adversary, not one who could be easily exploited. The menacing tone of Khrushchev's interview with Averill Harriman, which took place on 23 June, is infamous: "Your generals talk of maintaining your position in Berlin with force. That is bluff. If you send in tanks, they will burn and

---

91. Schick, *Berlin Crisis*, 89. For Eisenhower's claim that he was misunderstood, see Eisenhower, *White House Years*, 2:405–8.

92. Ann Whitman diary, 1 July 1959, *DDRS*, 1983, WH, no. 633, emphasis added. Eisenhower's warning is cited in n.a., telephone diary, 22 June 1959, *DDRS*, 1987, WH, no. 1057.

93. Speier, *Divided Berlin*, 51–54. Smith claims that these proposals "came dangerously close to effectively ending the free existence of West Berlin" and that, if the Soviets had accepted them, "West Berlin's hope of survival would have been destroyed"; see *Defense of Berlin*, 207, 208. The extent of the concessions are confirmed by a 1961 Department of State document: "When made, the July 28 Western proposal was considered to be the outermost limit to which the Western Powers might go." Western proposals at Geneva conference of foreign ministers (May–August 1959), 30 May 1961, *DDRS*, 1984, DOS, no. 912.

make no mistake about it. If you want war, you can have it, and remember it will be your war. Our rockets will fly automatically."[94] In retrospect, Khrushchev also claimed that he had thought Eisenhower was weak, because of the U.S. president's behavior at Geneva: "He was a good man but he wasn't very tough. There was something soft about his character."[95]

Despite Khrushchev's sometimes menacing rhetoric and his later recollection of his impressions of Eisenhower, he held a generally favorable image of the West. When the Geneva conference recessed, Khrushchev took the opportunity to reassert that the Soviets had not issued an ultimatum. On 19 June, he noted,

> As far as the deadline we have named is concerned, it should be said that if this does not suit the Western powers, the question can be discussed. We have never said that the deadline indicated in our proposals was the main or fundamental question. If it is unacceptable and a business-like approach is taken, it would be possible to agree on a different date. The only ones who can call our proposals an "ultimatum" are those who do not want to reach agreement.[96]

The Soviet image of the West became increasingly favorable after Eisenhower's invitation to Khrushchev to visit the United States. The general secretary argued that the president's 25 August press conference "shows that Mr. Eisenhower is prepared to work for the elimination of tension in relations among states. We see in this a good basis for the forthcoming fruitful exchange of visits with the President."[97] Khrushchev again praised Eisenhower on 31 August, noting that by making recent "cold war" statements, the president was doing "nothing more than giving former prejudices their due."[98] In short, Khrushchev's image of Eisenhower and the West remained generally favorable throughout the Geneva conference, and he did not seek to exploit any perceived weakness.

---

94. Averill Harriman, "My Alarming Interview with Khrushchev," *Life*, 8 July 1959, quoted in Speier, *Divided Berlin*, 30.

95. Nikita Khrushchev, *Khrushchev Remembers*, trans. and ed. Strobe Talbott (Boston: Little, Brown, 1970), 397.

96. *Pravda*, 20 June 1959, 2–3, and *Izvestia*, 20 June 1959, 1–3, translated in *CDSP* 11, no. 26 (29 July 1959): 14.

97. *Pravda*, 31 August 1959, 1, translated in *CDSP* 11, no. 35 (30 September 1959): 7.

98. *CDSP* 11, no. 35, (30 September 1959): 5, quoted in Jönsson, *Soviet Bargaining Behavior*, 158.

Camp David and Its Spirit: September 1959 to May 1960

Khrushchev's 4 August acceptance of Eisenhower's invitation to visit the United States marked the beginning of a period of relaxed tensions in U.S.-Soviet relations that was to last until the May 1960 U-2 incident. The Soviet leader arrived in the United States on 15 September and traveled around the country, returning to Washington ten days later. From there, Khrushchev and Eisenhower adjourned to Camp David for three days of talks, in which the Soviet leader agreed to remove any remaining suggestion of a deadline on the Berlin issue, and in which both leaders agreed to open negotiations.

The September meeting eased the Berlin situation. Eisenhower spoke increasingly of the "abnormal" situation in Berlin, suggesting that he did not believe entirely in the legitimacy of the status quo. Khrushchev's response was not to increase his demands, as deterrence theory suggests, but to make further accommodative offers. Khrushchev's image of the United States, and of President Eisenhower in particular, was favorable in the aftermath of Camp David, and this sense of goodwill continued throughout 1959.[99] This state of affairs began to change by early 1960, when domestic opposition led Khrushchev to adopt an increasingly coercive stance. The U.S. response—stinging speeches by Herter and Undersecretary of State Douglas Dillon—only further exacerbated Khrushchev's domestic opposition.

United States
At Camp David, Eisenhower took care to impress on Khrushchev that the United States would not participate in a summit "under any kind of duress." At the same time, however, he also noted Soviet attempts at conciliation. In his description of his meeting with Khrushchev, Eisenhower noted, "Mr. Khrushchev had explained that the two governments had understood differently the Soviet initiative in Berlin last November. The U.S. had mistakenly thought that Khrushchev was delivering an ultimatum." Eisenhower sounded this theme again in his 28 September press conference on the Camp David meetings, when he stated, "There is no fixed . . . time on this. No one is under duress, no one is under any kind of threat and as a matter of fact, [Khrushchev] stated emphatically that never had he any intention to give anything that was to be interpreted as duress or compulsion."[100]

99. This argument is based on Richter, *Khrushchev's Double Bind*, 119–22.

100. See, respectively, president's report of his private session with Khrushchev, 27 September 1959, *DDRS*, 1984, DOS, no. 444; and *New York Times*, 29 September 1959, 16, quoted in Schick, *Berlin Crisis*, 101.

At that same news conference, Eisenhower repeatedly referred to the "abnormal" situation in Berlin, a theme to which he would return. In response to a question on whether future negotiations would be "guided by the same standards and principles that we had before, namely, that any solution must guarantee Allied rights there, and protect the freedom of West Berliners," the president hedged:

> I can't guarantee anything of this kind for the simple reason, I don't know what kind of solution may finally prove acceptable, as I say, but you must start off with this. This situation is abnormal. It was brought about by a truce, a military truce, after the end of the war, an armistice, and it put strangely a few—or a number of free people in a very awkward position.[101]

Eisenhower remarked again in October that Berlin was an abnormal situation that had been created by the mistakes of Roosevelt and Churchill. It was now time to pay for those mistakes.[102]

On 16 October, Eisenhower reflected on the need for concessions and on his limited ability to compromise. His staff secretary described the remarks this way: "He added that if we are simply going to stand on the status quo there is no reason for a summit meeting. He commented that he thought that he could strike a bargain on his own with Khrushchev if he were to try to do so, but he knew our allies would not accept his acting unilaterally."[103] In short, while Eisenhower may have been a relatively unitary actor at home, he still had to contend with allied demands.

The good feelings generated by Camp David continued throughout 1959. When the U.S. moratorium on nuclear testing expired at the end of December, the administration announced that it would not resume testing without prior notice. Such conciliatory actions were based on Eisenhower's benign view of Soviet motivations and goals and on a sense of the illegitimacy of the Berlin situation.

---

101. *New York Times*, 29 September 1959, quoted in Richardson, *Germany and the Atlantic Alliance*, 272. Eisenhower's press secretary later clarified the president's comments: "The President of course did not mean that the freedom of the people of West Berlin is going to be abandoned or that Allied rights are going to be surrendered by any unilateral action." See *New York Times*, 29 September 1959, quoted in Smith, *Defense of Berlin*, 213.

102. Gray, memorandum of conversation with the president, 1 October 1959, *DDRS*, 1986, WH, no. 1107; Goodpaster, memorandum of conversation with the president, 22 October 1959, *DDRS*, 1982, WH, no. 2219. Also see Beschloss, *Mayday*, 230.

103. *DDRS*, 1982, WH, no. 2219, 3.

Soviet Union

One student of Soviet foreign policy concludes that on his return from Camp David, Khrushchev "confided to his colleagues in Moscow that he had taken the measure of President Eisenhower, and that it would not be difficult to extract concessions from him at a Summit meeting before the next Presidential election in November 1960."[104] The Soviet leader's statements at the time do not support such a conclusion. Rather, they suggest that Khrushchev's visit to the West proved that the U.S. leader took his demands seriously.

In the months following the meetings at Camp David, Khrushchev repeatedly praised Eisenhower's realism and expressed optimism over the state of U.S.-Soviet relations. He called the president "a great person" who "understand[s] great politics," "an intelligent man who realizes the seriousness of the international situation." Khrushchev further believed that "a certain relaxation in international tension has now been achieved."[105] For Khrushchev, this thaw was due to the fact that realists like Eisenhower were gaining control of foreign policy in the West. He told the Supreme Soviet on 15 January 1960 that "tension in international relations is beginning to show an overall tendency to wane, and the partisans of the 'cold war' are suffering defeat."[106]

Khrushchev did not attempt to exploit Western moderation. Rather, he argued that because realists had gained the upper hand in the West, the Soviets now could be more accommodating. On 24 September, even before retiring to Camp David, Khrushchev told a Pittsburgh audience, "if one approaches this business so firmly and takes uncompromising positions—I stick to my position and the US President sticks to his—then we will not have a business-like discussion." In his December speech in Budapest, Khrushchev said, "We are not speeding up a solution of the problem of West Berlin, we are setting no deadlines, present no ultimatums. . . ."[107]

Khrushchev's return to accommodative policies meant a return to his policies of early 1958—reductions in troop levels and an emphasis on strategic nuclear weapons as a means of reducing defense spending. In

---

104. Mackintosh, *Strategy and Tactics*, 219.

105. For the quotes see, respectively, Richter, "Action and Reaction," 438; *Pravda* and *Izvestia*, 8 October 1959, 1–2, translated in *CDSP* 11, no. 40 (4 November 1959): 4; and Embree, *German Question*, 200. Khrushchev's views were echoed in *Izvestia* and *Pravda*. See *CDSP* 11, no. 37 (14 October 1959): 4; and *CDSP* 11, no. 38 (21 October 1959): 3.

106. *Pravda* and *Izvestia*, 15 January 1960, 1–5, translated in *CDSP* 12, no. 2 (10 February 1960): 6.

107. For the quotes see, respectively, Richter, *Khrushchev's Double Bind*, 119; and Embree, *German Question*, 204.

early January 1960, the Soviet leader announced the reduction of the Soviet military by one-third, or 1.2 million troops. In response to Eisenhower's 29 December statement that the United States was now free from its moratorium on nuclear testing, Khrushchev pledged that the Soviet Union would "continue to abide by its pledge not to resume experimental nuclear explosions in the Soviet Union unless the Western powers begin testing atomic and hydrogen weapons."[108]

U.S. restraint gave Khrushchev some foreign policy successes to flaunt and helped offset domestic opposition, thereby allowing him to return to his earlier, more accommodative policies. Following Khrushchev's trip, Kozlov admitted in October that Soviet policy was "now showing fruit."[109] But Khrushchev was still not free of domestic opposition.

Suslov and Kozlov, in particular, opposed Khrushchev's conciliatory policy. Suslov argued in January 1960 for a hardening of Soviet foreign policy, complaining that "Western champions of the cold war . . . have not laid down their weapons. It would be dangerous to give in to complacency and over-confidence on this issue."[110] Michel Tatu argues that Kozlov also opposed Khrushchev's accommodative stance and that both Kozlov and Suslov omitted the customary references to the Soviet leader's "historic visit" to the United States in several speeches in early 1960.[111] Kozlov went so far as to publicly attack Khrushchev's benign image of Eisenhower: "The person who today does not recognize the actual existence of two sovereign states on the territory of Germany resembles an ostrich and by his short-sighted policy is not, of course, contributing to a relaxation of international tension."[112] As early as his 1 December speech, Khrushchev attempted to appease his domestic opposition: "We do not beg for peace, however. The desire for peace is by no means a sign of weakness on our part. The strength of the Soviet Union and the entire socialist camp is growing every day."[113]

Soviet policy began to harden in February 1960. It did so largely because control over tactics was passed to East Germany. On 3 February, the Ulbricht regime announced that the allied military missions in

108. *Pravda* and *Izvestia*, 15 January 1960, 1–5, translated in *CDSP* 12, no. 2 (10 February 1960): 7.

109. *Pravda*, 10 October 1959, quoted in Richter, "Action and Reaction," 449. Also see Tatu, *Power in the Kremlin*, esp. 33.

110. *Pravda*, 2 February 1960, quoted in Tatu, *Power in the Kremlin*, 79.

111. *Power in the Kremlin*, 79–80.

112. Quoted in Jönsson, *Soviet Bargaining Behavior*, 159.

113. Embree, *German Question*, 208. Also see Richter, *Khrushchev's Double Bind*, esp. 120.

Potsdam would now be accredited to East Germany, not the Soviet Union. The GDR issued new passes, recognition of which would have meant acceptance of East German authority. On the next day, the Warsaw Pact issued a declaration, repeated later in the week by Khrushchev, asserting that if there were no agreement with the West on an all-German treaty, the Eastern bloc nations would conclude a separate peace treaty.[114] The end result was a more coercive Soviet policy. In contrast to the predictions of deterrence theory, however, Khrushchev's underlying beliefs never changed. Rather, his accommodative policy provoked domestic opposition, leading gradually to a more coercive line.

United States

U.S. restraint continued even after Khrushchev's early comments suggested he was bowing to his domestic critics' call for a tougher policy. Ambassador Thompson went out of his way to attribute benign intentions to the Soviets. He sent two telegrams from Moscow on 1 January 1960 relating a New Years' Eve conversation at a Kremlin reception in which Khrushchev again threatened to conclude a separate peace treaty. Nevertheless, Thompson argued that Khrushchev was simply trying to "impress upon us [the] seriousness of [the] situation as he sees it," and the Ambassador attributed much of the Soviet leader's statements to the fact that "an alcoholic daze had settled over [the] entire company."[115] Eisenhower also continued his arms control efforts. At a press conference on 11 February, the president announced that he was willing to accept a ban on all nuclear tests in the atmosphere, ocean, and outer space, as well as all underground tests that could be monitored.[116]

The Western allies toughened their stance. On 11 January, in an address to the Berlin Chamber of Deputies, the West German chancellor said that if the West met the Soviet demands on Berlin, "new demands would follow today, tomorrow or the day after tomorrow. And the first capitulation will then be followed by other capitulations."[117] On 25 February, the French responded to the GDR's actions of 3 February and restricted the Soviet military mission in Baden-Baden to its headquarters, pending the issuance of new passes to the French mission in

---

114. See Smith, *Defense of Berlin*, 216–18; Richardson, *Germany and the Atlantic Alliance*, 273; and Hannes Adomeit, *Soviet Risk-Taking and Crisis Behavior: A Theoretical and Empirical Analysis* (London: Allen & Unwin, 1982), 188.

115. Thompson telegrams, 1 January 1960, *DDRS*, 1985, DOS, no. 337; *DDRS*, 1985, DOS, no. 336.

116. Ambrose, *Eisenhower*, 2:564; Eisenhower, *White House Years*, 2:480.

117. Quoted in Speier, *Divided Berlin*, 80.

Potsdam. The United States and Britain joined the French two weeks later. The United States also announced on 29 February, despite British objections, that high-altitude flights into Berlin would resume shortly.[118]

The shift in policy was clear by April, when Douglas Dillon delivered a blistering speech in New York. The problem of Berlin, according to Dillon,

> . . . represents a critical test of the integrity and dependability of the free world's collective security systems, because no nation could preserve its faith in collective security if we permitted the courageous people of West Berlin to be sold into slavery. . . . We have repeatedly informed Mr. Khrushchev that we will not negotiate under duress. Yet in his recent statements about his intentions to sign a separate peace treaty with the so-called German Democratic Republic unless an East-West agreement is reached on Berlin, he is skating on very thin ice. We are approaching the summit with every intention of seeking a mutually acceptable solution of the German problem, including Berlin. . . . But Mr. Khrushchev and his associates will be profoundly disillusioned if they assume that we will bow to threats or that we will accept their distorted picture of the German problem as a factual premise upon which to negotiate.[119]

Even if Eisenhower did not intend to dramatically alter U.S. policy, American rhetoric toughened noticeably in early 1960, tainting Washington's initially conciliatory stance. Much of this shift appears to have been driven by allied pressures.

Soviet Union

Khrushchev may have wanted to continue his conciliatory stance toward the West, but he faced opposition within the Kremlin. Ideological struggle with the Chinese, who rejected the concept of "peaceful coexistence," only increased the domestic pressure to get tough. Both the Chinese leadership and the Chinese press were more suspicious than Khrushchev of the intentions of the United States and of Eisenhower in particular. In May, Mao declined an official invitation to visit Moscow.[120]

---

118. The flights were canceled on 9 March, but the United States reserved the right to resume them in the future. See Smith, *Defense of Berlin*, 218–19.

119. *Documents on Germany*, 494, 496.

120. On the Sino-Soviet conflict, see Linden, *Khrushchev and the Soviet Leadership*, 101–4; Mackintosh, *Strategy and Tactics*, chap. 19; Slusser, *Berlin Crisis of 1961*, 68–74; and Tatu, *Power in the Kremlin*, 45–49, 103.

On 19 March, the Soviets said they would agree to a moratorium on tests in the atmosphere, oceans, and outer space if the United States would agree to a moratorium on low kiloton underground tests. This was a significant Soviet concession on the disarmament issue, since the ban would require the presence of U.S. inspection teams within the Soviet Union. Khrushchev was careful, however, to separate the Berlin and disarmament issues, claiming that a Western concession on the latter would not lead to a Soviet concession on the former.[121]

On the whole, Soviet statements and actions in early 1960 were mostly coercive. On 2 April, at a press conference in Paris, Khrushchev, who was accompanied by Suslov and Malinovsky, reiterated his threat to sign a separate peace treaty with the GDR. While still declaring himself "optimistic about the prospects of a summit meeting," the Soviet leader stated that the conclusion of a separate treaty would mean that "all countries now having garrisons in West Berlin on the basis of the surrender, the defeat of nazi Germany, would lose all rights connected with the occupation of the city. We have declared this more than once and we also reaffirm it today."[122]

Khrushchev repeated his threat in Baku on 25 April; if the upcoming summit did not produce an agreement, the Soviets would unilaterally end the occupation of West Berlin. The speech is also noteworthy for its interpretation of Dillon's speech and its intimation of the Soviet leader's plan to wreck the forthcoming summit.

The closer we come to May 16, the day the heads of government meet, the more one-sided the line some of the Western powers' statesmen are taking on the problems facing the conference participants. . . . One need not look far for examples. Let us take the recent speech by U.S. Under Secretary of State Dillon, which is presented as a statement of policy on the eve of the summit. This speech actually reeks of the cold war spirit. It suggests a collection of hackneyed fabrications concerning the Soviet Union and the socialist countries. . . . Dillon is trying to inject a spirit of animosity and suspicion on the very eve of the summit conference, when it is so essential that an atmosphere of trust be created and maintained between states. . . .[123]

---

121. See Khrushchev's press conferences of 29 February and 2 April 1960, in Embree, *German Question*, 230, 240.

122. Embree, *German Question*, 238, 239.

123. *Pravda* and *Izvestia*, 26 April 1960, 3–5, translated in *CDSP* 12, no. 17 (25 May 1960): 6–7.

Even Mikoyan was appalled by the U.S. speeches, stating that although he knew Dillon was a "sensible man," the American had said "incredible things" in his New York speech.[124]

In sum, Khrushchev had begun to toughen his policy in response to domestic political pressures. When the United States reacted with harsher rhetoric in the months leading up to the May 1960 summit, the Soviet leader's policies were further discredited. Facing opposition from domestic critics and other socialist countries, he shifted to a much tougher bargaining position even before the Paris meeting.

Confrontation: May 1960 to February 1961

The events of May 1960 only exacerbated the already deteriorating relations between the United States and the Soviet Union. The downing of a U.S. spy plane over Soviet territory fueled Khrushchev's domestic opposition and led to an increasingly tough Soviet strategy. The most visible sign of this hardening was the debacle at the May summit in Paris.

On the first of May, the Soviets shot down a U-2 reconnaissance plane but made no public statement about it. Only five days later, after NASA had issued a statement saying that a weather plane was missing, did the Soviets announce that the plane had been downed on May Day. President Eisenhower then authorized the State Department to issue a statement denying that the pilot had any authorization to fly over Soviet territory. Two days later, the United States issued another statement, reversing its earlier position by saying that although the president did not specifically authorize this flight, he did have general responsibility for all intelligence flights. Eisenhower confirmed at an 11 May press conference that he had taken personal responsibility for the incident. The Paris summit opened and closed on 16 May with Khrushchev demanding an apology and Eisenhower refusing.

The aftermath of the scuttled conference was one of confrontation and neglect on the part of the Soviets, who vowed to wait for a new U.S. administration. This shift was not due to change in Khrushchev's perceptions of the United States, although he did feel personally betrayed. Instead, it was a response to increasing domestic opposition to Khrushchev's failed policy of conciliation. Although Khrushchev had wrecked the May summit, Eisenhower correctly perceived the domestic pressures on Khrushchev and chose a conciliatory response.

---

124. *Pravda*, 24 April 1969, cited in Adomeit, *Soviet Risk-Taking*, 198–99.

Soviet Union

The decision to wreck the Paris summit was probably taken at the 4 May Central Committee meeting. Over the next few months, major changes occurred in the Soviet leadership, suggesting the extent of opposition to Khrushchev's policies. These changes further curtailed Khrushchev's power or, at least, his willingness to accommodate the West. Several of his supporters—including Aristov, Ignatov, Furtseva, and Pospelov— left the Secretariat for lesser posts, and Kirichenko's fall from grace as second secretary and heir to Khrushchev was formally completed. Kozlov and Suslov, both of whom opposed Khrushchev's recent shift to accommodation, were the real victors in the leadership shake-up. Most important, Kozlov became Party secretary and Brezhnev, a Khrushchev ally and Kozlov's major rival at the time, was transferred to the largely ceremonious position of head of state.[125] After these changes, the possibility that the Paris summit might have reached some agreement was remote. In early May, Khrushchev noted,

> the other side's latest moves, their speeches and some of their actions . . . unfortunately leave only scant hope that these Governments . . . are seeking concrete solutions. . . . There are signs that these [Paris] negotiations may not fulfill the hopes of the peoples of the world. . . . And if the conference is not held, so what? We've lived many years as we are, we can do without one for another hundred years![126]

Decisional conflict theory suggests that his domestic weakness should have motivated the Soviet leader to overestimate U.S. hostility. Alternatively, it suggests that his domestic vulnerability should have motivated Khrushchev to ignore U.S. threats and overestimate his ability to influence the West. Khrushchev's policy response was consistent with the second proposition, but not with the first. His perceptions of U.S. intentions and his advocacy of accommodative tactics did not change. The U-2 incident placed the moderate Khrushchev in a precarious position at home. In his 11 May news conference, he summarized his predicament: "The American militarists who sent the plane on a spying mission to this country have put me, as one responsible for the

---

125. See Linden, *Khrushchev and the Soviet Leadership*, 94–104; and Tatu, *Power in the Kremlin*, 61, 84–88. Tatu (70–71) contends that the changes were not unfavorable to the Soviet leader.

126. These statements, made on 4 May and 11 May, respectively, are quoted in Tatu, *Power in the Kremlin*, 56–57, 60.

arrangements of the United States President's arrival in the U.S.S.R., in a very difficult position."[127]

Khrushchev did not dramatically alter his perceptions of the U.S. president, however, choosing instead to attribute the incident to the ascendance of imperialist forces within the United States: "[A]pparently a complicated underground struggle between different political forces was going on in the United States of America!"; "[t]he following conclusion forces itself upon one: The aggressive imperialist circles in the United States of America have been undertaking recently the most active measures to disrupt the heads-of-government conference, or at any rate to prevent the reaching of an agreement for which the whole world is waiting."[128] Khrushchev went out of his way to absolve Eisenhower of responsibility, commenting on 7 May, "Even today I believe that the persons I met in the United States want peace and friendly relations with the USSR. . . . I am quite willing to believe that the President did not know that a plane had been sent to the Soviet Union and had failed to return."[129] Khrushchev continued to advocate reductions in defense spending, arguing that "[t]his [U-2] affair should not induce us to revise our plans so as to increase our appropriations for armaments and the armed forces, or to stop the cutback in military strength."[130]

When the U.S. president took personal responsibility for the incident, Khrushchev's position at home became more difficult still. In response, on 16 May Khrushchev disrupted the conference by demanding that Eisenhower denounce the flight, refrain from future flights, and punish those responsible. He canceled Eisenhower's planned visit to the Soviet Union and vowed to wait for the next U.S. government, or the one after that, to negotiate an agreement. On his way back from Paris, Khrushchev delivered a speech in East Berlin that repeated his willingness to wait six to eight months for a summit. He remained cautious, though, and concluded, "We are realists, and we shall never follow an adventurous policy."[131]

Khrushchev was responding to heightened domestic pressures. In a revealing rejoinder to Eisenhower's 16 May remark that he couldn't

---

127. Embree, *German Question*, 252.

128. For the quotes see, respectively, Embree, *German Question*, 259; and *Pravda* and *Izvestia*, 6 May 1960, 1–5, translated in *CDSP* 12, no. 18 (1 June 1960): 18. The first remark was made in a 20 May speech in Berlin.

129. *Pravda*, 8 May 1960, quoted in Tatu, *Power in the Kremlin*, 59.

130. Speech to the Supreme Soviet, 7 May 1960, quoted in Tatu, *Power in the Kremlin*, 76.

131. *Pravda*, 21 May 1960, 1–2, translated in *CDSP* 12, no. 21 (22 June 1960): 4. For the text of Khrushchev's statement in Paris, see Embree, *German Question*, 253–58.

speak for his successor, the Soviet leader responded, "Nor am I eternal."[132] That Khrushchev's views remained largely unchanged is apparent in a 28 May speech in which he again absolved Eisenhower and attributed the actions to imperialists within the United States: "Even now it is my opinion that the President did not know of these flights but that it was awkward for him, as the President, to confess that he did not know, that he was not aware of what was going on in the country."[133] On 29 May Khrushchev remarked, "I still believe that the President himself wants peace, but evidently the President's good intentions are one thing and his government's foreign policy quite another. The road to hell is paved with good intentions, and that is where Eisenhower will land."[134]

Domestic opposition became severe and open by May 1960. The tougher U.S. stance, and particularly the U-2 incident, had undermined the Soviet leader's claim that Eisenhower had peaceful intentions and that he and other realists had gained control in the West.[135] Tatu notes that June and July saw the triumph of collective leadership in the Soviet Union, the rise of Suslov and Kozlov as "strongmen," and the concomitant decline of Khrushchev's power.[136] The opposition to the chairman's policies became very vocal when a 23 May article in *Pravda* launched a thinly veiled assault on the chairman's perception of U.S. leaders: "Yes, we wanted to believe Eisenhower, we wanted to believe him for the sake of peace on earth. . . . We very much wanted to believe. But unlike certain simple-minded persons [*prostaki*] we were not exactly moved to enthusiasm by the President's foggy, evasive statements."[137]

Khrushchev's stand was assailed by his colleagues in the aftermath of the U-2 debacle. In late May Malinovsky noted, "The latest lesson of Camp David is too clear to allow us to forget history. No, we do not believe the imperialists. We are convinced that they are only waiting for a favourable opportunity to attack the Soviet Union and the other socialist countries, and the only thing that stops them is the risk of the total destruction of imperialism."[138] Suslov maligned "revisionists and other opportunists" who claimed that peaceful coexistence implied "a repudiation of the class struggle and a reconciliation of the

132. Quoted in Beschloss, *Mayday*, 288.
133. *Pravda* and *Izvestia*, 29 May 1960, 1–4, translated in *CDSP* 12, no. 22 (22 June 1960): 4.
134. Quoted in Beschloss, *Mayday*, 306–7.
135. See Richter, *Khrushchev's Double Bind*, chap. 6.
136. Tatu, *Power in the Kremlin*, 106, 109–14.
137. The article by Vsevolod Kochetov is quoted in Tatu, *Power in the Kremlin*, 66.
138. *Pravda*, 31 May 1960, quoted in Tatu, *Power in the Kremlin*, 77–78.

socialist and bourgeois ideologies," while Kozlov was only slightly more restrained.[139]

After the failed summit, Soviet policy hardened simply by ignoring the United States. Khrushchev announced on 27 June that his government was withdrawing from disarmament talks that had started in March. In late June and July, the Soviets issued a number of protests of military preparations in West Berlin and the FRG. Khrushchev also issued new threats in July regarding the upcoming session of the *Bundestag*. He warned that if the opening meeting of the legislature were held in Berlin, as it had been every year since 1955, he might sign a separate peace treaty with the GDR.[140]

The predominant Soviet strategy throughout the rest of 1960 was to refuse to deal with the outgoing U.S. administration. In the meantime, the initiative passed to Ulbricht, who was allowed to harass the West by imposing a series of restrictions on travel between East and West Berlin. The reason for the shift, in sum, can be found in domestic opposition, which became increasingly vocal after the U-2 incident. Yet even that act of betrayal did not lead Khrushchev to question Eisenhower's intentions. Khrushchev's behavior was consistent with both the argument presented here and motivational psychology. The Soviet leader could have been motivated by his domestic troubles to ignore U.S. signals of resolve, but his behavior is more simply explained as a rational response to those troubles: domestic opposition compelled him to alter course, but it did not change his underlying beliefs.

United States

After the Paris conference, Eisenhower noted the increasingly menacing tone of Soviet policy but did not attribute it to a shift in Khrushchev's preferences. The president agreed with his European allies that "Khrushchev was acting more like a student reciting a difficult lesson than as a person who was speaking his own convictions and beliefs. . . . For whatever reason, it was obvious the Chairman had concluded that his policy of conciliation had not paid off. It may have been costing him support in the Soviet hierarchy."[141]

Although Eisenhower recognized the strong domestic pressures facing Khrushchev, there was little he could do about Berlin while the Soviets waited for a new American administration. There were several protests of Soviet activity during August, and on 12 September the

139. Richter, *Khrushchev's Double Bind*, 133–35, quote at 135.
140. The meeting was postponed. See Speier, *Divided Berlin*, 115–17.
141. Eisenhower, *White House Years*, 2:556, 560.

United States sent a diplomatic note protesting the imposition of travel restrictions. As in the Eastern bloc, the initiative on the Western side also passed to the Germans. In late September, the West German regime informed Ulbricht that the interzonal trade agreement, negotiated in August and set to take effect in 1961, would be voided.[142] East German pressure on Berlin eased slightly in response but resumed on 7 November, when the GDR announced its right to inspect certain manufactured goods it classified as "war matériel" being shipped from West Berlin. The FRG then suggested restoring the trade agreement in return for the lifting of travel restrictions. Ulbricht initially resisted, threatening to blockade West German traffic to East Berlin, but he soon relented. The trade agreement was restored in late December.

The Kennedy Administration Takes Office: February to June 1961

The new U.S. administration's military policy, which emphasized increased conventional and nuclear abilities to deal with limited conflicts, soon overwhelmed any hint of accommodation on Berlin. The result was a mixed strategy, although one that started out much tougher than Eisenhower's policy. Kennedy's overall concern was to demonstrate his resolve before engaging in negotiations. Khrushchev had been hopeful that the new president would be more cooperative than his predecessor. He was sorely disappointed. Once Kennedy increased defense spending, Khrushchev renewed his coercive stance on Berlin.

United States

The new U.S. administration, to an even greater extent than the old one, was split in its perceptions of Soviet intentions regarding Berlin. The existence of this cleavage, represented by the disagreement between Thompson and Acheson, highlights the determining role of Kennedy's beliefs. Thompson and his supporters believed that the Allied position in Berlin was premised on three main interests: free access, the right to station troops, and the continued political and economic viability of democratic institutions in West Berlin. They thought Soviet actions, which were motivated largely by defensive goals, did not affect these basic interests and should not be opposed; resistance would only cause the Soviets to

---

142. The annual trade flow between the zones amounted to five hundred thousand dollars. See Adomeit, *Soviet Risk-Taking*, 201; Schick, *Berlin Crisis*, 131–32; and Speier, *Divided Berlin*, 123.

become desperate.[143] The ambassador warned of the deleterious effects of a policy of firmness and advised that negotiations would allow the chairman to "save face."[144] Other notable soft-liners in the Kennedy administration included Adlai Stevenson, Averill Harriman, Charles Bohlen, Walt Rostow, Theodore Sorenson, Arthur Schlesinger, Dean Rusk, and Robert McNamara.

The most outspoken hard-liner in Kennedy policy-making circles was Dean Acheson, who believed that the Soviets had offensive motivations and that the status quo had to be maintained at all costs. He—like Paul Nitze, General Maxwell Taylor, Lyndon Johnson, Henry Kissinger, and McGeorge Bundy—advocated a tougher response; negotiations would lead the Soviets to increase their demands. Acheson recommended that the president extend military terms of service and declare a state of national emergency, allowing Kennedy to call up the reserves.[145]

While the split between hard-liners and soft-liners remained much the same as under Eisenhower, U.S. policy shifted in 1961 because of the intermediate and tactical beliefs of the new president, who in his inaugural address reminded the nation that the Soviet Union had not "yielded its ambitions for world domination."[146] During the spring of 1961, Kennedy began a review of the government's Berlin policy. He sent Khrushchev a personal note suggesting that the two meet, and a summit was set for June in Vienna. Yet the president did not feel bound by his predecessor's concessions. As Averill Harriman, Kennedy's roving ambassador, unambiguously declared on 8 March, "All discussions on Berlin must begin from the start."[147] Any remaining trace of conciliation was obscured by the administration's military policy. In March, the administration asked Congress for additional funds to increase the capability and readiness of its conventional forces. On 25 May, on the eve of his summit meeting with Khrushchev, Kennedy requested a $3.4 billion increase in defense expenditures.

Kennedy was much more determined than Eisenhower had been to

---

143. Thompson, telegram to the secretary of state, 4 February 1961, *DDRS*, 1977, DOS, no. 74B, 1. Also see George and Smoke, *Deterrence in American Foreign Policy*, 434; and Smith, *Defense of Berlin*, 293–95.

144. Thompson, telegram to the secretary of state, 16 March 1961, *DDRS*, 1977, DOS, no. 46D, 3.

145. See George and Smoke, *Deterrence in American Foreign Policy*, 433–34; Smith, *Defense of Berlin*, 295–97; Theodore G. Sorenson, *Kennedy* (New York: Harper & Row, 1965), 399, 583–84; McGeorge Bundy, memorandum to the president, 4 April 1961, *DDRS*, 1986, WH, no. 2093; and Acheson, memorandum to the president, 3 April 1961, *DDRS*, 1985, DOS, no. 2547, 1.

146. Quoted in Beschloss, *Crisis Years*, 62–63.

147. *New York Times*, 11 March 1961, quoted in Smith, *Defense of Berlin*, 230.

maintain the status quo in Berlin and Germany. At the Vienna confer-ence in June 1961, he told Khrushchev that the goal of U.S. policy was the maintenance of the existing situation. In an insightful passage, Schle-singer notes that the U.S. and Soviet leaders saw the status quo very differently, and that both believed they were acting to preserve it. For Khrushchev, who saw the spread of the communist revolution as the status quo, Kennedy's stance on Berlin was an attempt to alter the situation. For Kennedy, Khrushchev's actions against Berlin were just as real a threat to what *he* saw as the status quo.[148] According to one student of the conflict, Kennedy ignored the advice of doves within his administration and "persisted in his fantasy that Khrushchev might be willing to live with the problem."[149]

Soviet Union
The general secretary expressed some early, if faint, optimism about the new administration in Washington, although that optimism was overshad-owed by his coercive actions. On 17 February 1961, he issued an *aide-memoire* to West Germany threatening that if Adenauer did not sign a peace treaty with the Soviet Union, Khrushchev would sign one with the GDR and unilaterally end the occupation of West Berlin. Even in the *aide-memoire*, however, Khrushchev expressed hope: "The defeat of the Republican Party in the United States election has everywhere been right-fully taken as the American people's condemnation of the perilous and futile policy which the Eisenhower government practised in its latter years."[150] In March, as the Nuclear Test Ban Conference resumed in Geneva, the Soviets demanded the replacement of the verification admin-istrator by a committee of three, each possessing veto power.[151] Yet in May Khrushchev accepted Kennedy's invitation to meet, and as late as 6 May he noted, "The coming into office of a new government in the United States fostered hopes in some people that the new United States leader-ship would show a more reasonable attitude to the resolution of interna-tional problems."[152] The State Department considered his 12 May speech his most moderate since before the U-2 incident.[153]

---

148. Arthur M. Schlesinger, *A Thousand Days: John F. Kennedy in the White House* (Boston: Houghton Mifflin, 1965), 307.

149. Beschloss, *Crisis Years*, 176.

150. Embree, *German Question*, 295.

151. At the June summit, Khrushchev said he would drop the demand for a *troika* only if the issue of the test ban were tied to a general and complete disarmament. See Schlesinger, *Thousand Days*, 309–10.

152. *Pravda* and *Izvestia*, 7 May 1961, 3–4, translated in *CDSP* 13, no. 18 (31 May 1961): 7.

153. Beschloss, *Crisis Years*, 162.

Any attempts at conciliation ended abruptly. While meeting with President Kennedy in Geneva on 4 June, Khrushchev decisively renewed the Berlin crisis. He presented the president with an *aide-memoire* that demanded a German peace treaty and free-city status for Berlin. The note unambiguously reintroduced an ultimatum with a six-month deadline. Khrushchev removed any possible remaining ambiguity in a television address to the Soviet people on 15 June: "We ask everyone to understand us correctly: The conclusion of a peace treaty with Germany cannot be postponed any longer. A peaceful settlement in Europe must be attained this year."[154]

Soviet rhetoric became increasingly menacing. For his 21 June speech marking the twentieth anniversary of Hitler's attack on the Soviet Union, Khrushchev wore the uniform of a lieutenant general, his rank from World War II. Accompanied by the defense minister, the commander in chief of Soviet ground forces, the commander of troops of the Moscow military district, and a former commander of a partisan unit in the Ukraine, the Soviet leader delivered a blistering speech warning both that the Soviet defense budget might increase and that the Soviets would resume nuclear testing as soon as the United States did.[155] In early July, while attending the Bolshoi with the British ambassador, Khrushchev reportedly asked, "Why should 200 million people die because of 2 million Berliners?"[156] In a speech to graduating students at Soviet military academies on 8 July, the chairman responded to the U.S. defense increases and announced an increase of 3.144 billion rubles ($3.4 billion) in Soviet defense spending and the suspension of reductions in the armed forces that had begun in January 1960. The military posturing continued the next day, Soviet Air Force Day, the first one in five years to include the display of new aircraft. Soviet Navy Day followed on 30 July and included the first public display of missile-launching submarines.[157]

East Germany took action in the summer of 1961 to prevent more citizens from fleeing to the West through Berlin. In late June, presumably with Soviet consent, Communist Party officials visited the homes of

---

154. *Documents on Germany*, 531. For the text of the 4 June *aide-memoire*, see Embree, *German Question*, 301–5.

155. Adomeit, *Soviet Risk-Taking*, 239–40; Schick, *Berlin Crisis*, 158; Slusser, *Berlin Crisis of 1961*, 10–11. Mackintosh (*Strategy and Tactics*, 263) suggests that the decision to resume testing was probably taken in March or April following the Kennedy administration's announcement of its new defense policy.

156. Quoted in Speier, *Divided Berlin*, 174.

157. See Adomeit, *Soviet Risk-Taking*, 240; and Raymond Garthoff, *Soviet Military Policy: An Historical Analysis* (London: Faber and Faber, 1966), 116.

East Berlin residents who worked in the Western sector of the city, advising them to find alternate employment in East Berlin. A month later, strict restrictions were placed on traffic to East Berlin from the surrounding areas, and the government announced that anyone caught trying to flee would be imprisoned for three years.[158]

Some scholars argue that Khrushchev underestimated Kennedy because of the new president's youth and eagerness to meet with the chairman.[159] In his memoirs, Khrushchev remembers Kennedy as "a better statesman than Eisenhower" and as a man who understood that "[s]tarting a war over Berlin would be stupid."[160] Yet the timing of Khrushchev's actions suggest that the Soviet leader was responding to Kennedy's conventional buildup. As Richter argues, Khrushchev's influence within the Presidium had been declining since the U-2 affair in May 1960, and therefore he was more vulnerable to international events.[161] Only a position of strength could convince the United States to recognize Soviet equality and could, in the process, vindicate Khrushchev's earlier policies.

The Berlin Wall: June to October 1961

Kennedy's experience at Vienna only reinforced his previous belief in the need for a revised military doctrine. Despite the existence of dissent within his administration, the president chose a middle line—a tough military policy accompanied by an ongoing call for negotiations on Berlin. U.S. intransigence caused Khrushchev to further increase his own coercive rhetoric and actions, but he still did not stray from his preference for an accommodative policy. The Soviet leader seized on the idea of building the Berlin Wall as a kind of compromise—a means of removing his earlier threat while saving face.

United States
Kennedy's encounter with Khrushchev at Vienna surprised and disappointed the president; the experience only reinforced his thinking on both Berlin and U.S. military doctrine. Sorenson describes the president at this time as being "calmly convinced that an unflinching stand for West Berlin's freedom would, in the long run, lessen the prospects for a nuclear war, while yielding on West Berlin would only weaken the future

---

158. Adomeit, *Soviet Risk-Taking*, 206.
159. For example, see Mackintosh, *Strategy and Tactics*, 264.
160. *Khrushchev Remembers*, 458.
161. *Khrushchev's Double Bind*, chap. 6.

credibility of our defenses."[162] At the same time that this experience
made him conscious of the potential dangers of inaction and of a military
strategy that relied heavily on the threat of nuclear weapons, Kennedy
remained sensitive to the dangers of overreacting and provoking the
Soviets into escalating the crisis.[163] Kennedy's views continued to represent a middle line between hard-liners like Acheson and soft-liners like
Thompson and Bohlen. Such disagreement illustrates the degree to
which Kennedy shaped U.S. policy.

Acheson remained the most bellicose of the president's advisors.
Three weeks after the Vienna conference, he prepared a paper for Kennedy in which he argued that Berlin was merely a pretext for Khrushchev to exercise his overarching objective—testing U.S. resolve. Any
perceived willingness to negotiate, according to Acheson, would be
taken as evidence of weakness by the Soviets and be exploited by them.
Acheson maintained that the appropriate policy was a massive nuclear
and conventional buildup. In a National Security Council meeting on 13
July, Acheson argued for the declaration of a state of national emergency, both as a means of deterring the Soviets and as a way of impress-
ing on the U.S. public the severity of the situation.[164] Acheson opposed
any negotiations with the Soviets, warning that they would view concessions as signs of weakness to be exploited.[165]

Thompson remained one of the most conciliatory members of the
administration. The ambassador continued to argue that Soviet aims
were limited and that they sought to improve their position in Eastern
Europe, not to threaten the United States. He prescribed a quiet military buildup accompanied by serious efforts at negotiation. Thompson's
views were shared by Sorenson and Schlesinger. Sorenson argued that
the declaration of a state of emergency would not only "engage Khrushchev's prestige to a point where he felt he could not back down from a
showdown, and provoke further or faster action on his part in stepping
up the arms race"; it would also encourage domestic opposition.[166] On 8
July, Kennedy asked Acheson to prepare a "political program" on Ber-

---

162. Sorenson, *Kennedy*, 586.
163. Sorenson, *Kennedy*, 590.
164. Despite his vocal opposition to the idea of negotiations, in his paper to the
president Acheson advocated offering the Soviet leader some face-saving concessions *after*
a military buildup. Schlesinger, *Thousand Days*, 320–21, 330.
165. See Bundy, memorandum to the president, 19 July 1961, *DDRS*, 1986, WH,
no. 2257; and Sorenson, *Kennedy*, 590.
166. Quoted in Schlesinger, *Thousand Days*, 327. For Schlesinger's misgivings on
U.S. planning, see Schlesinger, memorandum for Bundy, 18 July 1961, *DDRS*, 1978, WH,
no. 301A.

lin and he instructed McNamara to prepare an analysis of nonnuclear military options in the region.[167]

Despite this internal debate, U.S. policy in the summer of 1961 reflected Kennedy's preferences. As Khrushchev's and Eisenhower's had, Kennedy's strategy continued to be somewhat erratic and hybrid. The United States responded immediately to the Soviet *aide-memoire* on disarmament that had been presented to Kennedy in Vienna, but it was not until 17 July that the U.S. government made any reply to the Berlin *aide-memoire*. The delay occurred because it took six weeks to get a draft statement from the State Department and because the United States was speaking for its allies as well.[168] To a far greater extent than the other type I state in this study, czarist Russia, the United States was susceptible to bureaucratic and organizational delays. Nevertheless, the U.S. reply reflected Kennedy's policy preferences: the note strongly reasserted Western rights in Berlin and at the same time expressed a willingness to negotiate.

Following this official response, the Kennedy administration's bargaining strategy, which was largely formulated at the 19 July National Security Council meeting, was decidedly mixed. While the president requested additional funds for defense spending, authority to call up reserve forces, and a tripling of the draft (although he refrained from declaring a state of national emergency), he also pressed for negotiations with the Soviets.[169] The results of the National Security Council meeting were made public in Kennedy's 25 July television address, in which he outlined the military buildup, including an additional $3.25 billion for defense spending, and linked U.S. prestige to the Berlin issue. At the same time, however, Kennedy took care to reassure the Soviets: "We will at all times be ready to talk, if talk will help. But we must also be ready to resist with force, if force is used upon us. Either alone would fail. Together, they can further the cause of freedom and peace. . . ."[170]

Other confusing statements emanated from different parts of the U.S. government. On 30 July, Senator William Fulbright stated on national television that the East Germans would be justified in closing the border between East and West Berlin. In fact, he added, he did not understand why such a move had not yet been taken.[171] There is also evidence that the administration was considering behind-the-scenes

167. Schlesinger, *Thousand Days*, 326.

168. Schlesinger, *Thousand Days*, 322.

169. Sorenson, *Kennedy*, 591. Also see Kennedy's discussion of his strategy in his letter to Macmillan, 20 July 1961, *DDRS*, 1985, DOS, no. 946.

170. *Documents on Germany*, 556–57.

171. *New York Times*, 3 August 1961, cited in Smith, *Defense of Berlin*, 259–60.

negotiations with the Soviets on the issue of access to Berlin.[172] In short, the U.S. Berlin strategy was a combination of coercive and accommodative tactics in the summer of 1961. While there was significant domestic debate, policy reflected the president's preference for a largely coercive military strategy accompanied by a call for negotiations on Berlin.

Soviet Union

Khrushchev's blustering increased. John McCloy, Kennedy's special assistant for arms control and disarmament, visited the Soviet leader at his holiday retreat on the day after Kennedy's address. Khrushchev interpreted the president's speech as an act of hostility, an ultimatum, and threatened that if war occurred, Kennedy would be the last American president. He also told McCloy that he was sure that the Allies would not stand together over the Berlin issue.[173]

Khrushchev's anger was manifest in a 7 August televised speech that paralleled Kennedy's talk of 25 July. The speech suggested that the Soviet government might go beyond halting a reduction of forces to increasing troop strength by calling up reserves. While he called for an international conference and an easing of tension, Khrushchev placed great emphasis on Soviet prestige: "The experience of history teaches that when an aggressor sees that he is not being opposed he grows more brazen. Contrariwise when he meets opposition, he calms down. It is this historic experience that must guide us in our actions."[174] Concessions, Khrushchev argued, might invite Western aggression.

The next few days witnessed more menacing rhetoric and actions. On the ninth, Khrushchev publicly declared that the Soviet Union now possessed a 100-megaton nuclear weapon, and on the following day Marshal Ivan Konev was recalled from retirement to be commander of the Soviet forces in Germany. On 11 August the chairman gave a sometimes blistering speech in which he railed, "[I]f a war is unleashed, hundreds of millions might perish. What sensible person could find such arguments of the imperialists convincing? Under the pretext of defending freedom, which no one is threatening, the imperialists want to test our firmness; they want to do away with our socialist achievements. Your arms are too short, Messrs. Imperialists!"[175]

172. Record of meeting between Kennedy, Rusk, and Mr. Owen, 3 August 1961, *DDRS*, 1986, WH, no. 2258.

173. Schlesinger, *Thousand Days*, 329; Slusser, *Berlin Crisis of 1961*, 90–91.

174. Quoted in Smith, *Defense of Berlin*, v. Also see *Pravda*, 8 August 1961, 1–2, translated in *CDSP* 13, no. 32 (6 September 1961): 7.

175. *Pravda*, 12 August 1961, 1, translated in *CDSP* 13, no. 32 (6 September 1961): 11–12.

Even at this late date, though, Khrushchev clung to his prior beliefs and did not overestimate U.S. hostility. In the 11 August speech, his predilection for a peaceful settlement of the conflict was evident in his recognition of the need "to follow a sensible policy on our essentially small planet. . . . If the other side wished to cooperate, if it did not make the question of West Berlin the subject of a test of strength, agreement would certainly be possible."[176]

A barbed-wire barrier was erected on East German territory on 13 August. The GDR imposed a travel ban between East and West Berlin, and within several days the barbed wire had begun to be replaced by a concrete wall extending around the Western sector. Not long after, the Soviets announced the temporary suspension of releases of active duty troops to the reserves and the resumption of nuclear testing. They began intercontinental ballistic missile tests in the Pacific on 13 September. The building of the Berlin Wall, while at first glance a coercive tactic, also represented the acceptance by the Soviets of the status quo of a permanently divided Germany.

United States
It was not clear at the time that the crisis over Berlin that had been boiling for three years was over and that the physical division of the city provided a compromise settlement. The initial U.S. interpretation of the Soviet decision to allow East Germany to close the border between East and West Berlin was fairly benign. Sorenson notes that none of Kennedy's advisors at the time felt that the Soviet move interfered with the West's basic objectives in the crisis—maintaining a U.S. presence in and U.S. access to West Berlin and preserving the freedom of the residents of the Western sector to choose their own political and economic system.[177] The wall confirmed Kennedy's belief in the need for military preparedness, but he also stressed that he wanted "to take a stronger lead on Berlin negotiations."[178]

The first Western response occurred on 15 August, when the Western commandants in Berlin protested the building of the wall to the Soviet commandant. There was, however, no formal demand that the border be reopened. The U.S. response became more coercive the next day, when it was announced that soldiers due for release in the eight months after 1 October 1961 would be kept on active duty for an additional four months

176. *Pravda*, 12 August 1961, 1, translated in *CDSP* 13, no. 32 (6 September 1961): 11–12.
177. *Kennedy*, 593–94.
178. Quoted in Schlesinger, *Thousand Days*, 334.

and that twenty-three thousand reserve troops would be activated. An additional seventy-six thousand were called to active duty on 25 August. On 17 August, Kennedy sent fifteen hundred troops down the autobahn to exercise Western access rights, and the United States sent its first formal protest of the wall in a note to the Soviets. On the same day, the president agreed to send Vice President Johnson and General Lucius Clay to Berlin as a show of solidarity. Finally, on 19 August, a U.S. Army battle group was sent to Berlin.[179]

At the same time, the president went forward with negotiations. Talks between Rusk and Gromyko began in late September. These negotiations, when coupled with the U.S. military response, meant that U.S. policy after the building of the Berlin Wall was little different than before—largely coercive, but still mixed. The wall signaled an implicit compromise; the United States accepted the barrier in return for the Soviet withdrawal of the threat to sign a separate treaty.

Soviet Union
Many students of the Berlin crisis argue that the U.S. response, or lack of one, to the closing of the border confirmed Khrushchev in his belief that the West was divided and weak and encouraged him to erect a permanent barrier between East and West Berlin.[180] Although menacing Soviet tactics continued, Khrushchev was no more encouraged by U.S. restraint in August 1961 than he had been throughout the crisis. He tried to defuse the conflict by seeking negotiations with the United States. On 5 September, in an interview with a reporter, Khrushchev relayed a confidential message to Kennedy inviting the president to the Soviet Union.[181] On the twenty-ninth, the chairman sent Kennedy a twenty-six-page personal letter that marked the beginning of two years of private correspondence between the two leaders. He moved concurrently to lift the ultimatum that had been presented to the United States in the 4 June *aide-memoire*.

In retrospect, the Berlin crisis can be said to have formally ended on 17 October 1961. In a speech to the Twenty-second Party Congress, Khrushchev announced that since the West was being understanding and accommodative, the Soviet Union was removing the deadline.[182] The question had been settled, in effect, by the building of the wall through Berlin

---

179. Garthoff, *Soviet Military Policy*, 116–17.
180. For example, see George and Smoke, *Deterrence in American Foreign Policy*, 416; and Mackintosh, *Strategy and Tactics*, 266.
181. See Slusser, *Berlin Crisis of 1961*, 190–210.
182. Slusser, *Berlin Crisis of 1961*, 310.

and the U.S. acceptance of a divided city. With hindsight, it can also be argued that the outcome of the crisis was a tacit, mutual compromise.[183]

Conclusions

The underlying conflict lingered as a source of tension between the Soviet Union and the United States, leading at one point to a military confrontation to force entry of Americans into East Berlin. Further, the ambiguous outcome of the Berlin crisis often has been cited as a contributing cause of the October 1962 Cuban missile crisis.[184] The Soviet Union eventually signed its separate peace treaty with East Germany in 1964, but it was not until 1971 that an agreement was reached guaranteeing access to, and the independence of, West Berlin.

Contrary to the standard wisdom, initial U.S. restraint was not a misguided policy to pursue in the Berlin crisis. To the extent that a strategy can be discerned in Moscow's erratic posturing, it too was not misguided. While it is possible to think of strategies that might have been more effective—particularly clearer, less mixed ones—it is also possible to think of strategies that would have exacerbated the conflict, possibly leading to war. Specifically, that sequence of bargaining tactics suggested by deterrence theorists—coercion, then accommodation—would likely have failed because of the domestic nature of the adversaries.

Soviet and American strategies interacted with the domestic political situation of the opposing state to produce the largely cooperative outcome. Khrushchev's early conciliation supported Eisenhower's benign image of Soviet intentions. Even when Khrushchev shifted to more coercive tactics, Eisenhower correctly interpreted them as evidence of the Soviet leader's domestic opposition. In Moscow, initial U.S. restraint strengthened Khrushchev's hand against his domestic foes, but subsequent coercive tactics eroded the credibility of the Soviet leader's moderate prescriptions.

As in the two previous cases, the different ways in which the opponent's strategy produced a policy response are explained by the fundamentally different political institutions. The diffuse, if autonomous, nature of the Soviet state meant that Khrushchev was sensitive to political pressures from the elite, which led him to alter his policy preferences but not his

---

183. Snyder and Diesing, *Conflict among Nations*, 275, 497.

184. See Horelick and Rush, *Strategic Power and Soviet Foreign Policy*, 126–40; Schick, *Berlin Crisis*, chap. 7; Tatu, *Power in the Kremlin*, 230–34, 239–43; and Adam B. Ulam, *Expansion and Coexistence: The History of Soviet Foreign Policy 1917–67* (New York: Praeger, 1968), 669–70.

underlying beliefs. The unitary, autonomous American state structure meant that the president's beliefs determined the efficacy of Soviet strategy. Even though there was significant dissent, first Eisenhower's and then Kennedy's preferences largely determined U.S. policy. In short, a coalition politics approach best explains the bargaining process in Moscow, while a cognitive explanation illuminates the bargaining dynamics in Washington.

As in the Crimea and Fashoda crises, international structural and motivated bias approaches fail to explain the case adequately. A systemic explanation cannot account for the sources of actors' preferences, which are determined by domestic institutions and strategic beliefs. Nevertheless, the Berlin crisis demonstrates the importance of one systemic-level variable not previously considered—alliance dynamics. Both U.S. and Soviet leaders were constrained by relations with other states, especially their respective German clients. In this study, I focus on the domestic determinants of U.S. and Soviet foreign policy. As this chapter makes clear, however, domestic debates are often influenced by external factors such as alliance relations.

A motivated bias approach receives only limited and ambiguous support in the Berlin case. Khrushchev did not overestimate the hostility of his adversary; throughout the crisis, he maintained his benign view of the United States and its leaders despite increasing domestic opposition and U.S. threats. This outcome is compatible with a motivated bias explanation, but it is also more simply explained as a rational response to domestic political imperatives: Khrushchev shifted to coercive tactics because domestic pressures prevented conciliation, not because of motivated misperception. He persisted in his belief in Eisenhower's goodwill because there was insufficient reason to alter it. Domestic pressures required him to change his policy, not his preferences.

6

Conclusion

Other states' bargaining behavior interacts with, and is sometimes consciously used in, domestic debates. How that behavior influences those debates and shapes national policy depends on two factors: state structure and strategic beliefs. This chapter summarizes this study's findings and examines the strength of the competing theories outlined in chapter 2. It concludes by revisiting the practical and theoretical implications of my argument.

Existing Explanations

Not all the approaches examined in chapter 2 provide rival explanations for the outcome of international crises. Rather, the explanation developed in this book suggests that they are often complementary. Theories about the international structure set the parameters for state action, but they must be supplemented by a theory of the state that explains actors' preferences and intentions. Both cognitive and bureaucratic approaches provide such a theory, but their explanatory power depends on the domestic structure of the opposing state.

The International Structure

Systemic explanations of crisis bargaining are the most common. While the structure of the conflict determined the boundaries of bargaining in the three cases examined, it rarely provided determinate predictions about the relationship between bargaining behavior and conflict outcome. It was always necessary to examine the domestic origins of states' preferences in order to explain the evolution of the conflict.

Britain and Russia possessed roughly equivalent capabilities on the eve of the Crimean War crisis; both states possessed significant interests in the Ottoman Empire; and Russia was challenging the status quo in the region. Yet for several reasons, these structural factors are insufficient to explain the outcome. First, Russian interests in the Crimean conflict would not have been incompatible with British interests if Russia had not used coercive diplomacy and inflamed public opinion in Britain. Second, it is impossible to determine British interests independent of the outcome of the crisis without examining the domestic sources of those interests—the role of public opinion and the strategic beliefs of different members of the cabinet.

The Fashoda crisis provides the strongest evidence for a systemic approach. The local balance of power overwhelmingly favored London, and the European balance probably favored the British. Because the British were trying to protect the status quo in Egypt, many students of the crisis also argue that the balance of interests heavily favored London. Since the definition and legitimacy of the status quo in East Africa was so hotly disputed, however, it is impossible to establish *a priori* the supremacy of British interests, and the overall structure of the conflict, without examining the state of British and French public opinion, the strategic beliefs of national leaders, and the domestic institutions of the two states. Had Salisbury controlled British policy, for instance, the evidence suggests he would have accepted a compromise with the French. Even this strongest case for an international structural argument illustrates the need to supplement such an approach with a theory of the state.

As the Berlin crisis demonstrates, however, international factors also influence crisis bargaining in a way not considered in chapter 2. The dynamics of coalition maintenance constrained both U.S. and Soviet leaders. Indeed, alliance dynamics were not absent in the two earlier crises. It was France, not Britain, that provoked the 1852–54 Crimea crisis with Russia, and French policy in the 1898 Fashoda crisis depended in some part on the willingness of its Russian ally to come to France's defense. Future research on crisis bargaining should examine the ways in which these coalition dynamics interact with domestic debates. As Jeffrey W. Knopf notes in his study of the intermediate-range nuclear forces talks, "the presence of alliance partners creates different contexts within which two-level interactions can occur."[1]

Domestic Vulnerability and Motivated Bias

Work on motivated bias is an exception to the general neglect of domestic factors in the deterrence and cooperation literatures. While it highlights the importance of domestic political weakness, however, motiva-

---

1. "Beyond Two-Level Games: Domestic-International Interaction in the Intermediate-Range Nuclear Forces Negotiations," *International Organization* 47, no. 4 (autumn 1993): 600.

tional psychology proved the least useful explanation of the outcome of the cases examined, for two reasons.

First, there is little clear evidence that domestic weakness motivated national leaders to misperceive their opponent's behavior. In the Crimean War crisis, Lord Clarendon clearly perceived Russian offers of compromise and consciously decided to reject them for domestic political reasons. By the time Nicholas I offered concessions, the foreign secretary reasoned that public opinion in London was too enraged to allow compromise. Likewise, despite the precarious nature of Khrushchev's position during the Berlin crisis, it is not clear that he ever reverted to the defensive avoidance predicted by motivational psychology. Instead, even after U.S. actions and rhetoric hardened, the Soviet leader viewed Eisenhower as a "realist" who would cooperate. At most, Khrushchev failed to see that his policies were not succeeding in eliciting cooperation from the West.

Second, contrary to the predictions of a motivated bias approach, domestically vulnerable states sometimes responded cooperatively to initially coercive bargaining strategies. The Dreyfus Affair and the strikes in Paris divided public opinion and threatened the very existence of the French government in 1898. This domestic turmoil made it extremely difficult for Delcassé to concede to British threats, leading the French foreign minister to stall for time in the early stages of the crisis. However, it was also his domestic situation that ultimately made it possible for Delcassé to concede defeat. In short, the initially coercive British strategy succeeded against a domestically vulnerable opponent for domestic political reasons. Although domestic political factors were crucial to the evolution and outcome of all three crises examined, a hypothesis about domestic vulnerability fails to adequately capture the dynamics of conflict resolution.

Cognitive Psychology

The predictions of cognitive psychology—that policy makers interpret incoming information according to the content of their preexisting beliefs and that belief systems are resistant to change—received support in the three crises examined in this study. Palmerston's hard-line, defensive-deterrer view of the world as conflict-ridden and of Russia as inherently aggressive remained as unchanged throughout the Crimean crisis as did the unconditional compromiser Aberdeen's more harmonious view of the international system and benevolent image of his opponent. Khrushchev maintained his view of Eisenhower as a "realist" throughout the Berlin crisis. Finally, during the Fashoda crisis, the contingent compromiser,

Prime Minister Salisbury, remained as inclined to negotiate as Chamberlain remained hard-line in his policy toward the French.

In the Russian and American cases, a cognitive approach explains foreign policy. British restraint in the Crimean crisis reinforced Czar Nicholas I's faith in coercion as a tool of interstate influence and his belief that Britain would cooperate. A century later, Eisenhower perceived Soviet restraint in the early stage of the Berlin crisis and responded in kind. U.S. strategy only consciously shifted when the more hawkish Kennedy assumed office.

In the other states—Britain, France, and the Soviet Union—individual decision makers demonstrated the same tendency to interpret their opponent's behavior according to their preexisting beliefs, and cognitive psychology explains their policy preferences. In none of these cases, however, can a cognitive approach explain the outcome, since a single leader did not set foreign policy.

Bureaucratic Politics

In these states, policy changed even when individual perceptions did not. Bargaining strategies influenced the outcome of crises not through their impact on perceptions but through their influence on the domestic political process. In short, a bureaucratic approach explains the evolution and outcome of the conflict. Russia's coercive stance in the Crimean War crisis contributed to escalation by eroding support for the strategic arguments of the soft-line prime minister of Britain and his foreign minister and by reinforcing those of the hard-line opposition, especially the colonial secretary, Joseph Chamberlain.

In the Fashoda crisis as well, Delcassé's hard-line colonial policies were further undermined by British intransigence, leading the majority of the French public to advocate compromise. French strategy similarly interacted with the domestic political situation in London during the Fashoda conflict. The British prime minister favored compromise, but he was opposed by most members of his government and of Parliament and by a public inflamed by French aggressive policy in Africa. Salisbury recognized that his government could not survive any significant concessions.

Khrushchev's domestic political situation is also central to explaining Soviet behavior in the Berlin crisis. The Soviet leader's perceptions of the U.S. president as a reasonable man who could be trusted to deal responsibly with the Soviets changed little, even as his bargaining behavior shifted in the later phase of the crisis. This suggests that the shift from conciliation to coercion was in response to increasing domestic opposition to Khrushchev's policies.

The Russian and British cases suggest that bargaining behavior sometimes influences an adversary less through its impact on the perceptions of policy makers than through its influence on the domestic political incentives and resources of actors. Nevertheless, a bureaucratic politics perspective fails to explain the evolution and outcome of bargaining in states like czarist Russia where a single decision maker is relatively unconstrained by domestic factors.

State Structure and Crisis Bargaining

Neither cognitive nor bureaucratic approaches adequately explain the policy-making process, but both are important components of a larger theory of crisis bargaining. The organization of foreign policy authority—the structure of the foreign policy executive and its degree of autonomy from a national legislature—determines the channels through which bargaining occurs and, therefore, the usefulness of cognitive and bureaucratic approaches. A review of the findings of the case studies in this book follows, after which I briefly examine a number of areas in which the theory can be expanded.

The six states examined vary greatly in their policy-making processes, and this variation corresponds with variation in their domestic organization. In general, the more concentrated authority is within the executive element of government and the more autonomous the foreign policy executive is from the representative element, the less likely decision making is to enter the domestic political arena and the more likely policy is to be the result of a single leader's strategic beliefs. In contrast, the more diffuse authority is within the executive branch and the less freedom of action is enjoyed by the executive vis-à-vis a national legislature, the more likely crisis bargaining will display the telltale influences of bureaucratic politics: national leaders face domestic political imperatives, and the content of national policy reflects the process of coalition building among domestic elites. Table 2 presents the findings of the case studies in this book.

Although nineteenth-century Russia and the mid-twentieth-century United States differed in terms of their overall political structure, the organization of foreign policy authority was similar. In both type I states, the executive was a unitary actor. The czar also enjoyed total autonomy from any legislative constraint, while the U.S. president possessed considerable independence. Since he ruled within a democratic

TABLE 2. Findings

State and Time Period	Structure of Foreign Policy Executive	Degree of Executive Autonomy	Decision-Making Process
Russia 1852–54 (type I)	unitary	autonomous	cognitive
United States 1958–61 (type I)	unitary	autonomous	cognitive
Soviet Union 1958–61 (type III)	diffuse	autonomous	elite coalition building
France 1898 (type II)	unitary*	nonautonomous	societal constraints
Britain 1898 (type IV)	diffuse	nonautonomous	bureaucratic politics
Britain 1852–54 (type IV)	diffuse	nonautonomous	bureaucratic politics

* Note that the French foreign policy executive was a nearly, but not completely, unitary actor. See the discussion in chaps. 2 and 4.

state, the president was more susceptible to societal pressures. Nevertheless, because Congress had long yielded to the president on foreign policy, the holder of the highest office enjoyed remarkable freedom in an international crisis.

Different bureaucracies of the U.S. government could and did play a role in American foreign policy before the Vietnam War, but that role was largely limited to advising or influencing policy implementation. In his classic study of the Cuban missile crisis, Allison argues that governmental bargaining explains U.S. decision making.[2] In Allison's analysis of that case, however, the president sought the advice of the members of the Executive Committee of the National Security Council, or Excom, based on his personal relationship with them or on their technical expertise, not based on their institutional authority. Kennedy was persuaded by the force of these individuals' arguments, not by their power and authority. The president's authority was clear to the members of the Excom. Allison explains, for example, that the Excom rejected a nonmilitary path early in the crisis because of the president's opposition.[3]

2. *Essence of Decision*, chap. 6.
3. *Essence of Decision*, 202.

After an American U-2 plane was shot down over Cuba on 27 October 1962, Kennedy also vetoed the Excom's decision to bomb a Soviet surface-to-air missile site on the island.[4] In the decision-making arena, the president possessed the authority and the ability to act unilaterally.

The two British cases illustrate the opposite phenomenon. Cabinet rule within a parliamentary democracy presents a very different set of constraints: a diffuse executive highly restrained by legislative authority. The decision-making process in these type IV states least resembles the strong state of national security lore, and crisis decision making reflects both basic tenets of a bureaucratic process: domestic political imperatives condition policy-makers' preferences, and coalition politics prevail. An opponent's bargaining strategy influences a type IV state by affecting the distribution of power within its government.

In the two intermediary types of states, the decision-making process is a hybrid of cognitive and bureaucratic factors. In a type II state like the Third Republic in France, only one element of bureaucratic politics theory applies. Although the foreign policy executive is a unitary actor, he or she is susceptible to societal pressures because of the power of the legislature. In a type III state like the Soviet Union after Stalin, executive authority for foreign policy is diffuse but there is no effective national legislature to curb executive action. Therefore, only the second tenet of bureaucratic politics theory applies: policy is the product of coalition building and compromise among the foreign policy elite. This elite is nevertheless relatively immune from societal actors that have no access to the decision-making process.

In all the states examined, domestic institutions determined how crisis bargaining occurred. State structure also determined which theoretical approach—cognitive or bureaucratic—provided the best explanation of the bargaining process. To go beyond an analysis of the decision-making process and to explain or predict the outcome of a crisis, however, we must also examine the ways in which process, strategy, and preferences interact to produce policy outcomes. This book developed four sets of specific hypotheses on the relationship among these variables.

The first hypothesis addresses type I states where the executive is unitary and autonomous. In a type I state, strategy interacts with the beliefs of the foreign policy executive to determine the opponent's policy response and the outcome of the conflict. The initially coercive strategy prescribed by deterrence theory succeeds against a hard-line opportunist, who seeks only those goals that can be obtained without serious

---

4. Allison, *Essence of Decision*, 225; Stephen D. Krasner, "Are Bureaucracies Important? (Or Allison Wonderland)," *Foreign Policy* no. 7 (summer 1972): 425.

resistance. Initial coercion leads to escalation against a hard-line defensive deterrer, whose defensiveness produces an aggressive response. Such a strategy also leads to escalation against a contingent compromiser, who prefers accommodation to conflict, but who learns from an opponent's coercion to cease cooperating. Against an unconditional compromiser, any strategy succeeds. The initially conciliatory strategy prescribed by cooperation theory, in contrast, succeeds against any soft-liner. It is exploited by a hard-line opponent, however, resulting in diplomatic defeat for the cooperative state.

An adversary's bargaining behavior influences types III and IV states by affecting the distribution of power among their governing elites. The process by which it does so, however, differs in the two types of states. In type III states—those with diffuse, autonomous executives—the opponent's strategy influences elite support, while in a type IV state with a diffuse, nonautonomous executive, it influences elite, legislative, and public backing. Specifically, an initially coercive strategy erodes support for the ruler and boosts that of the opposition. For example, Russia's aggressive stance in the Crimean case undermined the soft-line Aberdeen and his foreign minister, Clarendon, and reinforced the arguments of their chief rivals, the more hawkish Palmerston and Russell. French strategy in the Fashoda conflict similarly sabotaged the soft-line Salisbury vis-à-vis his hard-line opponent within the cabinet, Chamberlain. Conversely, an initially conciliatory strategy supports the strategic arguments of the individual or group in power and undermines the opposition. Initial American restraint, for example, gave support to the moderate Khrushchev against his more hawkish colleagues in the Presidium, producing similar restraint in Soviet foreign policy in the early stages of the Berlin crisis.

Finally, the interaction of strategy, structure, and preferences in type II states reflects the unitary, nonautonomous structure. Like that of a type I state with a unitary, autonomous structure, the foreign policy chief's preferences determine policy in a type II state. Unlike the chief executive in a type I state, however, legislative and public pressures influence those preferences. For example, British coercion in the Fashoda crisis undermined Delcassé's aggressive colonial policy, forcing the foreign minister to retreat.

These hypotheses about crisis decision making in the four types of states are specific instances of two general propositions. First, the greater the consolidation of executive authority and the autonomy of the foreign policy executive from a national legislature, the less likely decision making is to enter the domestic arena and the more likely it is to be the product of a single chief executive's beliefs. In this case, cognitive psychology adequately explains the bargaining process; the chief executive interprets the opponent's bargaining strategy according to his or her preexisting beliefs. Second, the greater the diffusion of executive authority and the lower the degree of executive autonomy from the representative branch, the more likely the bargaining process is to enter the domestic sphere. In this case, bureaucratic factors explain the bargaining process; policy makers face domestic political pressures, and coalition building among domestic elites influences the content of a state's strategy.

While they support my state structure approach, the case studies in this book highlight three areas in which the argument can be expanded. First, while state structure tells us who can participate in decision making in an international crisis, it cannot always predict who actually will take part. In type I (unitary, autonomous) and II (unitary, nonautonomous) states, the foreign policy executive is comprised of a single office. In type III (diffuse, autonomous) and IV (diffuse, nonautonomous) states, many different offices and individuals comprise the executive and could, in theory, participate in crisis decision making. In the British and Soviet cases, the organization of the foreign policy executive determined that the members of the cabinet and Presidium, respectively, could have a voice in foreign policy making during a crisis. In neither state, however, did all the members of those executive bodies attempt to influence policy in a sustained way. Their influence varied depending on their personal prestige, institutional resources, leadership ability, and interest.

In his study of U.S. commercial policy in the late nineteenth and early twentieth centuries, David Lake suggests that executive leadership explains policy outcome. According to Lake, state structure can explain the constraints within which domestic bargaining occurs, but it cannot determine the outcome of the bargaining process, which also is determined by presidential leadership.[5] My argument is somewhat different: state structure determines the process by which decision making occurs; it also determines whose preferences matter. Those preferences, in turn, determine the state's policy response. Nevertheless, executive leadership remains important to determining who actually takes part in executive decision making.

A second area for further research concerns the means by which private actors gain access to the state. I argue in chapter 2 that during an international crisis private actors enter the decision-making process through a national legislature. The empirical test of this proposition demonstrates that it is largely, but not completely, accurate. Societal pressures sometimes enter the bargaining process through other channels. Before the Vietnam War, U.S. presidents enjoyed significant

---

5. *Power, Protection, and Free Trade*, esp. 13, 67, 73, 87.

freedom of action in foreign policy, particularly during a crisis. Because he and his party would have to stand for reelection, however, an American president was not free of domestic pressures. Even during a crisis, when he was largely immune from the immediate effects of domestic pressures, no U.S. president felt he could ignore public opinion.[6] Nonetheless, while the anticipation of negative public reaction may have influenced a president during a crisis, private actors did not mobilize or influence U.S. policy.

The French case raises similar questions. Both the French army and the colonial ministry played a domestic role in the 1898 Fashoda crisis that cannot be completely captured by a model of executive organization and executive-legislative relations. The head of the army resigned in the heat of the crisis, indirectly influencing French policy by influencing the fate of the government. At another point in the same crisis, the minister of colonies acted independently of the foreign minister and took a stronger anti-British stand than Delcassé. Both these episodes indicate, at the least, that Delcassé was not a totally unitary foreign policy executive.

More important, these events suggest that private actors sometimes have multiple points of access to the state, even during a crisis. For example, procolonialist organizations were warmly received in the colonial ministry. Similarly, the army's role in the Dreyfus Affair, in the Paris strikes, and in possible attempts to overthrow the government imply that some segment of that organization also served as a conduit for the transmission of colonialist sentiment. The existence of these additional "policy networks" linking state and society in the U.S. and French cases suggests the limits of my argument that during an international crisis private interests penetrate the state through a national legislature.[7] At the same time, however, both cases indicate that the legislature is the *primary* channel through which private actors influence national policy during a crisis.

Third and finally, a complete theory of the domestic politics of crisis bargaining would include the sources of public opinion. The state structure approach developed in this book can tell us when public opinion matters, but it cannot account for variations in the intensity of public opinion. In the Fashoda crisis, the British public would not tolerate compromise with the French, whereas French public opinion was far less aggressive toward Britain. Similarly, nothing in the argument developed in this book accounts for the vehemence of anti-Russian sentiment in Britain in the first part of the nineteenth century. A nuanced bureau-

---

6. See Allison, *Essence of Decision,* 194–96.
7. On policy networks, see Katzenstein, "Conclusion."

cratic approach is sufficient to explain the outcome—an initially coercive strategy erodes the public support for the strategic arguments of the dominant leader or coalition—but only knowledge of the source and content of public opinion can explain the intensity of the conflict.

Implications for Theory and Policy

The rest of this chapter explores the significance of my argument for the theory and practice of international conflict management in four principal areas: the domestic politics of conflict and cooperation, foreign economic policy, democracy and war, and domestic institutional change.

The Domestic Politics of Conflict and Cooperation

This study refutes the idea that domestic factors limit or prevent international cooperation. Many studies of arms control negotiations find that domestic factors impede collaboration.[8] Some students of political psychology also blame domestic politics for distorting policy-makers' perceptions of their adversaries.[9] My argument suggests that domestic political division, rather than inhibiting cooperation, may actually encourage it.[10] At the least, it suggests that domestic dissent sometimes leads a state to compromise, rather than to court conflict.

In two of the crises studied, severe domestic political weakness actually led to the success of an opponent's bargaining strategy. In the Fashoda crisis, the French public and press pressured Delcassé to back down. In the Berlin case, U.S. restraint initially undermined the opposition within the Presidium to Khrushchev's moderate policies. Motivated bias arguments cannot account for situations where a compromise emerged despite, or even because of, domestic division. Neither can most analyses of the domestic barriers to arms control that argue that domestic political factors place actors in a game of Deadlock.[11] While

---

8. See Evangelista, "Cooperation Theory and Disarmament Negotiations"; and Steven E. Miller, "Politics Over Promise: Domestic Impediments to Arms Control," *International Security* 8, no. 4 (spring 1984): 67–90.

9. See the works on motivated misperception cited in nn. 11–13 in chapter 2.

10. For similar arguments, see Richard C. Eichenberg, "Dual Track and Double Trouble: The Two-Level Politics of INF," in Evans, Jacobson, and Putnam, *Double-Edged Diplomacy*; Jeffrey W. Knopf, "Two-Level Games and Cooperation Theory: Insights from Nuclear Arms Control Talks" (paper presented to the annual meeting of the International Studies Association, Atlanta, GA, 31 March–4 April 1992); and Putnam, "Diplomacy and Domestic Politics," 444–45.

11. See Evangelista, "Cooperation Theory and Disarmament Negotiations."

domestic vulnerability was an important factor in the crises examined, it did not always preclude compromise.

This finding has significance for many contemporary bargaining issues. Too often, policy makers ignore the impact their strategy has on an adversary's domestic situation or inaccurately assume that domestic division breeds confrontation. They therefore incorrectly assume that policies that encourage domestic opposition to the opponent's government should be avoided. Several examples illustrate the potential of domestic conflict to encourage compromise. The political and economic effects of the United Nations' sanctions against Libya led many Libyans to call for Qaddafi's removal from office.[12] U.S. leaders were optimistic that efforts to sanction Iraq after Saddam Hussein's August 1990 invasion of Kuwait would have similar effects. Similarly, many analysts speculated publicly that the withholding by the United States of $10 billion in loan guarantees played a role in the Labor Party's overwhelming victory in the June 1992 elections in Israel.[13] This book argues that whether domestic division leads a state to compromise or leads to escalation of a conflict depends on how the opponent's strategy interacts with those domestic debates.

Foreign Economic Policy

The general argument presented here can be expanded from crisis bargaining to other areas of foreign policy with significant bargaining and negotiation dimensions. In chapter 2, I argued that private interests entered the decision-making process during an international crisis largely through the government's representative branch. While this is a crude measure by the standards established in the literature on international political economy, it offers a useful way to understand international crises. To the extent that other issue areas share the characteristics of crisis decision making—the perception of a short decision frame and a severe threat to the national interest—my conception of state structure may also provide an appropriate measure of the state's ability to act in those areas.

There are few other issues or events that so clearly threaten national security as a foreign policy crisis. Nevertheless, there are other issues—such as strategic trade or monetary policy—where societal actors cannot

---

12. See Chris Hedges, "Libyans' Patience With Qaddafi Ebbs," *New York Times*, 24 June 1992, A3.
13. For example, see Thomas L. Friedman, "Baker Calls for Peace Talks Again Once Israeli Chief Takes Office," *New York Times*, 25 June 1992.

easily distinguish their private interests from the national interest. In these areas, few interest groups become involved in the policy process. Joanne Gowa argues that the ability of a state to act in different issue areas is a function of the degree of publicness of the goods provided.[14] In this scheme, crisis decision making is a public good, since it is difficult to prevent any individual or group from reaping the benefits of national security once those benefits have been secured. For this reason, few private actors enter the policy-making process. In contrast, trade policy is excludable, according to Gowa, so collective action is relatively easy and interest groups are active. Monetary policy more closely resembles crisis decision making in this regard. It is more of a collective good, and policy making in this issue area therefore exhibits the difficulties of collective action. Krasner argues that unlike commercial policy, U.S. monetary policy is made in an environment insulated from domestic political constraints. The nature of these two issue areas, according to Krasner, provides one possible explanation for the different institutional contexts.[15] To the extent that it can be tied to national security, strategic trade is also less excludable than general trade policy and therefore more susceptible to the difficulties of collective action among private actors. Mastanduno argues, for example, that U.S. officials enjoyed significant domestic freedom in formulating and implementing export control policy because of its direct relationship to American national security.[16]

The interaction of strategy, state structure, and policy-makers' preferences explains the outcome of major power crises. While this argument is specific to decision making in major power crises, it is developed out of a larger literature on the role of the state and societal actors in the making of foreign economic policy. It is not surprising, then, that these factors would be influential in economic policy making. What is more surprising is that the two areas—national security policy and foreign economic policy—are similar in many ways. While the structure of the state for economic policy making often allows a greater role for private actors than does the national security structure, there are some areas—such as mone-

14. "Public Goods and Political Institutions: Trade and Monetary Policy Processes in the United States," in Ikenberry, Lake, and Mastanduno, *The State and American Foreign Economic Policy.*
15. "United States Commercial and Monetary Policy." Also see John S. Odell, *U.S. International Monetary Policy: Markets, Power, and Ideas as Sources of Change* (Princeton: Princeton University Press, 1982).
16. *Economic Containment: CoCom and the Politics of East-West Trade* (Ithaca: Cornell University Press, 1992); "Trade as a Strategic Weapon: American and Alliance Export Control Policy in the Early Postwar Period," in Ikenberry, Lake, and Mastanduno, *The State and American Foreign Economic Policy.* Also see Ikenberry, "Conclusion," 238.

198 Crisis Bargaining and the State

tary policy and strategic trade—that resemble crisis decision making enough to warrant comparison. Only further empirical research can determine the extent of this similarity.

Democracy and War

My argument on state structure also suggests that the recent wave of democratization around the globe may be a mixed blessing. It has become cliché to note that democracies are less likely to go to war, at least against other democracies, than are nondemocratic states.[17] However, few of the scholarly works that discuss this correlation between democracy and pacific foreign policy explain the causal links between the two variables; that is, few students of democracy and war understand what about a democratic state restrains it in the international arena.[18] The argument of this book provides some insight into the crisis behavior of democratic states. A state structure approach suggests that it is not the overall political structure of the state but the organization of the state for foreign policy making during an international crisis that is important.

Only a democratic state possesses an effective national legislature. As the British and French cases demonstrate, however, having a representative body that serves as a conduit for public opinion does not guarantee that public opinion will have a pacifying influence. Even in a conflict between two democratic states, such as occurred over Fashoda in 1898, public opinion can be warlike. More important, democracies are neither more nor less likely to be characterized by a unitary executive. Executive authority was nearly as concentrated in the United States during the Berlin crisis as it was in czarist Russia during the Crimean War crisis. In the cases examined in this study, it was not the fact that a state was democratic that propelled it toward war or prevented it from fighting. Rather, the ability of the state to determine policy depended on the structure of the executive and the degree of executive autonomy

17. For statements of this thesis, see Michael W. Doyle, "Liberalism and World Politics," *American Political Science Review* 80, no. 4 (December 1986): 1151–61; Zeev Maoz and Nasrin Abdolali, "Regime Type and International Conflict, 1816–1976," *Journal of Conflict Resolution* 33 (March 1989): 3–35; and Randall L. Schweller, "Domestic Structure and Preventive War: Are Democracies More Pacific?" *World Politics* 44, no. 2 (January 1992): 235–69.

18. Exceptions include David A. Lake, "Powerful Pacifists: Democratic States and War," *American Political Science Review* 86, no. 1 (March 1992): 24–37; Zeev Maoz and Bruce Russett, "Normative and Structural Causes of Democratic Peace, 1946–1986," *American Political Science Review* 87, no. 3 (September 1993): 624–38; and John M. Owen, "How Liberalism Produces Democratic Peace," *International Security* 19, no. 2 (fall 1994): 87–125.

from the legislature. This means that a parliamentary democracy was more susceptible to the whims of public opinion than was a presidential democracy.[19] When those whims are warlike, as they were in both British cases, parliamentary democracies can be extremely difficult to restrain, even in a conflict with a democratic foe like France.

Although the rising tide of democracy in Eastern Europe and Latin America is desirable, it will not necessarily mean a more peaceful international system. Nor will an increase in the number of democratic states mean that crises are less likely to escalate to war.[20] Rather than assuming that all democratic states will be more peaceful than nondemocratic nations, students and practitioners of international conflict management should be concerned with the political institutions created in these newly emerging democracies.

Institutional Change

Finally, understanding the source of institutional change is the first step in shaping domestic political institutions that effectively channel societal pressures and manage conflict. Some of the crises examined in this book demonstrate that domestic structures are not fixed; they can and do change in response to both external and internal factors. The degree of institutional change varies from incremental or adaptive, on the one hand, to revolutionary or episodic, on the other.[21] While many students of domestic institutions note that institutions change,[22] very little attention has been paid to why or how they change. This neglect is understandable, since "institutionalists generally focus on constraints and offer explanations of continuity rather than change."[23] It is nonetheless

---

19. For a related argument, see Waltz, *Foreign Policy and Democratic Politics*.

20. For critiques of the democratic peace thesis, see Christopher Layne, "Kant or Cant: The Myth of the Democratic Peace," *International Security* 19, no. 2 (fall 1994): 5–49; and David E. Spiro, "The Insignificance of the Liberal Peace," *International Security* 19, no. 2 (fall 1994): 50–86.

21. For two works that argue that domestic institutional change is likely to be "episodic" and "sticky" rather than incremental, see Ikenberry, "Conclusion," 224; Krasner, "Approaches to the State: Alternative Conceptions and Historical Dynamics," *Comparative Politics* 16, no. 2 (January 1984), 234–35.

22. See Ikenberry, "Conclusion"; Mastanduno, "Do Relative Gains Matter?"; and David Marsh and R. A. W. Rhodes, "Policy Communities and Issue Networks: Beyond Typologies," in Marsh and Rhodes, eds., *Policy Networks in British Government* (Oxford: Clarendon Press, 1992).

23. Kathleen Thelen and Sven Steinmo, "Historical Institutionalism in Comparative Politics," in Sven Steinmo, Kathleen Thelen, and Frank Longstreth, eds., *Structuring Politics: Historical Institutionalism in Comparative Analysis* (Cambridge: Cambridge University Press, 1992), 15. I am grateful to Andrew Cortell for bringing this quote to my attention.

regrettable, since such a neglect hinders our understanding of how domestic structures constrain foreign policy choices. Here I offer some preliminary hypotheses on the degree and origins of change in the organization of foreign policy authority within different states.

Institutional change has two major sources.[24] Exogenous roots of institutional transformation—those external to the political system—include war, international threats, revolution, large-scale political or economic upheaval, technological change, and—at least in a type I, unitary, autonomous state—the death of a national leader.[25] A dramatic example of this kind of change is seen in the difference between czarist Russia and the Soviet Union, a change precipitated by the Bolshevik revolution. Similarly, the deaths of Lenin and Stalin each led to subsequent changes in the organization of foreign policy authority. In Britain, in contrast, nineteenth-century legislative reforms that altered foreign policy institutions were largely rooted in socioeconomic and demographic changes.

In the United States, the level of international threat, especially foreign war, has been the most frequent source of exogenous change. The struggle between the legislative and executive branches for control of foreign policy has fluctuated in a cyclical pattern. In the first forty years of U.S. history, from 1789 to 1829, the American president dominated the foreign policy arena. From 1829 to 1898, during which time the perception of international threat remained low and the major problems facing the American government were domestic, the nation moved into a period of congressional government. After the Spanish-American War in 1898, and particularly after the two world wars of the early twentieth century, presidential dominance returned.[26] This "imperial presidency" was only challenged in the wake of the Vietnam War.

Indeed, the unitary, autonomous nature of U.S. foreign policy making in the 1958–61 Berlin crisis has long since ceased to exist. In 1993, Robert H. Michel, the House minority leader, warned the Clinton administration against becoming involved militarily in Bosnia, noting,

---

24. For a related argument, see Gabriel A. Almond, "Approaches to Developmental Causation," in Gabriel A. Almond, Scott C. Flanagan, and Robert J. Mundt, eds., *Crisis, Choice, and Change: Historical Studies of Political Development* (Boston: Little, Brown, 1973).

25. See Ikenberry's discussion of "crises and critical junctures" in "Conclusion," 233–36.

26. See David M. Abshire, *Foreign Policy Makers: President vs. Congress*, Center for Strategic and International Studies, *The Washington Papers* 7, no. 66 (Beverly Hills: Sage, 1979), 23, 29–30; and Cheever and Haviland, *American Foreign Policy and the Separation of Powers*, 39.

"You've got to build a case for whatever intervention with the American people first." This bipartisan sentiment was echoed by House majority leader Richard A. Gephardt: "I personally believe that the country benefits . . . by having a debate of our people beforehand through Congress."[27] Such statements are a far cry from the Congress's disinterest in foreign affairs during the Eisenhower administration.

Socioeconomic changes provided the exogenous impetus for the political reforms that occurred in Britain in 1867 and 1884—between the end of the Crimean conflict and the beginning of the Fashoda crisis. Collectively, these reforms changed the structure of the British state by significantly widening the franchise and increasing the power of political parties. In the process, Parliament changed its own role and the role of the cabinet in both domestic and foreign policy making.

The most common source of institutional change in this study was exogenous, but institutional change, especially incremental change, can also have *endogenous* roots. As David Marsh and R. A. W. Rhodes note about policy networks—one type of domestic institution important on a range of domestic and economic issues—"the analysis of change cannot be reduced to a simple environmental stimulus–policy network response model. Actors in the network shape and construct their 'world,' choosing whether or not and how to respond."[28]

Endogenous changes can be prompted by shifts in a society's prevailing political ideology that are wrought by changes in the electoral fortunes of a governing party or coalition,[29] by the institutionalization of routine or procedural change,[30] or by routine leadership changes that bring to power individuals with different preferences and skills than their predecessors. Institutionalization appears to be the most common endogenous source of change. The experience of the Vietnam War provided a large part of the impetus for congressional change in the United States, while socioeconomic trends propelled British reform in the nineteenth century. In both instances, however, institutions continued to change and evolve over time, and the catalyst for that change often came from inside the legislature itself.

Such endogenous change is most likely to occur in types II and IV

---

27. Quoted in Thomas L. Friedman, "U.S. Unlikely to Accept Any Serbian Conditions," *New York Times*, 6 May 1993, A16.
28. "Policy Communities and Issue Networks," 259.
29. Peter A. Hall, "Policy Paradigms, Social Learning, and the State: The Case of Economic Policymaking in Britain," *Comparative Politics* 25, no. 3 (April 1993): 275–98.
30. Nelson W. Polsby, "Political Change and the Character of the Contemporary Congress," in Anthony King, ed., *The New American Political System*, 2d version (Washington, DC: AEI Press, 1990), 43.

states—those in which the executive is responsible to a national legislature. In these states, the representative branch acts as a filter through which external events are viewed and interpreted. In the United States up until the 1960s—although it was largely a type I state on foreign policy issues—a functional national legislature existed. Even though Congress was not actively involved in crisis decision making, the United States was a type II state on most domestic issues. Congress therefore initiated a series of gradual changes in the 1960s and 1970s. While the source of change in states with an effective national legislature is most often endogenous, the form of change is most likely incremental. The representative element of government in such states serves both as the focus for incremental reform and as a brake on more revolutionary change.

Because the domestic institutions of most type I (unitary, autonomous) states have little endogenous foundation for innovation or transformation, these states are the most impervious to fundamental change. In czarist Russia, for example, there was no legitimate avenue for political dissent that might have led to political reform and institutional change. When change does occur in these states, it is more likely to be revolutionary than evolutionary, since it is most likely to be in response to some external crisis.

The six states examined in this study clearly indicate that institutions change over time. Further study of the role of external and internal sources of institutional change can contribute to the creation of effective, enduring domestic structures. Such political institutions, it is hoped, will help manage future international crises and resolve them short of war.

Index

Aberdeen, George Hamilton Gordon, earl of: advocacy of restraint, 67, 78, 86, 90; domestic pressures on, 7, 38, 48, 51, 53–54, 75, 82, 83, 86, 89–90, 188, 192; as irrational bargainer, 76; perceptions of Russia, 34, 68, 71, 75–76, 81, 84, 88–89; strategic beliefs of, 17, 54–55, 187; threatens resignation, 86; views on Ottoman Empire, 50, 65
Accommodation, 42
Acheson, Dean, 155, 173, 174, 178–79
Adenauer, Konrad, 154, 165
Ali, Mehemet, 73
Alliance dynamics, Berlin, 152, 162, 184, 186
Allison, Graham, 22, 190
Anti-party group, 138–39
Argyll, duke of, 71
Aristov, A. B., 169
Arms control, 195
Army, France, 121, 122
Autorité, 121

Bahr-el-Arab, 118
Bahr-el-Ghazal, 115, 118, 123
Balfour, Arthur, 103, 128
Baratier, Captain, 122
Bargaining strategy: in Berlin, 133–34, 183; in Crimea, 47, 92; in Fashoda, 95, 131–32; and information processing, 9; and learning, 9–10; and methodology, 42–43. *See also* Bureaucratic politics; Cognitive psychology; Cooperation

theory; Deterrence theory; International structural theories; Motivational Psychology; Reciprocity
Beach, Michael Edward Hicks, 103, 124–25
Berlin crisis (1948), 15, 134
Berlin ultimatum (1958), 147
Berlin wall, 177, 181–82
Binger, Gustave, 115, 116
Blue book, 119, 125
Bohlen, Charles, 174, 178
Bosnia crisis, 200–201
Bray-Steinberg, Count Otto von, 72
Brezhnev, Leonid, 169
Brunnow, Ambassador, 65, 69
Bueno de Mesquita, Bruce, 3
Bundy, McGeorge, 174
Buol, Count, 79, 85, 86
Buol Project. *See* Olmütz Proposal
Bureaucratic politics: in Berlin, 136–37, 179, 184, 188–89; in Crimea, 22, 51–52, 93, 188; and crisis decision making, 21–23, 36–38, 41, 42, 193; explanatory power of, 24, 44, 185; in Fashoda, 100–101, 188, 194–95

Camp David meetings, 161–62
Canning, Lord Stratford de Redcliffe. *See* Stratford de Redcliffe, Stratford Canning
Catholic Church, 48, 49
Central Committee of the Communist Party, Soviet Union, 7, 26, 39, 138–39, 169

Chamberlain, Joseph: advocacy of coercion, 124, 126, 128–29; on colonies, 99; domestic support for, 188, 192; strategic beliefs of, 104–5, 106, 188
Chamberlain, Muriel E., 54
China, 166
Clarendon, George William Frederick Villiers, 4th earl of: advocates restraint, 67; domestic pressure on, 7, 9, 20–21, 22, 48, 71, 75, 78, 84–85, 87, 88, 90, 187, 192; party affiliation, 53; perceptions of Russia, 51, 67–68, 71–72, 75, 76–77, 78, 84, 86–87, 90; on Seymour conversations, 65; strategic beliefs of, 56–57; on Stratford Canning, 81; as swing vote for coercion, 9, 18, 51, 75, 77, 87, 93; on Vienna Note, 81
Clay, Lucius, 182
Coercion, 42
Cognitive psychology: and crisis bargaining, 16–18, 31–35, 42 fig., 187–88, 192–93; as explanation of Berlin, 136–37, 184; as explanation of Crimea, 17, 51–52, 93, 187; as explanation of Fashoda, 100–101, 187–88; explanatory power of, 24, 44, 185
Collective Note, 88, 90
Collective responsibility, doctrine of, 53, 54, 102
Colonial Party, France, 101
Comité de l'Afrique, 106, 107
Committee of the Ministers, Russia, 59
Communist Party, Soviet Union. See Central Committee of the Communist Party, Soviet Union
Constantinople Note. See Turkish Ultimatum
Contingent compromiser, 34. See also Soft-liners
Cooperation theory, 1–2, 9, 10, 34–35, 192; and Berlin, 133; and Crimea, 47–48
Core beliefs, 32

Corwin, Edward S., 142
Council of Nationalities, Soviet Union, 138
Council of the Empire, Russia, 59
Council of the Union, Soviet Union, 138
Courcel, Baron, 114, 118, 126–27, 128
Cuban missile crisis, 2, 15, 183

Daily Mail, 123
Daily News, 83
Dawson, Douglas, 121
Deadlock, 195
Decisional conflict. See Motivational psychology
Decision-making theories. See Bureaucratic politics; Cognitive psychology; Motivated psychology
Defense Agency, Japan, 4
Defensive avoidance, 19. See also Motivational psychology
Defensive deterrer, 33, 60. See also Hard-liners
DeGaulle, Charles, 151
Delcassé, Théophile: autonomy of, 7, 95, 115–16, 126, 131, 194; domestic pressures on, 7, 14, 20, 101, 110, 113–14, 117, 120–22, 126, 131, 187, 188, 192, 195; on Marchand mission, 109–10, 112–13; and motivated misperception, 100, 112, 131–32; perceptions of Britain, 119–20; strategic beliefs of, 33, 41, 101, 108–9; uncompromising early policy of, 114–16; willingness to concede, 99, 118
Democratic peace, 11, 198–99
Dépêche Coloniale, La, 121
Derbyites, 53
Deterrence theory, 1, 9, 34, 191; and Berlin, 133, 146, 152, 154, 165, 183; and Crimea, 47–48; and Fashoda, 95
Dien Bien Phu, 143
Diesing, Paul, 21

Dillon, Douglas, 161, 166, 167
Doves. *See* Soft-liners
Dreyfus affair, 100, 113, 187, 194
Dulles, John Foster, 149–50, 150–51, 155

Eastern crisis: 1840, 57; 1877–78, 104; 1896–97, 104
Effendi, Fuad, 64
Egypt, 96
Eisenhower, Dwight D.: advocacy of restraint, 36; autonomy of, 134; disagreement within administration of, 6, 155; perceptions of Soviet Union, 144–45, 148, 149, 155, 172; relationship with Congress, 143–44, 156; strategic beliefs of, 134, 144–45, 188
Eisenhower, John, 156
Entente Cordiale, 130
Evangelista, Matthew, 4, 22
Executive Committee of the National Security Council (ExCom), 190

Firm-but-fair strategy. *See* Reciprocity
Formosa Resolution, 143
Franco-Turkish Treaty (1740), 48
Frieden, Jeff, 22
Fuad Effendi. *See* Effendi, Fuad
Fulbright, William, 179
Furtseva, E. A., 169

Gambetta, Léon, 108, 109
Gaulois, Le, 116, 121
Gelman, Harry, 39
Geneva Conference (1959), 157–58
Geoffray, *chargé d'affaires,* 111–12, 114, 119
Gephardt, Richard A., 201
German Party (*nemetskaia partiia*), 59
Germany, relations with France, 130
Goschen, G. J., 103, 125, 126
Gowa, Joanne, 197
Greek Orthodox church, 48
Grey, Edward, 96

Gromyko, Andrei, 157, 182
Groupe Colonial, 106–7, 108, 127

Halperin, Morton H., 22
Hard-liners, 17–18, 32–33
Harriman, Averill, 159, 174
Hawks. *See* Hard-liners
Henry, Colonel, 113
Herter, Christian, 157, 159, 161
Howard, H. E., 69
Hussein, Saddam, 20, 196

Ignatov, N. G., 169
Imperial presidency, 35–36
Intermediate beliefs, 32. *See also* Cognitive psychology
International structural theories: and crisis bargaining, 8, 13–16; as explanation of Berlin, 135, 184, 186; as explanation of Crimea, 14–15, 49–51, 50–51, 92, 185–86; as explanation of Fashoda, 14, 15–16, 95, 97–99, 120, 123, 131, 186; explanatory value of, 44
Ireland, 57
Irish Brigade, 53
Irrational bargainer, 17

Jervis, Robert, 20
Johnson, Lyndon, 174, 182
Journal des Débats, 121

Katzenstein, Peter J., 4
Kennedy, John F.: autonomy of, 134, 190–91; defense policy of, 174, 179; disagreement within administration of, 6, 36, 173–74, 178–79; perceptions of Soviets, 175, 177–78, 181; strategic beliefs of, 145–46
Kirichenko, A. I., 169
Kisselev, Count, 64
Kissinger, Henry, 174
Kitchener, H. Herbert, 97, 109, 110–11, 125
Knopf, Jeffrey W., 186
Konev, Ivan, 180

Kozlov, Frol, 141, 158, 164, 169, 171, 172
Krasner, Stephen D., 3, 197
Khrushchev, Nikita: autonomy of, 7, 39, 40, 137; correspondence with Kennedy, 182; and defense spending, 175; domestic pressures on, 8, 20, 39, 133, 134, 164, 168, 169, 170–72, 183, 184, 187, 188–89, 195; interview with Harriman, 159–60; and motivated misperception, 21, 44, 136, 169–71, 172, 184; and origins of Berlin crisis, 134–35; perceptions of United States, 44, 133, 140, 153, 160, 163, 167, 170–71, 172, 175, 177, 180, 187; strategic beliefs of, 139–40

Labor Party, Israel, 196
Lake, David, 193
Lalman, David, 3
Lansdowne, Henry Charles Keith Petty-Fitzmaurice, 5th marquis of, 90, 103
Lavalette, Ambassador, 65
Lebow, Richard Ned, 99, 132
Lenin, V. I., 200
Linden, Karl, 139, 140

Mackintosh, John P., 102
Macmillan, Harold, 148, 152
Mahdists, 96, 110
Malinovsky, Rodion, 141, 167, 171, 176
Manchester Guardian, 124
Mansfield, Mike, 143–44
Mao tse Tung, 166
Marchand, Jean-Baptiste, 96
Marchand mission, 108, 109–10
Marsh, David, 201
Mastanduno, Michael, 25, 197
Matin, Le, 116, 121, 127
May, Ernest R., 23
McCloy, John, 180
McCormack, John, 143
McNamara, Robert, 174, 179

Menshikov, Alexander, 64, 69, 70, 73
Menshikov mission, 62–73
Methodology, 41–45
Michel, Robert H., 200–201
Mikoyan, Anastas, 141, 147–48, 150, 152–53, 168
Mixed German committee, 157
Moldavia, 61, 73–74
Monetary policy, 196, 197–98
Monson, Edmund: perceptions of Delcassé, 116, 118; perceptions of French politics, 99, 111, 121–22, 123, 127–28, 129; perceptions of Russia, 98, 122
Morning Post, 124
Motivational psychology: and crisis bargaining, 18–21; as explanation for Berlin, 21, 44, 136, 169, 172, 181, 184, 187; as explanation for Crimea, 20–21, 44, 51, 92–93, 187; as explanation for Fashoda, 20, 99–100, 117–18, 120, 131–32, 187; explanatory power of, 44, 186–87, 195–96
Mouravieff, Count, 122
Munich, lessons of, 1
Murphy, Robert, 158

Napoleon, Louis, 91, 92
National Railway Workers' Union, 121
National Security Council, 26
Nesselrode, Karl Robert: autonomy of, 59; on Olmütz proposal, 86; on Ottoman Empire, 50; perceptions of Britain, 64, 72, 74, 88; perceptions of France, 74; and Seymour conversations, 62, 63; on Vienna note, 82–83
Nesselrode memorandum (1844), 49, 60
Nicholas I, Tsar: autonomy of, 6, 26, 35, 58–59, 92; critical of Nesselrode, 91; impact of British policy on, 6, 35; on the Ottoman empire, 50; perceptions of Britain, 52, 68–69, 88, 91; and Seymour

conversations, 62–63; strategic beliefs of, 48, 59–60, 188; and Turkish declaration of war, 85–86; on Vienna note, 82–83
Navy, Britain, 130
Nested games, 22
Nitze, Paul, 174
Nixon, Richard, 146
North Atlantic Treaty Organization, Ministerial Council, 150. *See also* Alliance dynamics, Berlin
Nuclear test ban, 156, 175

Official nationality, 58
Okawara, Nobuo, 4
Olmütz proposal, 85, 88
Opportunists, 33. *See also* Hard-liners
Organization of foreign policy authority: in Britain, 3–4, 6, 26, 29, 38, 39, 48, 52–54, 93, 101–2, 106, 131, 191, 201; coding of cases for, 29–30, 30 table; and decision making hypotheses, 2, 5–8, 30–41, 31 fig., 42 fig., 189–93; defined, 25–28; in democracies, 198–99; in France, 3, 7, 26, 40–41, 106–8, 131, 191, 194; in Russia, 6, 26, 27, 36, 48, 58–59, 189, 202; in Soviet Union, 7, 26–27, 39–40, 134, 135, 137–39, 183, 191; in United States, 6, 26, 27, 29–30, 35–36, 137, 142–44, 184, 189–91, 193–94, 200–202
Orlov, Count, 63, 91. *See also* State structure
Ottoman Empire: and balance of power, 49–50; declaration of war, 85; religious rights in, 48–49

Palmerston, Henry John Temple, Viscount: advocacy of coercion, 67, 75, 84; domestic support for, 7, 48, 192; party affiliation, 53; perceptions of Russia, 33, 76, 77, 84; resignation of, 54, 84, 89; strategic beliefs of, 17, 50, 55–56, 57, 187
Paris summit, 168

Parliamentary sovereignty, doctrine of, 52–53, 54, 101–2
Pavillon de Flore, 116
Peaceful coexistence, 140. *See also* Khrushchev, Nikita, strategic beliefs of
Peelites, 53
Peripheral beliefs. *See* Tactical beliefs
Policy networks, 28, 194, 201
Politburo. *See* Presidium
Political culture: as part of state structure, 28–29; in United States, 32, 135, 144
Pospelov, P. N., 169
Port Arthur, 104, 105
Presidium: and collective decision making, 7, 26, 39, 135, 137, 138, 139, 193; opposition to Khrushchev, 192, 195
Prest, John, 57
Prisoners' Dilemma, 15, 135

Qaddafi, Muammar, 196
Quai d'Orsay, 40, 107, 113, 116

Radical Party, 53
Rational bargainer, 17
Rayburn, Sam, 143
Reciprocity, 1
Reform Act: 1832, 53; 1867, 101; 1885, 101
Reshid Pasha, 73
Retribution, 91
Rhodes, R. A. W., 201
Richter, James G., 154, 177
Rifaat Pasha, 69
Risse-Kappen, Thomas, 4
Rosebery, Archibald Philip Primrose, earl of, 124
Rostow, Walt, 174
Rourke, John, 143
Rusk, Dean, 174, 182
Russell, John: advocacy of coercion, 67, 75, 84; domestic support for, 7, 48, 192; party affiliation of, 53; perceptions of France, 65; perceptions

Russell, John (*continued*)
of Russia, 65, 67, 68, 72, 76, 81–82, 90–91; strategic beliefs of, 57–58; to succeed Aberdeen, 54, 86; threatens resignation, 90
Russell, Richard, 156
Russian mobilization, 61–62, 64–65
Russian Party (*russkaia partiia*), 59
Russo-Turkish War, 87–92

Saab, Ann Pottinger, 73
Salisbury, Robert Cecil, marquess of: advocacy of restraint, 125, 126, 129, 132; domestic pressures on, 7, 38, 102, 110, 117, 123–25, 128, 188, 192; and motivated misperception, 99–100, 117–18, 132; perceptions of France, 99; strategic beliefs, 34, 103–4, 105–6, 187–88
Schlesinger, Arthur M., 174, 175, 178
Secretariat. *See* Central Committee of the Communist Party, Soviet Union
Seymour, George Hamilton, 62–63, 65–68
Sinope, Battle of, 89
Snyder, Glenn H., 21
Snyder, Jack, 139, 141
Soft-liners, 17, 33–34
Sorenson, Theodore, 174, 177, 178, 181
Stalin, Joseph, 134, 200
State structure: changes in, 29–30, 199–202; and decision making, 2–5, 24–25. *See also* Organization of foreign policy authority
Stevenson, Adlai, 174
Strategic trade policy, 196, 197–98
Stratford de Redcliffe, Stratford Canning, 68, 70–71, 74, 80, 83
Suslov, Mikhail, 141–42, 164, 167, 169, 171
Supreme Soviet, 138
Systemic theories. *See* International structural theories

Tactical beliefs, 22. *See also* Cognitive psychology
Taiwan Straits crisis, 143
Tatu, Michel, 164, 171
Taylor, Maxwell, 174
Tocqueville, Alexis de, 137
Temperley, Harold, 50
Thompson, Llewellyn, 165, 173–74, 178
Tit-for-tat. *See* Reciprocity
Times (London), 83, 124
Treaty of Kutchuk-Kainardji (1774), 48
Treaty of Unkiar Skelessi (1833), 49
Trouillot, Georges, 112, 115, 116, 122, 125, 194
Turkish Ultimatum, 79
Twenty-second Party Congress, 182
Two-level games, 22, 28

U-2 incident, 168, 169–70, 171, 177, 191
Ulbricht, Walter, 164–65, 172, 173
Unconditional compromisers, 34. *See also* Soft-liners
Union Coloniale Française, 106, 107
Upper Nile region, 96, 98, 118, 142–43

Victoria, Queen, 117
Vienna Note, 79–80, 85, 88
Vietnam War, and changes in state structure, 3, 29, 35, 190, 193, 200, 201
Violent interpretation, 81, 83

Wallachia, 61, 73–74
War Powers Resolution, 29
Warsaw Pact, 165
West Niger, conflict over, 105
Whig Party, 53
Wilson, Woodrow, 142
World War I, lessons of, 1–2